June 5
65

America's Best
Lake, Stream, and River Fishing

America's Best Lake, Stream, and River Fishing

By Heinz Ulrich

New York: A. S. Barnes and Company, Inc.
London and Toronto: Thomas Yoseloff Ltd.

A. S. Barnes and Company, Inc.
11 East 36th Street
New York 16, New York

Thomas Yoseloff Ltd.
123 New Bond Street
London W.1, England

Library of Congress Catalog Card Number: 62–10179

Printed in the United States of America

1218225

Contents

Illustrations

PHOTOGRAPHS, following page 192:

Brookie. Brookies. Bass. String of fish. Pickerel. Another pickerel. Boy and catch. Equipment check. Brown trout. Landlocked salmon. Smelt dippers. Fishing village. Sunfish and yellow perch. Trout. Family fun. Landing one. Largemouth bass. Bass, sunfish, and catfish. Channel catfish. Sockeye salmon. Steelhead and salmon. Sturgeon. Brook trout. Another brook trout. Mess of trout. Carp. Rainbow trout. The art of bait casting.

Where to Fish

The section that follows lists the best spots for fresh-water fishing in all our 50 states. Places are listed not only for their fishing but also for their facilities, so that anyone planning a fishing vacation should find all the information he needs here. Since the listing of each body of water is accompanied by the name of a nearby town or city, the fisherman need only refer to any state road map—obtainable at gasoline stations or by writing to the Texaco Touring Center, 135 East 42nd Street, New York 17, New York. By using a road map he should be able to locate any water without difficulty. Travel routes will be listed of course, so the angler should have no trouble getting to any location he chooses.

The "Where to Fish" section treats each state separately. It gives the best of each state's fishing, including what the waters are, what fish are there and how good the fishing is. Also listed is such varied information as where to get Indian guides to fish Pyramid Lake; where to go swamp fishing; where to sign on for Colorado, Salmon, and Snake River floats; how to start a pack trip into the Rockies for golden trout; where to fish from an enclosed air-conditioned dock for crappie; how to arrange a flatbottom Ozark float; where to barge-fish in an oxbow lake; and how to obtain canoe routes for an Adirondack fishing trip. Fishing in national forests and national and state parks is listed in this section, along with the names and locations of hundreds of streams, rivers and lakes.

Additional information on fishing in national parks can be obtained from:

National Park Service
Washington 25, D. C.

Further information on fishing and camping in national forests is available from:

Forest Service
U.S. Department of Agriculture
Washington 25, D. C.

For more details on forests, write to the individual forest supervisors.

Alabama

Tourist information from:

State Chamber of Commerce
468 South Perry Street
Montgomery 1, Alabama

Fishing information from same source.

Fish in Alabama: largemouth bass, smallmouth bass, white bass, bluegill, crappie, walleye pike, blue catfish, yellow catfish, channel catfish, sauger and other rough fish.

The Alabama fresh-water fisherman has his pick of fine reservoir lakes, rivers, and deltas in this 51,609-square-mile Gulf of Mexico state. The Tennessee River makes a tremendous U-turn beginning in the northern part of Alabama. After flowing south along the eastern borders of Kentucky, Tennessee, and into Alabama, the big river turns and begins flowing north along the western portions of Tennessee.

Fishing the bend of the Tennessee River in Alabama usually means fishing in one of its reservoir lakes, including Guntersville Lake (69,000 acres) near Guntersville, Wheeler Lake (67,000 acres) near Decatur, Wilson Lake (16,000 acres) near Florence and Sheffield; or fishing the section of Pickwick Lake (43,000 acres) that is in Alabama. The Tennessee River favorites are largemouth and smallmouth bass, white bass, bluegill, crappie, walleye, blue catfish and channel catfish coming large. Boats are available at all of these lakes, and motel accommodations can be found in Florence, Sheffield, Decatur and Guntersville.

Lake Martin is a very popular fishing area near Alexander City, with Kowaliga Beach (on Route 63, along the lake) a rapidly growing recreational area where fishing boats can be rented. Motel accommodations are plentiful at nearby Alexander City.

Bass of large proportions are found in Lake Martin's 40,000 acres of water, along with other sports fish, crappie and the 3 kinds of catfish.

Lay Lake (6,000 acres) and Mitchell Lake (5,800 acres) are near Clanton, and Lake Jordan (4,900 acres) is a short way to the south near Montgomery. These lakes are the Coosa River chain of reservoirs. Smallmouth, largemouth and white bass as well as crappie and catfish are the sports fish. The area is somewhat underdeveloped, but there is lodging at Clanton and nearby Montgomery.

Bartletts Ferry Lake above Phenix City on the Georgia border has largemouth, smallmouth and white bass as well as catfish. A fisherman can find lodgings at Phenix City. A new lake will appear further south above Fort Gaines when the W. F. George Dam is completed.

Especially interesting is delta fishing in the southern portion of the Mobile and Tensaw rivers. Here an angler never knows if he will hook a weakfish, catfish, bass or ladyfish, for salt- and fresh-water fish mix freely.

Alabama, like so many other southern states, is experiencing an extraordinary increase in fishing. The TVA and other projects are adding thousands of acres of clear, warm water, ideal for fish propagation. These new lakes teem with sports fish waiting to smash at an angler's tackle. Fish in Alabama have plenty of natural food, and they grow to monstrous size, as the 4-pound 12-ounce, world-record bluegill testifies. Until 1955 Alabama also held the smallmouth-bass record.

The state has good fishing which is getting better yearly.

Alaska

Tourist information from:

    State of Alaska
    Division of Tourist and Economic Development
    Klein Building
    Juneau, Alaska

Fishing information from:

State of Alaska
Department of Fish and Game
Subport Building
Juneau, Alaska

Fish in Alaska: king salmon, silver salmon, lake trout, rainbow trout, steelhead trout, cutthroat trout, Dolly Varden trout, Arctic char, brook trout, northern pike, grayling, sunfish and others.

Writing about fishing in Alaska—586,400 square miles, bigger than Texas, Oklahoma, Louisiana, Mississippi, Alabama and Florida combined, or bigger than the total land areas of Great Britain, France, West Germany and Italy—is not writing about fishing in a state, but about fishing in an area larger than many major nations. Couple this vast area with a population of slightly more than 150,000 and add that the waters are cold and clear, and it won't take you long to realize that in Alaska there are fishing opportunties so excellent that they are unequaled anywhere else in America.

One of the major problems for the continental fisherman who wants to fish Alaska is in getting there. Airplanes are the chief means and flights leave daily from Seattle and once a week from Minneapolis and New York. An adventurous way is by the Alcan Highway. Dawson Creek in British Columbia is the jump-off place, from which it's a 1,500-mile trip to Fairbanks. The 200 miles of the road through Alaska parallel the Tanana River, and an angler can stop and catch grayling and trout. Cars starting from the United States should be in good condition, and a repair kit and an extra set of tires are recommended. There are camp sites and accommodations along the way. One tip: don't make a spring trip until the end of May, because thaws make traveling terribly difficult.

Many Alaskan fishing waters are not easily accessible, and some of the best can only be reached by airplane. Bush pilots will fly fishermen into the back country, where there is exciting fishing. Or the fisherman can make arrangements in Alaska's big cities for all-expense trips into the back country. Arrangements can also be made through:

Northwest Orient Airlines
1885 University Avenue
St. Paul 1, Minnesota

or

Outdoor Vacations Inc.
Columbia, Missouri

(This company also has fishing and hunting trips to all parts of the world.)

Northern Alaska, above the Arctic Circle, offers fishing throughout the Brooks Range Mountains. Planes fly from Bettles to the inaccessible lakes where fishing is for whitefish, grayling, and pike. Rainbow trout are so thick in many of the lakes that it is often hard for an angler to find a lure that will not take them. Further south near Chitina is the Chitina Lakes area, where there is excellent grayling fishing. Northern pike are, of course, found throughout the interior of the state and abound in this area. Guides and lodging can be found at Chitina.

The Japanese Current of the Pacific Ocean keeps Alaska's southern border amazingly warm. Many places in the continental United States get far colder than this section of Alaska. Sitka had a record low temperature of only −5°, and it has an average January temperature of 32.4°, Juneau's record low was −15°, its January average temperature being 27.5°. Summer temperatures occasionally go into the 90's.

The area around Juneau, Alaska, is a salmon festival, with giant king salmon going up to 80 pounds in the summer and scrappy silver salmon up to 20 pounds starting in August. The far southwest corner of the state has cutthroat, Dolly Varden, and rainbow trout in rivers and lakes such as Mirror Lake on Revillagigedo Island. Salmon are taken all through the area.

North of Sitka and east of Juneau is the Glacier Bay National

Monument with 20 glaciers, including famous Brady and Muir glaciers. The Monument has 15,320-foot Mount Fairweather and is a worthwhile trip.

Anchorage, on the coast, has complete tourist facilities and is a good jump-off place for back-country fishing. Trips are made from here to Mount McKinley National Park, where North America's highest peak (20,320-foot Mount McKinley) is located. Fishing in the park is primarily for grayling. South of Anchorage on the Kenai Peninsula there are lake trout, grayling, steelhead and salmon. A highway from Anchorage to Homer makes the area accessible.

Iliamna Lake, the biggest lake in Alaska (1,057 square miles), is on the Alaska Peninsula. There are no roads leading to it, and fishermen are flown to the lake town of Iliamna, which has an airfield. Fishing here is for lake trout, Dolly Varden, rainbow trout and grayling. Excellent catches of steelhead, king salmon and silvers are also common in the area. Fishing is exceptionally good in the Kvichak River.

Further out of the Alaska Peninsula is Katmai National Monument, where lodging is at South Naknek. Fishing in this vast area of lakes and mountains is for king salmon (summers), sockeye salmon (beginning July) and silver salmon (in the fall). Mackinaw trout, lake trout, Dolly Varden, rainbows, steelhead, northern pike and grayling are here. Offshore Kodiak Island has excellent fishing for salmon, steelhead and Dolly Varden. Lodging and guides are at Kodiak.

Further west off the Bering Sea in Bristol Bay is Dillingham, a town with a population of 600. Dillingham centers an area of excellent fishing and has many lakes nearby, including Lake Nunavaugaluk, Lake Aleknagik, Lake Nerka, Lake Beverley, Lake Kulik, Lake Nuyakuk and others. This area is very productive for Arctic char, grayling, northern pike and Mackinaw trout. Rainbow trout are in the lakes and the Agulowalk River. There is also fine salmon fishing here.

Alaska is the perfect place to fish. For any angler who longs for the once-in-a-lifetime chance to enjoy fishing as it was in pioneer days, this frontier country is the place to go.

Magazine dealing with Alaska outdoors:

Alaska Sportsman   Cost: $3.00 per year
P. O. Box 118
Ketchikan, Alaska

Arizona

Tourist information from:

Arizona Travel Bureau
State Highway Department
Phoenix, Arizona

Fishing information from:

Arizona Game and Fish Department
Phoenix, Arizona

Fish in Arizona: Arizona Native Trout, brown trout, rainbow trout, brook trout, white bass, smallmouth bass, largemouth bass, channel catfish, bluegill, crappie and rough fish.

Everyone is discovering the 113,909-square-mile state of Arizona. First, a few major-league baseball teams ventured there for spring training on an experimental basis, and others soon joined them. Then some vagabond travelers settled there to live, and word spread so fast that the state's population has doubled in 10 years. And so it has been with fishing—a few boys dunked hooks in Arizona and came up with whoppers, and now everyone wants a chance.

Warm-water game fish are Arizona's chief fishing attraction, but some pretty fine trout fishing also adds to the lure of the state.

The most famous body of water here is, of course, the Colorado River, which makes up much of the western border and also runs through much of northern Arizona. It is here that world-famous Grand Canyon is located. There is fishing in the streams of Grand Canyon National Park, but of course the chief attraction is the scenic splendor of the 217-mile-long and 4-to-14-

mile-wide chasm that the river cut into the land. Hotels, motels, sightseeing and pack trips are all part of the attraction of Grand Canyon.

Lake Mead (246 square miles) has stored the waters of the Colorado River where Boulder Dam blocked the river. Lake Mead is one of the best bass lakes in the country, and catches of crappie and bluegill are plentiful, too. Camping facilities and boats are supplied at Pierce Ferry and Bonelli Landing. Temple Bar, 80 miles from Kingman, Arizona, has an air strip, cabins, camping and boat rentals.

Further south on the Colorado River is 70,000-acre Lake Mohave. Rainbow trout hide in its upper reaches near Willow Beach, where the cool water from the river runs into the lake. Bass can be taken throughout the lake, along with crappie and bluegill. Camping facilities, cabins and trailer village, boats and a tackle shop are at Willow Beach, while Katherine Landing near Bullhead City has a motel in addition to these facilities.

Havasu Lake on the Colorado has warm-water game fish and is noted for its large crappie, while Topock on the north of the lake is in a swampy area well known for its bird hunting, where fishing is good except when the water level drops. Site Six and High Island areas on the lake have boats and camping facilities.

The Salt River in east central Arizona, like the Colorado, has some steep canyons along its path. The Salt River has been dammed, so that the reservoir lakes will give good sport. Roosevelt Lake (16,000 acres) is known for its fine largemouth bass. Tonto National Monument with prehistoric cliff dwellings is just east of Roosevelt Dam. The other lakes in this chain include the Apache, Canyon, and Saguaro; and they all offer warm-water game fish and boats, guides, and camping facilities. Phoenix is a few miles west of Lake Saguaro.

The Gila River was dammed by Coolidge Dam, to form San Carlos Lake. This lake periodically has its troubles because of droughts, but when it has ample water there are good warm-water game fish. Globe is near the lake.

The mountain streams of Arizona have cold, clear water which supports trout. Six-hundred-acre Big Lake and 200-acre Crescent

Lake, near Springerville, are located in the Apache National Forest on the center of the eastern border. These lakes, along with many fine trout streams in the vicinity, are filled with rainbow and brown trout. Thirty-three public camps and picnic areas are in the state park; and lodges, cabins and motels are found in the nearby towns of Springerville, Greer and Alpine. Near Alpine there are rainbow and brown trout in 150-acre Luna Lake. The Apache Indians have developed 250-acre Hawley Lake for trout fishing and will soon open up Lake Pacheta for fishing and boating. These lakes are in the Apache Indian Reservation, which has free camping and a trailer site as well as a log-cabin style motel for the accommodation of visitors.

The Mount Baldy Wilderness Area is famous for over 200 miles of trout streams, some of which hold the rare Arizona Native Trout, a yellow-bellied trout native only to Arizona. McNary is a town in the vicinity where information can be supplied.

The state is actively making efforts to stock and improve fishing, and has built new lakes and improved old ones wherever possible. It has good trout fishing as well as good warm-water fishing, and with the aggressive conservation program fishing should continue to be good for years.

Magazine dealing with Arizona outdoors:

Arizona Wildlife Sportsman Magazine
804 North 4th Street
P.O. Box 3407
Phoenix, Arizona

Arkansas

Tourist information from:

Publicity and Parks Commission
412 State Capitol Building
Little Rock, Arkansas

Fishing Information from:

Arkansas Game and Fish Commission
Game and Fish Commission Building
Little Rock, Arkansas

Fish in Arkansas: largemouth bass, smallmouth bass, white bass, rock bass, crappie, bluegill, rainbow trout, brown trout, walleye, longnose gar, alligator gar, channel catfish and rough fish.

Arkansas (53,102 square miles) is traditionally known as the Land of the Ozarks and offers fine fishing in its 9,000 miles of streams and 500,000 acres of lake waters.

Trout fishing is found in the northeast section of the state in the Ozark Mountains and the Ouachita Mountains near Hot Springs National Park, with the Norfolk, White and the Spring rivers the best trout streams in the state. The Ouachita River below Blakely Mountain Dam near Hot Springs and the Little Missouri River below Narrows Dam have rainbow trout.

Float trips in safe and comfortable shallow draft, flatbottom fishing boats are avaliable on the Arkansas, Black, Buffalo and White rivers. Guides and boats can be hired generally on a flat day charge for trips that can go from 1 day to 2 weeks.

Float trips on the Buffalo and White rivers can be arranged through the Cotter Trout Dock or the Hurst Fishing Services in Cotter.

The Buffalo River is a smallmouth-bass stream with excellent catches of bluegill and walleye. The White River has rainbow trout, some brown trout, largemouth and smallmouth bass, walleye pike, perch and bluegill. This once "wild and woolly" section of the country is quite tamed now, and the natives even wear shoes.

Alligator gar are found along the lower section of the White River, where the water gets slower and muddy. They are also in the St. Francis River and in the Ouachita River near Camden. If an angler gets a 100-pounder he shouldn't go reporting records, because the fish regularly get this big and much bigger.

The sport of shooting gar with bow and arrow has become popular.

The Arkansas River running through the state has largemouth bass and bluegill in sections and rough fish throughout, but the old Mississippi which makes up the eastern border of the state and the Red River in the southwestern portion near Texarkana have rough fish.

Another popular fishing site is the 45,000-acre Bull Shoals Lake on the Missouri border. There are boats and guides for fishing largemouth bass, whitebass, crappie and channel catfish. Camping facilities are available throughout Bull Shoals State Park.

Also located on the Missouri border is Norfolk Lake, which has four types of bass: largemouth, smallmouth, white and rock. Channel catfish, walleye, bluegill, crappie and pan fish are plentiful, too. Mountain Home has facilities for the visitor.

Further south in Arkansas in the Ouachita Mountains is the lovely 48,000-acre reservoir, Lake Ouachita. This lake is located in Ouachita National Forest, a short drive from the resorts of Little Rock and Hot Springs. Fishing can be arranged by Frank Harris at Navy Fishing Village, Lena Landing, Lake Ouachita, Buckville, Arkansas. Beds at the lodge are available for only $1.50 a night, or cabins may be rented. Incidentally, baby sitters are available for 35 cents an hour. There are also 14 camp sites to choose from in the park. Boats for the lake are at Joplin, Brady Mountain and Tompkins Bend. Fish are largemouth, smallmouth and rock bass, walleye, crappie, bluegill and channel cats.

Lake Conway (65,000 acres) is a few miles north of Little Rock. There are boats and camping on the lake, where fishing is for a full line of warm-water game fish, including largemouth bass.

Peckerwood Lake, above Stuttgart, and Lake Erling in the far southwestern corner of the state hold a supply of warm-water game fish.

Some other interesting lakes in Arkansas are the oxbow lakes near the Mississippi River, which were formed as a result of a channel change in the old river. Lake Chicot (4,100 acres)

by Lake Village is the largest. This lake has alligator gar, channel catfish, largemouth bass, bluegill and crappie. The Horse-
shoe Lakes near Chatfield and West Memphis have warm-water
fish.

Arkansas boasts primarily warm-water game fishing, with the
extra dividend of some trout fishing in the north of the state.
The best fishing, however, is done on one of those float trips,
where you sit back in a comfortable deck chair and float downstream in a 20-foot flatbottom, throwing out an assortment of
lures as your guide points out the hot-spots. When you're busy
fighting on a lunker, you know it's Arkansas fishing at its best.

California

Tourist information from:

   California Chamber of Commerce
   350 Bush Street
   San Francisco, California

Fishing information from:

   State of California
   Department of Fish and Game
   722 Capitol Avenue
   Sacramento 14, California

Fish in California: king salmon, silver salmon, Kokanee salmon,
steelhead, rainbow trout, sea-run cutthroat trout, cutthroat trout,
brown trout, brook trout, sturgeon, bass, crappie, perch and
other fish.

The Pacific Coast's 158,693-square-mile state of California is
the third largest in the country, and it has better fishing today
than it has ever had in the past. California has always been
noted for fine steelhead and salmon fishing, but what has really
improved is the mountain-lake fishing and the warm-water inland fishing. One hundred years ago only one species of perch
made up the warm-water fish of California, while today there

are largemouth and smallmouth bass, crappie and bluegill—all
of which have been introduced by man. Also there are new
waters that the forty-niners never dreamed existed, and the
mountain lakes that were barren of fish until a few years ago
are now regularly stocked by airplane.

The California coastal area offers salmon and steelhead fishing in many of its northern streams. One of the best known is
the Klamath River and its tributaries which include the Trinity,
Salmon and Scott rivers. Fish are taken from the mouth of the
Klamath River near Klamath, all the way upstream to the Copco
Dam, just below the Oregon border. Steelhead fishing is best
upstream, while king- and silver-salmon fishing is better near
the mouth of the river. Seasons for salmon include a small spring
run and a fall run, which is far more productive. Steelhead are
present from July to October and also during the less productive January and February run. Sea-run cutthroat trout are in
the river from the fall until the spring. Facilities are good in
the area and the Six Rivers National Forest has camping grounds
for outdoorsmen.

The Eel River empties into the Pacific near Fernbridge and is
the best-known steelhead stream in California. The Eel River
and its tributaries, the Van Duzen River, Middle Fork and South
Fork, have good salmon fishing too. King- and silver-salmon runs
favor the fall and winter. Some of the best summer steelhead
fishing is in the Van Duzen River and the Middle Fork of the
Eel (near Dos Rios). The South Fork of the Eel runs along
Highway 101 through beautiful redwood country, and it has the
best winter steelhead fishing. Camping is in various state parks,
including Richardson Grove State Park (boats here) along Route
101, or at Grizzly Creek Redwood State Park along Route 36.

Some of the smaller rivers that have salmon and steelhead
runs . . . the Smith, Mad, Mattole, and Ten Mile rivers.

The Sacramento River, which flows by Sacramento and empties
into San Francisco Bay, has some salmon and steelhead fishing
upstream as far as the Redding Dam. Salmon fishing in this
river does not compare with the more northerly streams. Also

the San Joaquin River to the south has a fall king-salmon run.
Best fishing in this river is for channel catfish and sturgeon.

The Shasta Reservoir Lake, formed by the damming of the
Sacramento, is located on Route 99 just above Redding. This
tremendous lake (29,500 acres) is full of good fishing, offering
mackinaw trout, brown trout, rainbow trout, largemouth bass,
bluegill, sturgeon and Kokanee salmon. Sometimes when driving
to the lake from the south a person gets the feeling the waters
are going to be crowded, but with a lake this size a fisherman
always has vast stretches of water to himself. The lake is in the
southern portion of the Shasta-Trinity National Forest, which
takes in the towns of Weed, Dunsmuir, Redding, Callahan, Etna,
Trinity Center and Dorris. The area offers 43 campgrounds.

The Trinity Alps take in part of the Trinity-Shasta National
Forest. There are many small high lakes and streams for fishing
in this wilderness area. Some include Lower and Upper Canyon
Creek lakes, which are 8 miles from Dedrick up Canyon Creek.
The lakes have brook trout, rainbow trout and brown trout.
Grizzly Lake (42 acres at an elevation of 7,100 feet) has fine
rainbow fishing. A 70-foot waterfall drops from the lip of the
lake to form Grizzly Creek below. Rainbow trout are caught
here. The Department of Fish and Game at Redding will mail
interested sportsmen lists of guides and packers.

Clear Lake (40,000 acres) is near the towns of Clear Lake
and Lakeport, which have hotels, motels, cabins and boats for
the fisherman's use. Angling is for warm-water game fish, including bass, crappie, bluegill and channel catfish. Clear Lake
State Park offers many camping units in its 550 acres.

The northeast corner of California is a primitive area that
includes the Warner Mountains and Surprise Valley—an area
some people think is the nearest we can come today to seeing
nineteenth-century America. Fishing lakes include Goose Lake on
the Oregon border and Big Sage Reservoir near Alturas. Facilities
are very scarce here, however.

Near Susanville is Honey Lake, a noted fishing spot that is
part of the Lassen National Forest, which has its headquarters
in Susanville. There are many lakes in the southern portions of

the Cascades, and fishing thoughout the area is for steelhead, brown and rainbow trout.

Lake Tahoe (21,500 acres) is located on the California-Nevada border near Reno, Nevada, and Truckee, California. Mackinaw trout are taken by deep trolling; other fish are rainbow trout, brown trout, brook trout and Kokanee salmon. This is a resort area with all facilities.

Further south near the Nevada border south of Bridgeport is Mono Lake. This eastern section of California, which is in the Sierra Nevada Mountains area, has mountains going as high as 14,496 (Mt. Whitney) and has over 5,000 lakes for fishermen. Some of the lakes are over 10,000 feet above sea level and can be reached only by pack train. Golden trout run in them.

Yosemite National Park is located just west of Mono Lake. The park has 250-foot sequoias almost 4,000 years old and fine alpine country. There is fishing in Tenaya Lake and in streams like the Merced River.

The Granite Creek area is located southeast of Yosemite National Park. Trout fishing is the sport in Granite Creek, East and West forks, Jackass and Cora creeks, while lake fishing is in the alpine lakes, found at elevations of 8,000 to 10,000 feet. There is some golden-trout and brook-trout fishing in these lakes, many of which are higher than the timber line (9,500 feet).

Bishop, which lies in the heart of many high lakes, including the Treasure Lakes and Golden Lake, has a contest on opening day giving prizes for the best rainbow trout taken. Major streams here are Bishop and Pine Creeks, and golden trout are one of the specialties of the area. Convict Lake (140 acres of rainbow trout waters) is near Bishop.

Located just below the Kings Canyon National Park and the Sequoia National Park is the Mineral King area of California. Fishing for rainbow trout can be had in the East Fork of the Kaweah River. A typical mineral king lake is 17-acre Upper Franklin Lake, which is 2½ hours by trail from Mineral King. At an elevation of 10,500 feet, it is noted for its eastern brook-trout fishing. Upper Monarch Lake at 10,600 feet is all of a 1½-hour climb from Mineral King Road, and fishing is for brookies. Fish are stocked here by plane. The five Mosquito Lakes are also a long mountain climb for the quiet, isolated brook-trout fishing in them.

The Kern River near Bakersfield is a good trout stream and is stocked annually. Other fish to be taken in the river include brown trout, smallmouth bass and channel catfish.

Southern California offers fishing in the Colorado River along the Arizona border for bass, crappie, bluegill and channel catfish. The Salton Sea near Indio has facilities for fishing and boating. Salton Sea State Park offers camping accommodations in an area over 200 feet below sea level. The transplanted Corvina from the ocean adds sport here and fish go to 25 pounds. Another ocean fish of the Salton Sea is the perchlike Sargo, transplanted by the Department of Fish and Game. The Sargo is good eating, abundant and goes to 2 pounds. Another lake in the south is Henshaw Reservoir Lake (6,000 acres) near Julian, which has warm-water game fish, including bluegill, crappie and many hard-fighting black bass.

The state of California offers countless opportunities for the fisherman and outdoorsman. Information on its 19 national forests full of fine fishing waters can be obtained from:

U. S. Forest Service
630 Sansome Street
San Francisco 11, California

Information about California national parks and monuments can be received by addressing a post card to:

National Park Service
180 New Montgomery Street
San Francisco, California

With the exception of the desert areas, there is fishing in all sections of California, and a sportsman never has trouble finding water to fish in the Golden State. A weekly newspaper dealing with California outdoors:

Western Outdoor News
2603 West 54th Street
Los Angeles 43, California

Colorado

Tourist information from:

Colorado Department of Development
State Capital
Denver 2, Colorado

Fishing information from:

State of Colorado
Department of Game and Fish
Denver 1, Colorado

Fish in Colorado: rainbow trout, cutthroat trout, brook trout, brown trout, Mackinaw trout, grayling, whitefish, largemouth bass, Kokanee salmon, walleye pike, yellow perch, channel catfish and rough fish.

The 104,247-square-mile state of Colorado is where Presidents fish when they desire trout. Mountains rise 10,000 to 14,000 feet every few miles in the western half of the state, and drainage from them makes swift, cold streams and lakes ideally suited for trout.

Colorado's northwest corner has the Yampa and the Little Snake rivers, which have brown and rainbow trout as well as whitefish. Trappers Lake is the only lake in the area where boats are available, and the fishing is for cutthroat, brown and rainbow trout. There are facilities at Meeker and Craig. Steamboat Springs, Colorado, the famous winter resort, has fishing in the Stillwater and Chapman reservoirs, as well as the many streams. There is fine camping in the Routt National Forest, which has its headquarters in Steamboat Springs.

Grand Lake, Shadow Mountain, Granby and Willow Creek reservoirs are located north of Granby, with boats at Grand Lake, Granby, and Shadow Mountain. Fish found in the reservoirs are brown and rainbow trout, and since 1951 Granby has had Kokanee-salmon fishing as the result of stocking. Facilities are plentiful throughout this area. Rocky Mountain National Park is here, and spectacular mountain peaks rise to 13,000 feet in the park. Some camp sites can accommodate over 100 tents. Denver is only a short drive southeast.

The Colorado River has its headwaters in this section of the state, and then it flows almost 250 miles southwest into Utah. The river has rainbow and brown trout as well as channel catfish along a route which passes such famous resorts as Glenwood Springs.

The Colorado River is joined by its tributary, the Gunnison River, at Grand Junction. The Gunnison is one of the state's most popular trout streams and gives up fine catches of browns and rainbows. Wet-fly and nymph fishing is productive. Black Canyon of the Gunnison National Monument has campgrounds, as does the Colorado National Monument, which is just west of Grand Junction.

Pikes Peak centers a resort area that includes Pike National Forest, which has camping, picnicking and fishing throughout the area. One camp site, the Lost Park, is at an elevation of 9,900 feet, and there is fishing in Lost Creek. Pikes Peak itself is 14,109 feet. The principal resort here is Colorado Springs, with guest and dude ranches in the area. Fishing in the Pike National Forest includes many mountain streams such as Monument, Geneva, Bureno and Kirby creeks. The South Platte River starts here and is filled with brown and rainbow trout. There is fine fishing below Cheesman Dam.

The Arkansas River forms to the west and then flows south to Salida, where it pivots east and runs to Kansas. The Arkansas is a brown and rainbow stream in Colorado and has good fishing near Buena Vista. Here, too, are Twin Lakes near Leadville, which have already given up the record Mackinaw trout for Colorado—a 29-pounder. There are boats on the lake, and fishing is also good for brown and rainbow trout.

The eastern-plains half of Colorado has the Arkansas River dammed west of Lamar to form the John Martin Reservoir. Bass, crappie, channel catfish, walleye pike, and other warmer-water fish can be taken here.

The Rio Grande is another great river that has its headwaters in Colorado, north of Monte Vista. Fish found in the river are brown and rainbow trout. Monte Vista is the headquarters for the Rio Grande National Forest, which offers hiking, camping, hunting and fishing.

Southwest Colorado has the Mesa Verde National Park, home of the scenic ruins of thirteenth-century cliff dwellers.

Colorado offers a visitor fine mountain fishing in almost 10,000 miles of streams and 2,000 lakes, ponds and reservoirs. Some of the waters are subject to heavy fishing, but an angler need only head into the mountains for the solitude of a fine trout stream and some truly excellent fishing.

Magazine dealing with the Colorado outdoors:

Colorado Outdoors   Cost: $1.00 per year
1530 Sherman Street   Published bimonthly
Denver 1, Colorado

Connecticut

Tourist information from:

Development Commission
State Office Building
Hartford 15, Connecticut

Specific fishing information from:

State of Connecticut
Board of Fisheries and Game
2 Wethersfield Avenue
Hartford, Connecticut

A nonresident's license is necessary.

Chief fish: largemouth bass, smallmouth bass, chain pickerel, rainbow trout, brook trout, brown trout, perch, walleye, shad and rough fish.

Connecticut is a small, highly industrial New England state, 5009 square miles in area, that is not particularly known for fishing spots. However, with the state's active stocking program and with enough native fish, fishing is adequate, and good accommodations are available almost everywhere.

Candlewood Lake, a 10-mile-long lake in the state's southwestern corner, is a favorite spot for New York City escapees. This lake has bass, pickerel and pan fish and is well worth the 1½-hour drive from New York City. Boat rentals are available at New Fairfield.

Lake Lillinonah, a few miles west of Candlewood, and Lake Zoar have largemouth and smallmouth bass and pan fish. Liveries, motels and dining facilities can be found in these spots. Other bass spots are Waumgumbaug Lake, Black Pond and Highland Lake. Amos Lake near Preston City is well known for its chain-pickerel fishing.

The best trout fishing is at Beach Pond (near Voluntown), Wononskopomuc Lake (near Salisbury), Uncas Lake, and Norwich Pond. Trout also can be taken from the Housatonic and Farmington rivers.

The center of the state's fishing activity is the Connecticut River. Shad are a big sport here, and are caught on their spring spawning migrations. The shad in the Connecticut River hit red flies and red beads, while in other rivers on the East Coast shad will not take any bait or lure. The May run of shad is exciting sport for the Connecticut Yankees. Also bass, northern pike and chain pickerel come out of the northern reaches of the river. Boat liveries are at Enfield, Haddam, Middletown, Old Saybrook and Windsor.

Connecticut's active stocking program is keeping sports fishing very much alive throughout the state.

Delaware

Tourist information from:

State Development Department
Capitol Building
Dover, Delaware

Specific fishing information from:

Board of Game and Fish Commission
Dover, Delaware

Chief fish: largemouth bass, chain pickerel, perch, brook trout, brown trout, crappie, bluegill, sunfish, carp and rough fish.

Delaware (2,057 square miles) is the nation's second smallest state and is one eastern seaboard state that has fresh-water fishing to a limited degree. Fresh-water fishing takes a definite back seat to coastal fishing in Delaware, but it is nevertheless available for those who prefer it.

The state stocks trout in the streams of New Castle County, and there are over 50 fresh-water lakes and ponds where warm-water sports fish can be caught. The Nanticoke River also provides sport for the angler.

Some of the lakes and ponds where fishing and boating are available include: Becks Pond, Lums Pond, State and Craigs Pond near Kirkwood, Moores Lake and Silver Lake near Dover, Coursey Pond, McCauleys Pond near Frederica, Silver Lake, Haven Lake and Griffiths Lake near Milford. The Phillips Landing Recreational Area near Bethel, Trap Pond, Trussum Pond near Laurel, and Lake Como near Smyrna have fishing–boat launching facilities and picnicking areas for those fishermen who prefer to bring their families.

Florida

Tourist information from:

Development Commission
Caldwell Building
Tallahassee, Florida

Fishing information from:

Florida Game and Fresh Water Fish Commission
Tallahassee, Florida

Fish in Florida: Largemouth bass, bluegill, crappie, warmouth, channel catfish, alligator gar, longnose gar, chain pickerel, tarpon, snook and rough fish.

Ask any 100 fishermen, "What is the most popular state for warm-water fishing?" and 95 will answer, "Florida." I concur.

Florida consists of 58,560 square miles, and there are up to 30,000 lakes here besides 17 giant springs and 166 rivers for fishing.

Beginning in the northwest section, there is Lake Seminole, a reservoir lake completed in 1957 that has developed into an excellent bass spot.

Twenty miles to the east of Panama City near Wewahitchka is the Dead Lakes region. This is an area of cypress trees, swamps, Spanish moss . . . and big bass. Other fish taken from the Dead Lakes are crappie, bluegill, warmouth, chain pickerel, gar, and channel catfish. The flooded area west of the Apalachicola River makes up much of this area. Fishing camps here number over a dozen. Two camps to be noted are Lake Grow Hunting and Fishing Lodge and Magnolia Lodge of Wewahitchka.

Tallahassee, the state capital, is surrounded with good fishing lakes. There are Lakes Talquin, Jackson, Iamonia and Miccosukee. Many small lakes are known for bass, crappie, bluegill and channel catfish. Tallahassee is a fine resort town. Boats in the area can be hired at Blouts Camp for fishing on Lake Talquin and 10 other spots. Gidden's Fishing Camp is one of 3 places on Lake Jackson, while Iamonia Fishing Lodge on Lake Iamonia and Reeves' Fish Camp on Lake Miccosukee make up some of the other facilities. The Apalachicola National Forest is southwest of Tallahassee. It is a pine forest and near fishing in Silver Lake.

The Suwanee River of northwest Florida has fishing camps at Suwanee, Mayo, and Oldtown. Fish include bass, bream, crappie, warmouth, chain pickerel, and channel catfish. Also caught here and in most other Gulf rivers are the prehistoric alligator gar and longnose gar. The river has overnight camping and swimming facilities in Manatee State Park, 20 miles above the Gulf.

The Osceola National Park is near the Georgia border in the eastern half of the state, 30 miles due west of Jacksonville. The park is located in extremely flat country with many cypress swamps and one lake, Ocean Pond, for fishing. Fish are bass, perch and bream. There is a public campground on the north side of the pond.

The St. Johns River of northeast Florida is famous for both fresh-water and salt-water fishing. The downtown railroad bridge in Jacksonville is the legal separation between salt and fresh water; but of course fish don't know that, and salt-water fish are taken miles upstream. The St. Johns runs north and parallels the east coast for about 200 miles, with its mouth at Jacksonville.

South of Sanford the river is 3 feet in depth and is navigable only with outboards. This is a world-famous bass river that also has striped bass and tarpon through much of its water. There are boats at Green Cove Springs, Palatka and St. Augustine. St. Augustine is a fine place to stay, and a visit to Marineland, the oceanarium, is always a fascinating experience.

Lake George, part of the long St. Johns River, has boats for hire at Georgetown. Sportsmans Lodge has boats and 54 living units north of the lake at Welaka. Other boats are rented at DeLeon Springs, DeLand, Orange City and Sanford.

The area around Gainesville is noted for many fine bass lakes, including Orange Grove, Levy, Santa Fe and Lochloosa lakes. Ocala National Forest is there, and in it numerous lakes, ponds and streams for fishing. There are overnight camping facilities at Juniper and Alexander Springs, boats at Juniper Springs and Kingsley Lake. There is a scrub-pine area full of small lakes with big bass in them. It is somewhat underdeveloped and offers fine fishing.

Traveling south through the center of the Florida peninsula, there is an area, Lake County, known for its limitless lakes. The Leesburg vicinity of the state has Lakes Tsala, Griffin, Apopka (the second largest lake in the state), Panasoffkee and Harris. Big Lake Apopka is 10 miles southeast of Leesburg near Winter Garden and is served by 4 fishing camps. Lake Harris also is served by 4, while Lake Griffin has a dozen camps. Lake Pana-soffkee and the Withlacoochee River have 17 boat liveries for rentals and a dozen fishing camps, including Harry's Lodge, on the lake at Panasoffkee.

Just to give some idea of the number of lakes in this region, Orlando has 37 within the city limits.

The area centering around the resorts of Haines City, Winter Haven, Lake Wales and Lakeland has an endless supply of lakes. The major ones here include Tohopekaliga Lake and Lakes Kissimmee, Hatchineha, Marion, Alfred and Pierce. This is the heart of the citrus belt, and the annual midwinter citrus exposition is held at Winter Haven. The big lakes here, as in the rest of Florida, have boat rentals available. Tampa is only 25 miles west of Lakeland.

Sebring, home of the annual sports-car race, is on Lake Jackson, and there are large Lake Istokpoga and other smaller lakes to the south. Sebring has boats for Lake Jackson, and Lake Istokpoga has several boat liveries on its shores.

The lakes from Gainesville down past Sebring can all be counted on to produce black bass. Many of the small lakes and small streams produce surprisingly large fish, and the rule for this area is: If you're near water, fish it—you'll get a bass. Other fish taken are crappie, bluegill, warmouth, chain pickerel and some good-sized channel catfish.

Forty miles above Tampa on the Gulf of Mexico coast is Homosassa Springs, an area where fresh- and salt-water fish mix freely. There are fishing camps at Homosassa for fishing the Homosassa River.

Lake Okeechobee (730 square miles) is the biggest in the state of Florida. It is a clear, shallow, warm-water lake that for years caused Floridians trouble because of its nasty habit of spilling over its borders during the rainy spell. The lake has bass in endless supply, and all the other Florida game fish are represented, including bream, crappie, channel catfish, chain pickerel and shad. Fishing equipment should be sturdy here, for weeds are thick and strong. Boats for fishing can be hired at Canal

Point, Pahokee, Moor Haven and Okeechobee. The Seminole
Indian Reservation is on the northwest shore. West Palm Beach
is only 30 miles east of Belle Glade on the lake, and many
times salt-water fishermen make the short trip inland when they
want a change of pace.

Lake Okeechobee is thought of as the northern tip of the Everglades. Clewiston is a fishing center on the lake which supplies
guides and accommodations. The Clewiston Inn caters to fishermen with guides and boats for fishing the lake or the Everglades.

The furthest southern major expanse of fresh-water fishing in
Florida is in the endless miles of swamps, waterways, swamp
grasses, marshes, and mangrove swamps that make up the Everglades. Throughout the swamp, fishing is good in the sloughs,
creeks, and drainage canals, including the Miami Canal, North
New River and Hillsboro Canal. Fishing camps are situated on
the Miami Canal outside of the city. The west part of the swamp
has fishing camps at Immokalee (located on Route 29, which cuts
right through the swamp). This road travels on to the Everglades
in the famous Ten Thousand Islands region for salt-water fishing.

The Everglades National Park is located on the southern portion of the great Everglades and is 2,300 square miles in area.
Royal Palm Ranger Station in the park owns a 60-room motel
with boat rentals and guides for visitors and fishermen. Bass,
crappie and bream are the chief fish taken throughout the Everglades.

The Florida Keys, still further south, are a salt-water fishing
center.

Florida is the state a fisherman thinks of when the weather
gets cold, lakes freeze over and fishing seasons are closed by
law. One week of Florida black-bass fishing can break up any
winter and make the year a memorable one.

Magazine dealing with Florida outdoors:

Florida Wildlife   Cost: $2.00 a year
Florida Game and Fish Commission
Tallahassee, Florida

Georgia

Tourist information form:

Georgia Department of Commerce
100 State Capital
Atlanta 3, Georgia

1218225

Fishing information from:

State Game and Fish Comission
401 State Capital
Atlanta, Georgia

Fish in Georgia: rainbow trout, brook trout, brown trout, largemouth bass, smallmouth bass, white bass, crappie, bluegill (bream), carp, flathead catfish, channel catfish, gar and rough fish.

Georgia (58,876 square miles in area) is the largest southeastern state and has fine, varied fishing.

The state has some 300 trout streams in its northern section. An angler will not find the kind of trout fishing to make him quit Maine or Colorado; but nevertheless Georgia has trout, and provides the southern sportsman with an excellent chance to get out and enjoy some sport with these fine fish. Some trout streams here include Jones Creek, Montgomery Creek, Nimblewill Creek and Rock Creek located near Black Mountain. Above Gainesville, Georgia, there are the Chattahoochee River, Dukes Creek and Chestattee River. West of Morgantown are the Jacks River and Fightingtown Creek, while the trout streams around Hiawassee include the Hiawassee River and Corbin Creek.

The Soque River and Goshen Creek are located near Clarksville.

Elevations go as high as the 4,784-foot Brasstown Bald Mountain in northern Georgia, and the swift-running streams in these mountains enable trout to survive. The Georgia Fish Commission deserves many thanks, too, for it works diligently to maintain the species.

The state is primarily noted for warm-water game fish, and

any angler looking for largemouth bass will never be disappointed. Northern Georgia holds Burton Lake, Lake Blue Ridge, Nottely Lake, Lake Rabun, Nacoochee Lake, Tallulah Lake and Tugaloo Lake. Fishing camps are plentiful here, with 4 on Lake Burton alone, including Wilkel's, La Prade, Jones' and Hill's. Tallulah Falls and Tallulah Gorge are between Tallulah Lake and Tugaloo Lake. Smallmouth and largemouth bass, crappie, bluegill, and catfish are the regular catches.

The Chatuge Reservoir lies in North Carolina and Georgia. Boats can be hired in the town of Hiawassee for good bass and crappie fishing.

Further east along the South Carolina border just a few miles above Augusta is Clark Hill Reservoir. Bass, bluegill and crappie are the fish in this huge 78,000-acre reservoir, with 3 state parks dotting the area.

Lake Sidney Lanier, a 47,000-acre reservoir with 670 shoreline miles near Gainesville, offers fine bass and other warm-water game fish. This lake was completed in 1955, but it already shows signs of being another prize Georgia bass lake. Atlanta is but a few miles south of the big lake.

Allatoona Lake, offering warm-water game fish, is near Cartersville, which is located a short way northwest of Atlanta and has 2 state parks to provide for camping.

Bartletts Ferry Reservoir on the Chattahoochee River borders Georgia and Alabama. The border towns of Lanett, Alabama, and West Point, Georgia, are at the north of the lake, and warm-water fish abound. Further south on the river a new lake will appear at Fort Gaines when W. F. George Dam is complete.

The Chattahoochee River was dammed again at the Florida border, and Lake Seminole is complete. The Woodruff Dam was finished in 1957, and from reports is developing into a bass lake of importance. There are 3 state parks on the lake.

Sinclair Lake near Milledgeville supplies boats, guides and other facilities. The fishing here is for smallmouth bass, largemouth bass, bluegill, crappie and some extra-large catfish.

A unique and unusually exciting fishing area is located in southeastern Georgia—the famous or infamous Okefenokee

Swamp. The town of Waycross acts as a gateway to the swamp. Roads in the Okefenokee are as much as 30 miles apart, and the swamp is a sanctuary for birds, reptiles and fish. There is excellent sport here for the rugged visitor, and Camp Cornelia near Folkston is a fishing center where guides are obtainable for sorties into the big swamp. Guides are a must here, and in one day a guide can teach you how to walk on the decayed vegetation called houses. He will also show the angler how to bring home a mess of bass.

Although Spanish moss, cypress trees and swamp grasses are everywhere, the Okefenokee is technically not a swamp, for it drains outward. The Suwannee River has its headwaters here.

Georgia holds a long-standing world record—a 22-pound 4-ounce largemouth bass which was taken in Lake Montgomery. Unfortunately, this lake is dry now, but the new reservoir lakes make up for this loss many times over. It wouldn't surprise me if the next record-breaking bass were to come out of one of the new Georgia lakes.

Hawaii

Information from:

Board of Commissioners
    of Agriculture and Forestry
Division of Fish and Game
P.O. Box 5425
Pawaa Station
Honolulu 14, Hawaii

Fish in Hawaii: goldfish, carp, bass, trout and goby.

Hawaii, our 50th state, consists of 7 islands of Pacific paradise totaling some 6,434 square miles—islands that have some of the best salt-water sports fishing in the world off its shores. Big catches of striped marlin, blue marlin, yellowfin tuna and gigantic dolphins are a regularity. Also jack cravelle, oceanic bonito, amberjack and wahoo are sports fish that every angler can go after.

Fresh-water fishing is limited, even though there are many spectacular waterfalls and streams on the islands. This fishing is the result of the importation of various species. First imported were goldfish from China in 1867. These were planted in drainage canals, where they thrived but changed back to their darker natural colors. Next came carp, and these still thrive there. Bass were imported at the turn of the century, and now populate the reservoirs of the islands, including Wahiawa on Oahu. Trout were brought in later, and some still survive in the streams of Kauai. Goby is a small, edible fish that natives dip nets in streams and canals to catch.

Although all this angling can be enjoyable, salt-water game fishing far surpasses the limited fresh-water sport on the islands.

Idaho

Tourist information from:

Department of Commerce and Public Relations
Room 434
State House
Boise, Idaho

Fishing information from:

Idaho Fish and Game Department
518 Front Street
Boise, Idaho

Fish in Idaho: king salmon, Kokanee salmon, grayling, golden trout, cutthroat trout, brown trout, Mackinaw trout, steelhead, Kamloops (rainbow) trout, Dolly Varden trout, brook trout, smallmouth bass, sturgeon and rough fish.

When an angler thinks about Idaho's 83,557 square miles, he thinks about salmon or trout—big ones. Records bear him out, for a 32-pound, world-record Dolly Varden trout came from Lake

Pend Oreille, the same lake which gave up the world-record Kamloops (rainbow) trout—a huge 37-pounder. Another fish he thinks about is the white sturgeon, for the Snake River gave up a 360-pounder—the biggest fish ever taken in fresh water. Every year monstrous sturgeon are taken; in 1959 one 9 feet 7 inches long and weighing 320 pounds was brought in after a 2-hour struggle.

The Rocky Mountain state of Idaho comes as far south as the Nevada border and runs north to an almost triangular point at the Canadian border. Priest Lake, one of the state's famous fishing sites, is located in the north, just south of the Canadian border, in the narrow strip of land between Montana and Washington. Fishing here is for native cutthroat trout, Dolly Varden, Mackinaw and salmon. Mackinaw trout up to 51 pounds have been taken from the lake's clear, cold water. The lake offers visitors 3 marinas with boats, resorts, 2 pack-and-saddle outfits (one is Sheridan and Sons at Priest Lake) and 2 national forests camp sites. Excellent stream fishing adds to the lure of the area.

The 43-mile Lake Pend Oreille is southward near Sandpoint. This lake goes to a depth of 1,150 feet and is known for its two world records—the Kamloop and Dolly Varden trout. Other fish taken include cutthroat, perch, crappie, bass, bluegill and whitefish. Boats complete with a guide rent for about $6.00 an hour and much less without the guide. Motels and resorts are around the lake, and there are camp sites in the wilderness areas. One resort, Talache Ranch Lodge near Sandpoint, has a complete line of hunting and fishing facilities.

Further south and nearer to the Washington border by Coeur d'Alene is 125-mile-long Lake Coeur d'Alene. This is a resort area that has all kinds of facilities. Cutthroat-trout fishing is tops in the lake, which also has Kokanee salmon and smallmouth bass. The area offers a variety of fishing, for the St. Joe, Coeur d'Alene and Spokane rivers all have cutthroat trout and Dolly Varden trout. There is good bass fishing in many small lakes of the area, and another specialty is Fernan Creek, which is a fishing spot reserved strictly for children.

The world-famous Snake River flows across the southern portion of Idaho to Caldwell, where it swings north and makes up the western border of Idaho as far north as Lewiston. The Snake offers fishing for steelhead, king salmon (Chinook) and monstrous white sturgeon.

Another equally famous Idaho river is the Salmon, often called the River of No Return. This river is in the middle of the state, and its South Fork and Middle Fork draw fishermen from all over the world to try for the big salmon and trout. Outfitters such as Lea Bacos Guide Service, P.O. Box 2602, Boise, Idaho, arrange white-water float trips on the Salmon and Snake rivers. Trips can be arranged through Smother's Salmon River Lodge, Shoup, Idaho.

Don L. Smith of North Fork, Idaho, is another old hand at guiding floats on the Salmon. One of his fishing specialties is a six-day, 120-mile float trip on the Salmon which allows plenty of time to fish and wander into the tributaries along the wilderness route of the trip. The cost is $250 per person for 4 or more, and it includes food. Rainbow trout, Dolly Varden and cutthroat trout are caught in this river. Prize Chinook salmon running over 20 pounds are taken constantly. A trip on the Middle Fork is more expensive than one on the North Fork, because all equipment has to be flown in.

The winter resort of Sun Valley near Ketchum offers good stream- and lake-fishing opportunities in the Big and Little Wood rivers and Silver Creek. Many high mountain lakes can be reached by 1-day pack trips from here.

Southern Idaho has memorable fishing in many places. The Island Park–St. Anthony area is a well-known resort section, with lodges, motels and inns. The North Fork of the Snake River has good rainbow-trout fishing, which is best below the dam of the Ashton Reservoir. The Teton River, accessible by rubber boat, holds cutthroat and rainbows. Bitch Creek has rainbows, and Henry's Lake Outlet has brookies, rainbows and cutthroats. Lake fishing here includes 8,000-acre Island Park Reservoir, with rainbows and salmon, and 5,500-acre Henry's Lake, with big native cutthroat and brook trout. Island Park Reservoir has boats for rentals. The Targhee National Forest offers a choice of camp sites for its visitors with pack trips that regularly head into the forest.

Bear Lake, located on the Utah border, is a resort area that offers fishing for rainbow trout, lake trout and whitefish.

The state of Idaho gives the modern angler an excellent chance to fish in waters that are as good now as they were in the old days. And the modern angler with light equipment can have sport better than he ever dreamed possible—for what old-timer ever had the fun of holding a 20-pound trout on a light fly rod or a spinning rod?

Magazine dealing with Idaho outdoors:

Idaho Fishing and Hunting Guide—An annual
611 Hays Street   Cost: 75 cents
Boise, Idaho

Illinois

Tourist information from:

Department of Information Service
Room 406
State Capital
Springfield, Illinois

Fishing information from:

Division of Fisheries
102 State Office Building
Springfield, Illinois

Fish in Illinois: Largemouth bass, smallmouth bass, bluegill, sunfish, crappie, channel catfish, bullhead, carp, northern pike, walleye, yellow perch, rock bass and other fish.

Illinois, the "Green State," stretches south from Lake Michigan almost 500 miles to Mound City and is 56,400 square miles in area. Fishing in the state centers on 341 fishable streams with over 7,000 miles of water, and 344 public fishing lakes.

In the north in Lake County near the towns of Fox Lake and Antioch are the Fox Chain-O'-Lakes, which include Fox, Pistakee, Channel, Petite, Catherine, Bluff, Grass, Marie and Nippersink lakes. These lakes have largemouth bass, northern pike, walleye pike (not in Bluff Lake), rock bass, crappie, channel catfish, and sunfish. Fishing is only adequate here, but there are camping and boating facilities; and the lakes are only 40 miles from Chicago, which makes them a popular escape area.

Silcam Spring Lake, a smallmouth-bass lake, is located in Adams County near Kellerville in the middle western part of the state. Rice Lake, in the center of the state near Banner, has 1,000 acres noted for largemouth-bass fishing. Walleye and bluegill and crappie are here too. The Kickapoo State Park lakes near Oakwood consist of 11 small lakes where largemouth bass, bluegill, crappie, channel catfish and carp run. In the southern extreme of the state, there is Murphysboro Lake near Cairo, Crab Orchard and Little Grass lakes near Carbondale—all of which hold largemouth bass, sunfish, crappie and bullhead. Crab Orchard is the biggest lake in the state, 103 shore-line miles, and it is a Federal-controlled land that has complete camping and boating facilities.

The Mississippi River makes up the entire border of Illinois. Fish caught here include northern pike, walleye, bass, sunfish, channel catfish and others. The Ohio and Illinois rivers flow into the Mississippi and have the same general sports fish. State parks with fishing facilities are Fort Kaskaskia and Mississippi Palisades for the Mississippi River, and Cave-in-Rock and Fort Massac for the Ohio River. On the Illinois River are located Buffalo Rock, Illini, and Pere Marquette parks. A suggested trip for power boats on the Illinois River is from Starved Rock Park to Havana, Illinois. Other smaller streams are the Apple, Rock, Kankakee and Sangamon rivers. Most of the state's sports fish are found in these waters.

Crappie, the Number 1 fish of the state, are plentiful everywhere.

Magazine dealing with Illinois outdoors:

Outdoors in Illinois
State Office Building
Springfield, Illinois

Published biannually
Distributed free on request

Indiana

Tourist information from:

Department of Commerce and Public Relations
333 State House
Indianapolis, Indiana

Fishing information from:

Indiana Department of Conservation
State House
Indianapolis, Indiana

Fish in Indiana: largemouth bass, smallmouth bass, bluegill, crappie, carp, northern pike, walleye pike, rainbow trout, brown trout, brook trout, bullhead, channel catfish, cisco and other rough fish.

"The Hoosier State" of Indiana (36,291 square miles) is bordered by Lake Michigan on the north, the Ohio River on the south and has some interesting fishing in between.

The lakes of Indiana are not large, but there are over 1,000 of them available for fishing. The northeastern section of the state has the best sports fishing.

Northern pike, smallmouth bass, rock bass and channel catfish run in the St. Joseph's River near Elkhart. The Elkhart River in the same area has bass. The Little Elkhart River and Emma

Creek are considered to be two of Indiana's best brown and rainbow streams. Pigeon River, Fawn River and Curtis Creek in La Grange County are fine trout streams.

Wawasee Lake near Syracuse (2,600 acres) is one of the biggest lakes in the state. It has northern pike, walleye pike, largemouth and smallmouth bass and crappie. Boats and camping facilities are here. Lake James (1,000 acres) over in the far northeast corner of the state near Angola has virtually the same species of fish as Wawasee Lake. Most of the northeastern lakes offer good fishing for northern pike and bass.

Hamilton Lake (765 acres) near Hamilton has largemouth bass, bluegill, northern pike and crappie. Lake Gage, in the same area, is considered one of the best fishing lakes in the state. It has rainbow trout, walleye pike, largemouth and smallmouth bass and northern pike. Cisco (chub) netting is popular here, as it is in the other lakes of the area.

The Wabash River makes up a good portion of the western border of the state and then cuts across it. This river and its tributaries—the Mississinewa, the Eel and the Tippecanoe rivers —have good channel catfishing. The Tippecanoe also has northern pike, smallmouth and rock bass in its northern waters, while the Eel River is a bass river.

In the northwest there is Pine Lake near La Porte, which has over 500 acres with largemouth bass and bluegill. Lakes Shafer and Freeman near Monticello cover 2,800 acres and are in a resort area that has camping, boating and guides available. The catch here would be channel catfish and silver bass. Bass Lake near Knox has 1400 acres and is good for bass, walleye, crappie and bluegill. Lake Michigan fishing is for big perch or for smelt, which are netted.

The White River running southwest from Indianapolis is noted for its white perch and large channel catfish, while Hovey Lake near Mount Vernon has pan fishing. Streams, rivers and lakes of the southeast generally produce crappie and channel catfish.

The best fishing in Indiana is in its northeast section, where the waters are cold and clear, and in the bigger lakes.

Iowa

Tourist information from:

Iowa Development Commission
200 Jewett Building
Des Moines 9, Iowa

Fishing information from:

Iowa State Conservation Commission
East Seventy and Court
Des Moines, Iowa

Fish in Iowa: largemouth bass, smallmouth bass, white bass, yellow bass, northern pike, pickerel, walleye pike, crappie, bluegill, catfish, rainbow trout, brown trout and rough fish.

Corn grows tall, women beautiful and fish big in the 56,280-square-mile state of Iowa. This state is bordered by the Mississippi River on the east, and the Sioux and Missouri rivers on the west.

Its rivers and most of its 16,000 miles of running water are too silted to support trout; but in the northeast, near the Wisconsin-Minnesota borders there are some trout waters, some of which include Waterloo Creek near Dorchester, Village Creek near Lansing, Paint Creek near Waterville, Bloody Run near McGregor and Buck Creek near Garnavillo. Even these northern streams are not conducive to trout propagation, because they have to be restocked constantly.

There is good canoeing in the Yellow River at Yellow River State Forest near McGregor. Smallmouth bass and catfish can be caught here.

Clear Lake in the north contains 3,600 acres of fine fishing water near the town of Clear Lake. Species there are largemouth bass, northern pike, walleye, and yellow bass. White bass, channel catfish, bluegill and crappie are present in adequate numbers, too. The lake is widely known for its yellow-bass fishing. The state park at the lake provides a lodge, camping, a trailer park and boats.

Further west along the Minnesota border, there are the lakes of East Okoboji (2,000 acres) and West Okoboji (4,000 acres). Fishing is for largemouth bass, crappie, bluegill, northern pike, walleye, yellow perch and bullhead. The state park on West Okoboji has a lodge, overnight camping, a trailer camp and boats.

The same general area contains Spirit Lake, a 5,500-acre shallow lake with fine largemouth bass, crappie and bluegill. Other lake fish can be caught here, too. Lodging is plentiful in the area, and boats are available at the lake.

Five Island Lake near Ruthven has 950 acres, but is only 3 to 5 feet deep. This water is known for its perch and bullhead fishing. The lake has boats available.

Coming a little south but still in the northwest of the state, near the city of Storm Lake, is Storm Lake, 3,000 acres with what are considered the best walleye pike in the state. Other fish include white bass, crappie, channel catfish and bullhead. A state park provides boats and picnicking facilities.

Further south along the Raccoon River is Black Hawk Lake (950 acres) near Lake View. This is a popular fishing lake, and catches of crappie and bullhead are good. Then, too, the largemouth bass, walleye, and pan fish of the lake always keep an angler busy. A state park provides boats, baits and cabins.

The middle and southern portions of Iowa do not have large lakes available for fishing, except some oxbows of the Mississippi and Missouri rivers. Best known is Lake Odessa near Wapello, with largemouth bass and crappie.

The Mississippi River on the eastern border of Iowa runs through some steep limestone bluffs in the north, and the best fishing is behind some dams, for walleye. Largemouth bass, crappie, carp and other rough fish also run in this river.

The Des Moines River runs vertically through the center of the state and provides fine chances for canoeing. There are smallmouth bass, walleye and northern pike in the northern sections of the river, and channel catfish and flathead in the southern portions. The East Fork of the Des Moines is a fine sportsfishing stream.

The Big Sioux River of the western border has channel catfish, but its water is too polluted to support other sports fish. The Little Sioux River to the east has walleye. These rivers both drain into the Missouri, which continues south as the western border of the state. Fish caught in the Missouri River are mostly channel catfish, blue catfish, crappie and bullhead, but occasionally other sports fish are taken. Fishing should get better in future years, for pollution control is now exercised on the Missouri.

Iowa offers a real fishing bargain in the State Conservation Commission book, *Iowa Fish and Fishing*—an excellent survey of angling in the state. A $2.50 check to the Commission will bring this 377-page book, which clearly reflects the active efforts of the conservation interests in Iowa to improve fishing conditions.

Periodical for Iowa outdoors:

> Iowa Conservationist   Cost: $1.00 a year
> The State Conservation Department
> East 7th and Court
> Des Moines 8, Iowa

Kansas

Tourist information from:

> Industrial Development Commission
> State Office Building
> Room 122 S
> Topeka, Kansas

Fishing information:

> Kansas Forestry, Fish and Game Commission
> Pratt, Kansas

Fish in Kansas: flathead catfish, channel catfish, bullhead, white bass, largemouth bass, crappie, bluegill, sunfish, walleye, drum and rough fish.

The "Sunflower State" of Kansas (82,276 square miles) has several major rivers with an abundance of warm-water game fish. These are the Arkansas River, running through the heart of the state, and the Smoky Hill-Kansas and the Cimarron rivers in the western part of the state. Countless other tributaries and feeder streams flow into these major rivers, and fish taken are flathead catfish, up to 70 pounds, and giant channel catfish. The smaller rivers and streams have crappie, sunfish, bluegill and bullhead.

Kansas lists thousands of ponds, 39 state-controlled lakes and 8 federal reservoirs. The bigger bodies of water are the Cedar Bluff Reservoir (6,600 acres of water south of Wakeeney), the Kirwin Reservoir (5,000 acres near Kirwin), and Webster Reservoir (4,000 acres southwest of Stockton)—all in the northwest part of the state. Fish in these reservoirs and in other larger bodies of water in the state generally include white bass, walleye, crappie, largemouth bass, channel catfish, bluegill and bullhead.

Southwest Kansas has 3,000-acre Kearny Reservoir, east of Lakin, which is also known as Lake McKinney. Clark County State Lake near Kingsdown holds 337 acres of water and is one of the deepest lakes in the state. Finney County State Lake (324 acres) is periodically restocked with warm-water game fish, including bass, bluegill, crappie and channel catfish.

Kanopolis Reservoir in central Kansas is a 3,500-acre body of water. It is near the town of Marquette and offers cabins, camping and picnicking. Lovewell Reservoir near Lovewell is 3,000 acres. Harington City Lake (364 acres) and Lake Council Grove (343 acres) offer camping facilities. Fish found in the big lakes of the northeast are bass, crappie, bluegill, catfish, walleye and drum.

In southeast Kansas is Fall River Reservoir, 2,600 acres of water near Eureka, Kansas. Then Lake Bluestem (El Dorado City Lake) is 870 acres. Smaller lakes in the area include Cowley, Butler, and Neosho county state lakes and Eureka City Lake. Marais des Cygnes Waterfowl Refuge on the Marais des Cygnes River near Pleasanton has three shallow lakes with 1,500 acres of water. Fishing here is good in the spring and early summer before aquatic vegetation limits the sport.

Kansas lakes will drop considerably during a dry spell; all acreage figures are for full lakes.

This state is proud of its big catfish, and they highlight its fishing.

Kentucky

Tourist information from:

Department of Public Relations
Capital Annex
Frankfort, Kentucky

Fishing information from:

Department of Fish and Wildlife Resources
Capital Annex
Frankfort, Kentucky

Kentucky has 32 state parks, of which 13 have motels or cottages, fishing and boating. For further information write to:

Division of Parks
Capital Annex
Frankfort, Kentucky

Fish in Kentucky: walleye pike, bluegill, channel catfish, flathead catfish, crappie, smallmouth and largemouth bass, white and striped bass, muskellunge, sauger, rainbow trout and rough fish.

The "Bluegrass State" of Kentucky (40,395 square miles) has 14,000 miles of running water, an endless number of ponds, and 5 major reservoir lakes, all offering good fishing.

The Ohio River forms the whole northern border of the state, and its tributaries constitute the state's drainage system. The west has the Green River and its two tributaries, the Nolin and the Barren rivers—all three of which are well known for muskie.

These and other rivers were once the main arteries of transportation in Kentucky and are still important to industry and sportsmen.

Float trips are famous on the river, and fishermen get big bass and catfish in the waters. Bowling Green is an excellent jump-off place for fishing the rivers. The Green River flows through Mammoth National Park, famous for its gigantic caves.

The Kentucky River joins the Ohio at Carrollton, and this river—as well as its tributaries, Eagle Creek, Elkhorn Creek and the Red River—is a bass river. The Red has some muskie. The rivers are floatable up to Irvine, but there are not many boats available, so an angler should bring his own.

Part of the early run of the Cumberland River is in southern Kentucky, in Cumberland National Forest into Lake Cumberland. After this the Cumberland flows through Tennessee and into western Kentucky as part of Lake Kentucky again, before disappearing into the Ohio River. The southeastern portion of this river has bass, crappie and walleye pike. Fishing is popular in winter for the late winter run of walleye. The tributaries, Rockcastle River and the Laurel River, which run through Cumberland National Forest are especially famous for these fish. The big lake has fine fishing for largemouth bass, smallmouth bass, Kentucky rock and white bass, walleye, crappie, bluegill and catfish. Below Cumberland Dam, rainbow trout have been stocked, and in the western part of the state the river has channel catfish, bass and perch.

All the important lakes in the state are reservoirs. Kentucky Lake in the west has 2,380 miles of shore line and has largemouth and smallmouth bass, white bass, crappie, walleye and pan fish. Crappie fishing in the spring is superb. Boats are available at Murray, Benton, Eddyville, Golden Pond, Grand River, New Concord and Gilbertsville. Tourist facilities are plentiful.

Reservoir Lake Cumberland began in 1951 with the completion of Wolf Creek Dam. This 105-mile-long lake has 1,255 miles of shoreline and has an average depth of 90 feet. It is a bass lake of supreme importance. Walleye are another important sports fish here, with 5- 10-pounders common, and trophy 20-

pounders have already been taken. Also taken are catfish, crappie, bluegill and pan fish. Boats are available at Albany, Burnside, Corbin, Jamestown, Monticello and in Cumberland Falls State Park.

Herrington Lake is a 31-mile long 3,600-acre lake in the center of the bluegrass region of the state. The lake is known for its white bass (or striped bass, as they are sometimes called), and spring runs of white bass up the Dix River regularly get anglers their 60-per-day limit. Tourist facilities are good, and boats are at Burgin, Danville and Lancaster.

Dale Hollow Reservoir is one of the best-known bass lakes in the county. The world-record smallmouth bass—11 pounds 15 ounces—came from here in 1955. Crappie and bluegill are also in this lake, which is located on the Kentucky-Tennessee border. Accommodations and boats are at Albany.

Dewey Lake, completed in 1949, is in the eastern part of the state and is 165 miles long and has 860 acres of water. This is an uncrowded area where accommodations and boats are found at nearby Prestonsburg. The lake has bass, crappie, bluegill and rough fish in good supply.

Bass fishing is an all-year sport in Kentucky, with bass jigging popular in the winter. Kentucky fishing—winter, spring, summer or fall—is good and should get better every year. With all the relatively new water developments, more record bass will come out of these lakes soon.

Louisiana

Tourist information from:

    Department of Highways
    Box 4245 Capitol Station
    Baton Rouge 4, Louisiana

Fishing information from:

    Louisiana Wild Life and Fisheries Commission
    Baton Rouge 4, Louisiana

Fish in Louisiana: largemouth bass, smallmouth bass, white bass, spotted bass, yellow bass, pickerel, crappie, bluegill, channel catfish, blue catfish, gar, carp and other rough fish.

No closed season in Louisiana.

If Napoleon had been a fisherman we would never have been able to buy Louisiana, for no fisherman would ever sell such a hot-spot. The state is 48,523 square miles and has bass, bass and more bass throughout its waters.

Some fine fishing in Louisiana is in the dozen or so oxbow lakes near the Mississippi River. These lakes came about through a change in the river course, and some of them still have a water connection with the great river. One of the oxbows is Lake Providence, which is near Highland in the north of the state, and on which there are boats, restaurants and a 30-unit motel. Lake Bruin near Newellton and Lake St. John near Spokane hire out boats for fishing.

Lake Concordia near Ferriday is a well-known bass lake. On this oxbow, catches are best in the spring and late fall. There are complete accommodations here.

Going further south along the river there is Lake Old River near Morganza. The various fishing camps on the lake have built large rafts that are anchored, and the lake fishing is done from them. The fee for fishing is small, and the catches of bluegill and crappie are good.

The oxbow Lake False River near New Roads is only a few miles from Baton Rouge and is one of the most popular lakes in the state. This is a clear, deep lake, almost 100 feet in places, and it supports a vigorous bass population. Other warm-water game fish can be caught here, too.

A unique experience for the Louisiana angler is fishing in the state's many swamp areas, where bass can be taken in 1 or 2 feet of water. This is mostly top fishing in among the grasses, where the bass can be seen smashing up at a lure. One such area is near Marksville, where there are overflow lakes, bayous, and plenty of swampy fishing areas. Marksville has accommodations, and Marksville State Park is in the area.

Morgan City is another swamp-fishing center, and throughout much of the southern section there is ample opportunity for marsh fishing. Sometimes ducks and geese are so thick in southern Louisiana that it is hard for a nonresident to believe what he sees. There are many waterfowl refuges in southern Louisiana.

There are many fine lakes in the state. In the northwest corner on the Texas border is Caddo Lake, where cypress trees and aquatic vegetation create a good basis for fish life, and there are sizable catches of smallmouth bass, crappie, channel catfish, gar and pickerel.

Near Shreveport, Cross Lake has excellent white-bass fishing. Catches of bass, catfish, crappie and bluegill also run high. There are guides at Rainbow Camp in Shreveport. There are plenty of bayous here where bass lurk and hit hard. South of the city, Wallace Lake is another good spot for fishing.

Lake Bistineau near Minden has Lake Bistineau State Park, where there is camping and boating. Fish in the lake are all of the warm-water game-fish variety. Not too many miles east of the lake is Driskill Mountain, a mere 535 feet high. This is the highest spot in Louisiana, which clearly shows how close to sea level the land is. Couple this lack of elevation with the fact that over 40 per cent of the nation's drainage funnels through Louisiana, and it is easy to understand why there is so much marsh and swamp land and so much water.

The rivers that bring the water through the state are, of course, headed by the great Mississippi River; but the lesser rivers, Atchafalaya, the Sabine and Calcasieu, all carry their share of water. Fishing for gar, catfish and other rough fish is common in the rivers. The Red and the Tensas rivers have bass fishing along their routes.

Considered by many to be the finest fishing lakes in the state are those in the Black Lake area, including Black, Clear and Saline lakes. There are fishing lodges here, and one lodge is Black Lake Lodge in Chestnut, Louisiana. Cabins, boats and guides are available for the visiting fisherman, and fishing is for largemouth bass, white bass and bluegill, with crappie and catfish common.

Catahoula Lake in the central section of the state has fine bass and other warm-water game fishing.

There is even excellent fishing in and near the city of New Orleans.

There is salt-water fishing in Lake Pontchartrain, and in Pearl River and other streams there are fine bass, bluegill and goggle-eye.

Louisiana has an endless supply of warm water, most of it seething with fish. About the only fishing problem is keeping back the rough fish, for in some areas they tend to overpopulate and stunt other species. But one thing an angler can depend on when venturing to Louisiana is the plenteous bass that wait for him in every corner of the state.

Further information on Louisiana outdoors:

Fishing and Boating in Louisiana
    by Grits Gresham   Paperback book: $2.25
Published by Tom Publications
Box 1703
Shreveport, Louisiana

Maine

Tourist information from:

Maine Development Commission
State House
Augusta, Maine

Lists of fishing camps and guides from:

Maine Publicity Bureau
Gateway Circle
Portland 4, Maine

Fish in Maine: Atlantic salmon, landlocked salmon, lake trout, rainbow trout, brook trout, brown trout, bass, pickerel, white perch, pan fish, rough fish, and largemouth and smallmouth bass.

The fisherman who complains about a fishing let-down in the hot months will find the state of Maine (33,215 square miles) a haven. Here the weather never gets so hot that the fish have to dive to survive, and they remain hungry and active all summer long.

Maine, like many northern states, is heavy with lakes—over 2,500 of them. Many have been left by the retreating glaciers of prehistoric times. The streams and rivers that feed these lakes are cold-water and full of trout, but many of the lakes have landlocked salmon which thrive in them. These salmon originally came into the lakes from the sea but were cut off, and instead of dying they flourished in the fresh water. The Conservation Department has been busy artificially planting salmon throughout the state, and consequently the fish are found in many more lakes than they lived in originally. Some of the best salmon waters include Eagle, Long, Chesuncook, Moosehead and Sebago lakes, to mention just a few.

Other fish found in the state include the exotic Atlantic salmon, which comes in from the sea to spend the summer in 7 of the state's rivers. These are:

1. Machias
2. East Machias
3. Narraguagus
4. Dennys
5. Sheepscot
6. Pleasant
7. Penobscot

Trout abound in Maine's cold water. The brookie can be picked up in most of the cold, fast streams. Rainbow trout live in the lakes, and the Wyman Dam pool in the Kennebec River at Bingham is a world-famous spot for big ones. Brown trout have rapidly found the state's waters to their liking and have propagated rapidly. The majestic togue, the lake trout, is a resident of Maine's waters who can add excitement to any fisherman's day.

Another Maine fish is the black bass; but the smallmouth bass is more common, for the colder waters are more to his liking. Pickerel are also plentiful, and in one county it is even permissible to sell them. The white perch is a hard-fighting pan fish that is in generous supply along with sunfish and other pan fish.

To get a picture of the best fishing waters of the state, divide Maine into three sections. The most northern would include all the land south of the Canadian border down to a line running from the south of Chesuncook Lake to Calais. Here is some of the best trout and salmon fishing anywhere. The connecting lakes—Long, Mud, Cross, Square, Eagle, St. Froid and Portage lakes—make up the fish river chain. Other fine spots include Chesuncook, Pemadumcook and Millinocket lakes, and Sourdnahunk Lake and Stream. Much of the area is rugged, and the fisherman planning a vacation should write for a guide. Fishing camps that can be used as a headquarters are located at Musquacook Lakes, Munsungan Lakes or Millinocket. White-water canoeing, camping and fishing in exciting waters are a prime lure of the area.

The central section of the state would run from where the first section stops south to a line going from Rangeley to Augusta and out to the ocean. It is here that most of the Atlantic salmon rivers are located. The eastern central portion is where fishing for bass, pickerel, and white perch gets as popular as the pure trout-salmon fishing in the northern region.

There is excellent salmon fishing in Grand Lake (16,000 acres), one of the original salmon lakes. To the east the waters of Grand Lake spill into Big Lake, which is an excellent bass lake. Spednic Lake is another famous bass lake. Eastern Grand Lake (11,500 acres) is a salmon and togue lake. The town of Topsfield is located in the center of this area, and all the lakes and streams can be reached from there. Pickerel and white perch are in most of the lakes of this area, many of which also have brook trout.

Cold Stream Pond, north of Bangor, is a salmon and togue center. Also out of Bangor, lakes such as Phillips Lake, Green

Lake, Branch Pond or Graham Lake can be reached for salmon, brook, brown or lake trout as well as for bass or pickerel. Then, too, the Penobscot River running by Bangor is an Atlantic salmon river.

Located near Waterville, Maine, there are the six lakes that make up the Belgrade Lakes Region, which is famous for its largemouth and smallmouth bass.

Off in the western portion of this central district of Maine there is Moosehead Lake (75,000 acres), which is 40 miles long and 20 miles wide, the largest lake in the state. Salmon, trout and togue are in this clear, cold water. Greenville is a jump-off town for fishing in the big lake and in the surrounding rivers and streams. A little further south is the Dead River Region with its many ponds of cold, clear water that invigorate trout all summer long. In this area is Tim Pond, and the Chain of Ponds.

South of the line running from Rangeley to Augusta is the southern section of Maine. The town of Rangeley off in the west, on Rangeley Lake, is the center of a salmon and trout area the elevation of which is about 1,200 feet above sea level. Besides the big lake there are many other lakes, streams and ponds for trout. Quite good accommodations are to be found here.

Near the coast of the southern section, good bass fishing can be had around the towns of Readfield and Mount Vernon. The city of Augusta and Winthrop are in the center of some good trout- and bass-fishing waters. In the area further south famous Sebago Lake (30,000 acres), the second largest in the state, dominates fishing. Sebago is the spring salmon-fishing center because it is one of the first lakes to free itself of ice. Sebago was an original salmon lake, and fishing has remained good. During the summer months excellent smallmouth-bass fishing gives an angler plenty of play, and white perch, brown trout and pickerel are plentiful, too. Other smaller nearby lakes and streams also have good fishing, and an angler may venture into the area at any time and expect to find a wide range of accommodations.

Maine's world-record catches of fish—including a 4-pound

12-ounce white perch from Messalonskee Lake and a 22-pound 8-ounce landlocked salmon from Sebago Lake—clearly indicate the excellence of this state's fishing.

Maryland

Tourist information from:

Department of Information
P. O. Box 706
State Office Building
Annapolis, Maryland

Fishing information from:

Maryland Game and Inland Fish Commission
State Office Building
Annapolis, Maryland

also

Department of Tidewater Fisheries
State Office Building
Annapolis, Maryland

Fish in Maryland: largemouth bass, smallmouth bass, crappie, sunfish, brook trout, brown trout, rainbow trout, bullhead, catfish, pickerel, walleye, perch, crappie and other fish.

Maryland, a 10,577-square-mile state that borders the Atlantic Ocean, is famous for its Chesapeake Bay fishing, but it also offers fresh-water fishing within its borders.

There are two major rivers running through the state, the Susquehanna and the Potomac. The Potomac and its tributaries, including the Monocacy and Anacostia rivers, have largemouth and smallmouth bass and other warm-water fish, including catfish, sunfish, crappie and perch. The lower regions of the Potomac have salt-water fish, including striped bass. Boats in the river are available at Williamsport, Brunswick, White's Ferry, Great Falls and other towns.

The Susquehanna River in its lower regions has salt-water fish, including shad. There is good fishing where the Octoraro Creek empties into the river below Hopkins Cove. Pickerel, crappie, catfish and big bass are here, too. Largemouth hot-spots are the grassbeds on the flats of the river. The upper river is a small-mouth-bass stream.

Another river that empties into Chesapeake Bay, the Patuxent, has pickerel, shad and crappie.

Some of the biggest and best-known trout streams which are stocked regularly include Bear Creek near Grantsville; Hunting Creek near Thurmont; Evitts Creek near Flintstone; Little Antietam Creek near Hagerstown; Fishing Creek near Lewistown; and Middle Creek near Wolfsville. The Savage River near Grantsville is also a popular trout stream.

Bass streams include Flintstone Creek near Flintstone; Deer Creek near Harford County; Gunpowder River near Bradshaw; and Seneca Creek near Dawsonville.

Lakes, ponds and reservoirs include the Baltimore City reservoirs, Loch Raven, Pretty Boy Lake, Lake Roland and Lake Liberty, which have all the Maryland fish distributed through them. Big Pool and Little Pool reservoirs near Hancock have warm-water fish. Herrington Lake, Deep Creek Lake, Savage River Reservoir and Piney Reservoirs near Grantsville also have warm-water fish. In the east near the Delaware border there are Garland Lake, Smithville Pond and Chambers Lake with largemouth bass, crappie and sunfish. Deep Creek Lake near Oakland is the biggest lake in the state, with 65 miles of shore line. Its specialties are pickerel, pike, walleye, perch and bass.

The high spot of Maryland fishing is definitely Chesapeake Bay, and many of the biggest fresh-water fish taken in the state come from the brackish waters of the bay and its surrounding rivers.

Magazine dealing with Maryland outdoors:

The Maryland Conservationist
The Maryland Game and Inland Fish Commission
State Office Building
Annapolis, Maryland

Massachusetts

Tourist information from:

Department of Commerce
334 Boylston Street
Boston 16, Massachusetts

Fishing information from:

Division of Fish and Game
73 Tremont Street
Boston 8, Massachusetts

Fish in Massachusetts: Brook, brown and rainbow trout, large-mouth and smallmouth bass, pickerel and northern pike, walleye pike, bluegill, bullhead, crappie, white perch, yellow perch and other fish.

Massachusetts is a highly developed state of some 8,257 square miles. Fishing here has a long history, dating back to the Colonial Ordinances of 1641–47, which first established every citizen's right to fish in ponds of over 20 acres. There are now some 468 lakes, ponds and reservoirs open to the state's sportsmen.

Unfortunately Massachusetts is one of those states whose local reservoir managers still feel fishermen pollute water, so consequently some of its best lakes are still cut off from sport. However, many reservoirs have opened up, such as the New Bedford, Middletown and Putnamville reservoirs, to mention a few. Rod and gun clubs in the state should continue their fight to open all the reservoirs to sports fishing.

The Quabbin Reservoir (25,000 acres) north of Springfield is the biggest body of water in the state, and it has a 15-mile east branch and a 12-mile west branch. The reservoir has black bass, northern pike, walleye, perch, rainbow trout, brown trout, brook trout, bluegill and crappie. Boats and guides are here, but anglers should remember there is a small charge in addition to the regular license for fishing this water.

Other lakes include Lake Cochituate (614 acres) near Middlesex, with pan fish and stocked rainbows and brown trout. Onota Lake (665 acres) near Pittsfield is periodically stocked with rainbow and brown trout. This lake in the heart of the Berkshire vacation area also gives up bass, pike and pickerel. Big Benton Pond (332 acres) near Otis is a pickerel lake. Also Lake Pontoosuc (480 acres) near Pittsfield has chain pickerel and yellow perch. Lake Quinsigamond near Worcester has pan fish and is stocked with trout. Webster Lake (1,278 acres) near Worcester, is a bass lake.

The southeastern portion of the state has many ponds, including Assowompsett Pond near Middleboro, which have warm-water game fish. The Cape Cod area has fresh-water ponds and streams throughout its 100 miles of vacation-land. They include the trout-stocked ponds of Wakeby Pond near Mashpee, and Crystal Lake and Cliff Pond near Orleans. There are also many warm-water game fish in these and the many other ponds of the area. The Mashpee River is a trout stream.

The Connecticut River runs through the state, and from it are taken bass, walleye, pickerel and northern pike.

The Merrimack River is in the northeast of the state and flows through Lowell. This river has bass as its chief prize. The Deerfield River in the northwest running along the famous Mohawk Trail is a trout stream. The Westfield River further south near Pittsfield follows the Berkshire Trail and is also stocked with trout. Near Sturbridge, McKinstry and Hatchet brooks are stocked with trout, as are many other streams in the state.

General facilities are good throughout Massachusetts, and one never has to go far to find lodging.

The state is carrying on an aggressive fish-management program whose aim is to stock as many streams and ponds as possible. Consequently, vacationers should have easy access to a stocked stream anywhere in the state.

A free booklet, *Stocked Trout Waters of Massachusetts,* published annually by the Division of Fish and Game lists all recently stocked waters.

Magazine dealing with Massachusetts outdoors:

Massachusetts Wildlife   Bimonthly
Information and Education Section   Free subscription on
Fisheries and Game Field Headquarters   request
Westboro, Massachusetts

Michigan

Tourist information from:

Michigan Tourist Council
Stevens T. Mason Building
Lansing 26, Michigan

Fishing information from:

Michigan Conservation Department
Lansing 26, Michigan

Fish in Michigan: muskellunge, northern pike, walleye pike, largemouth and smallmouth bass, bluegill, crappie, yellow perch, smelt, brook trout, brown trout, rainbow trout, lake trout and others.

The state of Michigan (58,216 square miles) includes in its fishing opportunities 11,037 lakes, more than 36,000 miles of streams along 3,121 miles of shore line bordering four of the Great Lakes.

Fishing is found throughout the state, and some of the best opportunities are in the Great Lakes. Lake Superior (31,810 square miles) offers some lake-trout fishing, but most of it has been ruined by the lamprey scourge. This fishing will get better, for the chemical "lampricide" has begun to control the lamprey eel. Isle Royal National Park (130,000 acres) is an island located 50 miles off the Keweenaw Peninsula of upper Michigan. This island has ferries running to it from Cooper Harbor or Hancock. There is fishing here for brook trout, rainbow trout and small-mouth bass.

Lake Michigan (22,400 square miles) is considered practically a private lake by Michigan natives. Fishing here is for yellow perch, which is the Number 1 fish, while many largemouth and smallmouth bass are taken on the shores of the lake. The northern sections of Lake Michigan have rainbow trout (lake steelhead) and brown trout. Other fish are walleye and smelt. Smelt fishing is especially popular in the northern sections and also in the lower sections of the lake near Chicago, where the fish are taken in dip nets and gill nets by hundreds of fishermen lining the shores.

Lake Huron (23,010 square miles) has fine smallmouth-bass fishing along its Michigan shore line. Walleye are plentiful in the lake and in Saginaw Bay, a renowned walleye hot-spot. Smelt netting is another popular sport in the spring.

Lake St. Clair, which lies just east of Detroit between Lake Huron and Lake Erie, is well known for its big, hard-fighting muskie. Many a mighty muskie has been taken within sight of the Detroit skyline. However, the most popular fish of this lake is yellow perch, which is plentiful and grows big. Other fish of this lake include bass, walleye and pan fish.

Lake Erie (9,940 square miles) touches the southeastern tip of Michigan. It has black and white bass, walleye and perch.

The Upper Peninsula has fishing in streams and lakes, and there is fine brook-trout fishing throughout the area. The brookie is a native of the Upper Peninsula and has always thrived there.

This northern section of Michigan has two national forests. Hiawatha National Forest is in the center of the peninsula and has many small lakes that have trout and walleye. Big and Little De Noc bays on the southern part of the forest bordering Lake Michigan are excellent walleye-fishing spots. Northern pike, perch and smelt round out the other sports fish of the bays. Within the park Indian Lake (8,000 acres) near Manistique has good northern pike, walleye, perch and rock bass. Further to the east there is Manistique Lake (10,130 acres) near Curtis, which has northern pike, perch, walleye, rock bass and smallmouth bass. Still further to the east and directly north of the Mackinac Straits, now spanned by the famous Mackinac Bridge, is the Marquette National Forest, which is noted for its trout fishing and camping.

Throughout the Upper Peninsula there are canoe trails such as the Black River near Bessemer (for experts only), the Ontonagon near Ontonagon, the Escanaba River near Gwinn—all of which are trout streams. Canoe fishing trips on the Brule and Menominee rivers can bring good catches of walleye, northern pike, yellow perch and smallmouth bass.

Michigan fishing in the lower peninsula has hot-spots like West Michigan's 17,000-acre Lake Charlevoix near Boyne City. Fish caught here are lake trout, brown trout, bass, northern pike, bluegill, yellow perch and smelt. This lake has complete facilities nearby and boats on its shores.

Shortly south from here on Highway 31 are Torch Lake and Elk Lake near Rapid City. These are two fine hot-spots for lake trout, while the muskie, northern pike and walleye of the lakes can add to the fisherman's pleasure.

Still following Route 31 south along Lake Michigan there is the 9,700-acre Crystal Lake near Frankfort. Here smelt were first introduced to the Great Lakes states in 1912. These little sports fish took so well that they were soon transplanted to the Great Lakes, and the rest is history. Other fish in Crystal Lake include lake trout, perch and rock bass.

Southwestern Michigan has many small lakes, most of which have fishing for bluegill and black crappie.

Eastern Michigan, starting near Cheboygan, has many fine fishing opportunities, including Mullett Lake (16,600 acres) and Topinabee Lake, both of which are easily accessible from Cheboygan. Lake fishing is primarily for walleye, northern pike and bass, while there is muskie fishing in the Cheboygan River. Black Lake (10,130 acres), above Onaway offers camping in Onaway State Park on its shores. Fishing is for smallmouth bass, walleye, northern pike, rock bass and perch.

Further south near Spruce is Hubbard Lake (8,800 acres), where there are brook trout, walleye, bass and yellow perch. Guides, boats, camping and motels are in the area for the visitor.

As part of its attraction, the Huron National Forest has 18 completed camp sites and a winter-resort area besides trout fishing and canoeing in the Au Sable River and Pond. Brook, brown and

Minnesota

Tourist information from:

Division of Publicity
Department of Business Development
State Office Building
St. Paul 1, Minnesota

Fishing information from:

Division of Game and Fish
Department of Conservation
St. Paul 1, Minnesota

Fish in Minnesota: walleye pike, northern pike, muskellunge, sauger, largemouth bass, smallmouth bass, lake trout, brown trout, rainbow trout, brook trout, crappie, bluegill, carp, perch, catfish and others.

Minnesota has 84,068 square miles, of which 4,059 square miles are fresh water. This adds up to the largest and best fresh-water fishing in America. It would be hard to conceive going more than 1 mile in any direction in Minnesota and not coming to some fishing water, for there are more than 5,000 lakes of over 40 acres in this state, which bills itself as the "State of 10,000 Lakes."

The far northeastern portion of the state bordering Lake Superior is the area of the Superior National Forest. Here there are thousands of lakes teeming with such northern specialties as walleye pike and northern pike. Canoe fishing and camping are favorites of the area, and trips can be arranged through many outfitters including: Bill Rom, Canoe Country outfitters, Ely, Minnesota; or the Lac La Croix Fishing Lodge, 1200 East White Street, Ely, Minnesota. Much of this country is wilderness, and guides should accommodate out-of-staters on trips. Fish can be caught in the thousands of small lakes or the big ones such as Vermilion Lake (38,000 acres) near Tower, Kabetogama Lake (20,000 acres) near Ray, Basswood Lake (13,000 acres) near Ely, and Pelican Lake (12,000 acres) or in the Kawishiwi River. Basswood Lake

rainbow trout are regularly stocked into the Au Sable. There
Higgins Lake (9,600 acres) and Houghton Lake (20,000 ac
near Roscommon. Houghton Lake has fishing for walleye, no
ern pike, bluegill and Michigan's favorite—yellow perch—wl
the smaller Wiggins Lake has smallmouth bass, rock bass, wl
fish and lake trout. Lodging and boats are available here, j
as they are at most of the state's major lakes.

A few miles west of the Huron Forest is the city of Cadilla
which is also headquarters for the Manistee National Forest. Th
forest has over a dozen finished camp sites and has many lake
where fish are plentiful. Some of the best fishing is in 1,100-acr
Lake Cadillac, where bass, perch, northern pike, walleye, bluegil
and crappie make up the sport. Nearby is 2,580-acre Mitchell
Lake with largemouth bass, walleye, bluegill, rock bass and perch
waiting for the fisherman.

Southeastern Michigan has good quantities of bluegill and
crappie in its many lakes and ponds.

Some of the state's finest fishing opportunities are in its 45
recommended canoe trails, where canoeing, camping and fishing
are supreme. Some trails on the Lower Peninsula include the
Thunder Bay River near Lachine, the Muskegon River upstream
from Muskegon, and the Tittabawasse River upstream from
Saginaw. Never leave a fishing pole home on these trips, for
there are opportunities for pike, bass or other gamesters along the
way.

For a complete list of trails write to the Michigan Tourist
Council for their free booklet *Canoe Trails of Michigan*. On the
same card ask for a *Michigan Campground Directory* and *Fishing in Michigan*, and all the information for a wonderful trip will
be at your fingertips.

Whether the sportsman's wish is Great Lakes fishing, pond
fishing, stream fishing, float trips or shore-line smelt netting,
Michigan is a state that has all the facilities to give him the sport
of his choice. With the help of this state's excellent Chamber
of Commerce, an angler can really plan his trip to Michigan to
the last detail.

has earned a reputation as one of the best smallmouth-bass lakes in the country, while the Kawishiwi River is noted for its northern-pike fishing. Other fish of the area include walleye pike, largemouth and smallmouth bass, crappie and carp.

The fishing in the beautiful cold, clear water of Lake Superior has been ruined by lamprey eels. This lake, which still holds the record for lake trout—a 51½-pounder—has been hit by this scourge and cleaned of fish; but now that science has found a lampricide, the lake will soon show vast increases in trout fishing.

Further west along the Minnesota-Canadian border is 345-square-mile Rainy Lake. Fish here include largemouth and smallmouth bass, northern pike, walleye and crappie. Complete facilities are at International Falls. One unusual fishing opportunity is provided by Northernaire Floating Lodges, Mr. Phyl Kuluvar, International Falls, Minnesota, who rents houseboats to fishermen and hunters.

The gigantic Lake of the Woods (1,346 square miles of water) is on the Canadian border near Baudette. The lake has fine walleye, northern pike, lake trout, smallmouth bass and pan fish. Muskie exceeding 30 pounds regularly come from the lake. Baudette has all facilities for a visitor; however, it is fair to say that the best fishing in the lake is on the Canadian side.

South of Lake of the Woods are the Upper Red Lake and Lower Red Lake, which are well known for their walleye fishing. Northern pike and muskellunge are very much a part of the sports-fishing picture here, too. Waskish is the resort town that services the lakes with resorts, guides and boats.

The Chippewa National Forest lies west of Grand Rapids, and throughout the forest there are some fine muskellunge-fishing opportunities. The biggest lake here is Leech Lake (112,000 acres), which has muskellunge, northern pike, walleye and crappie. Other lakes include Lake Winnibigoshish (48,000 acres), Cass Lake (16,000 acres), Sand Lake and Whitefish Lake. Facilities are plentiful and may be found in any of the following towns: Squaw Lake, Cass Lake, Walker, Grand Rapids and Deer River. The Chippewa National Forest also provides camp sites for those who like to live out. This area, including all the lakes down to Mille Lacs Lake, makes up what probably amounts to the walleye pike center of the country.

Mille Lacs Lake (126,000 acres) east of Brainerd is another one of those monstrous cold lakes that make Minnesota fishing famous. The Minnesota specialties are the pike brothers—walleye and northern—with walleye fishing especially good here.

Park Rapids has the Straight River, which is famous for its big brown trout.

The resort town of Detroit Lakes is surrounded by many lakes, including Detroit Lake. Fish caught are northern pike, walleye pike, largemouth bass, bluegill and crappie. South from Detroit Lake is Lake Minnewaska (12,000 acres) near Glenwood. This lake has the same fish as those in Detroit Lake.

Southern Minnesota has fishing, too, and there are such lakes as Lake Washington near Mankato, Swan Lake near Nicollet, Lake Shetek near Currie, and Heron Lake near Windom. These and many others generally can be counted on to produce largemouth and smallmouth bass, walleye, northern pike, carp and pan fish.

Even the highly populated Minneapolis-St. Paul area has much good fishing surrounding it. Fishing is in lakes such as Forest Lake, White Bear Lake, famed Lake Minnetonka and many smaller ones. The fish generally are largemouth and smallmouth bass, walleye, northern bluegill and crappie.

The Mississippi River has its headwaters in Chippewa National Forest west of Lake Winnibigoshish and flows through the lake past Grand Rapids to Minneapolis–St. Paul, then makes up the eastern border of the state. Near Wabasha it is Lake Pepin. The upper Mississippi has muskellunge fishing, and there is smallmouth-bass fishing down to Minneapolis. Other parts of the river offer northern pike or walleye pike, while the Lake Pepin area has pike, walleye, smallmouth and largemouth bass, crappie, bluegill and some muskie. Throughout Minnesota the "ole muddy river" of the south is a cool, clear stream full of fine fishing.

The St. Croix River makes up much of the eastern border of the state before joining the Mississippi near St. Paul. The St.

Croix has good fishing for smallmouth bass, largemouth bass, northern pike, walleye pike, bluegill and crappie. The tributaries of the river have brown-trout fishing. Two other good fishing rivers that are especially noted for their smallmouth bass and walleye are the Kettle and Snake rivers.

One-third of all the fishing licenses sold in the state of Minnesota are to out-of-staters; therefore, it is no secret that the fishing of Minnesota is among the best there is in the country. And when you see some of the catches of walleye pike, northern pike, muskellunge and smallmouth bass the boys bring home, it's no wonder that fishermen come back year after year to the "State of 10,000 Lakes" to do their fishing.

Local information from:

Detroit Lakes Civic and Commerce Association
Detroit Lakes, Minnesota

International Falls Chamber of Commerce
International Falls, Minnesota

Park Rapids Headwaters Associations
Park Rapids, Minnesota

Mississippi

Tourist information from:

Economic Council
P. O. Box 1849
Jackson 5, Mississippi

Fishing information from:

Mississippi Game and Fish Commission
Jackson, Mississippi

Fish in Mississippi: largemouth bass, white bass, bluegill, crappie, walleye pike, channel catfish, gar, sunfish and rough fish.

Mississippi (47,716 square miles) has the Ole Mississippi

River making up its corkscrew western border and the Gulf of Mexico bordering it on the south. Warm-water fishing is everywhere within the state, and the best of it takes place in the new reservoir lakes, the oxbow lakes along the river, and the areas close to the Gulf.

In the northeastern corner is the TVA's Pickwick Lake, over 50 miles long. Facilities for fishing and vacationing are at Iuka. Largemouth bass, white bass, walleye pike, crappie, bluegill and channel catfish are the specialties.

A short way south of Memphis, Tennessee, is the 33,000-acre Arkabutla Reservoir. Coldwater, Mississippi, has boats available for fishing largemouth bass, white bass, crappie and channel catfish.

Thirty miles south is Sardis Lake, a 58,000-acre reservoir. Sardis State Park borders the lakes shores and offers camping facilities, with boats available to fish for the usual line of warmwater game fish.

The 65,000-acre Grenada Reservoir is located in Grenada. This lake has on its shores two state parks and Holly Springs National Forest. There are camping, boating and guides around the lake. The fish are largemouth bass, white bass, crappie, bluegill and channel cats.

The Bienville National Forest, east of Jackson, is in the midst of a pine and hardwood forest. There is one improved campsite in the park, and fishing is in the streams.

The oxbow lakes, formed by a change in the Mississippi River, are Moon Lake near Clarksdale, Lee Lake near Greenville, Eagle Lake near Vicksburg and Lake Mary near Woodville. Boats can generally be found on these lakes, where the fishing specialty is bass. Many of them have gar, while the Mississippi River itself has rough fish.

Many of the streams of the state, especially in the northeast, are muddy and sluggish, and fishing is only for catfish and gar. The city of Vicksburg has an annual gar rodeo, in which 100-pounders are taken regularly.

Fishing in the bayous and cypress swamps along the Pascagoula River in the southeast and the Pearl River in the west is for bass and gar. There is also delta fishing where bass and channel catfish mix with the fish of the Gulf.

Mississippi is a state for warm-water fishing—a state where bass grow big.

Missouri

Tourist information from:

Division of Resources and Development
Jefferson Building
Jefferson City, Missouri

Specific fishing information from:

Conservation Commission
903 Elm Street
Columbia, Missouri

Fish in Missouri: largemouth bass, smallmouth bass, rock bass, white bass, drum, bluegill, carp, channel catfish, flathead catfish, crappie, pickerel, walleye pike (jack salmon), trout and rough fish.

Missouri, "Land of the Ozarks" has 16,000 miles of fishable streams and 152,000 acres of impounded waters for fishing within its 69,674 square miles. The Mississippi River makes up the eastern border of the state, and the Missouri River travels across its girth and then makes up the northwest border. The Gasconade River is a major tributary of the Missouri. Many streams and rivers in the state are excellent for float trips, and lakes and reservoirs are plentiful.

The Missouri River is known for its channel catfish. The streams that feed the river have bass in them, and the Salt River has crappie and sunfish. In the Mississippi River crappie, sunfish, channel catfish and rough fish can be caught.

The best-known Missouri streams are the Ozark mountain group, which includes the White, Eleven Pond, Current, Black, Gasconade, Meramec, Osage and St. Francis rivers. These are excellent smallmouth-bass waters. Float trips are famous in the

state, and an Ozark float is the pride and joy of Missouri fishermen. Some streams regularly floated in Missouri are the White,
Gasconade, Osage Fork, Big Piney and Little Niangua rivers, all
in the Ozarks. For the complete list of outfitters write to the
Division of Resource and Development for the free booklet
Floating and Fishing in Missouri. There is good fishing along the
way for channel catfish, trout, bass and jack salmon (walleye
pike).

Other waters include the One Hundred and Two and the
Platte rivers in the northwest; and further east the Grand,
Chariton, Cuivre, Fabius and Salt rivers have crappie, bass,
sunfish and catfish.

There are some excellent large lakes in the state, the biggest
of which is Lake of the Ozarks. A 60,000-acre lake surrounded
by over 30 resort hotels, it is the result of the damming of the
Osage River and has largemouth bass, white bass, walleye pike,
crappie and channel catfish.

Lake Taneycomo (2,200 acres of water) in southwest Missouri
is near Branson, Forsyth and Rockaway Beach. From it come
excellent catches of bass, crappie, catfish and bluegill. The construction of the Table Rock Reservoir on the White River a few
miles above Lake Taneycomo has led conservationists to believe the lake can be converted into a trout lake. A hatchery
has been built, and stocking has begun.

Bull Shoals Lake, a reservoir of 45,000 acres on the southwest
border of the state, is one of the best largemouth-bass lakes
anywhere. It is also good for crappie and white bass. Below the
dam big rainbow trout up to 20 pounds are taken. Table Rock
is a little west and its 43,000 acres of water are now being developed for tourism. Walleye are expected to be the principal
sports fish.

Clearwater Lake and Lake Wappapello are located in the
southeastern section of the state. They are excellent for crappie
and channel catfish, and the area around them is developing into
a summer vacationer's haven. Another reservoir, Lake Norfolk
on the Arkansas border, is good for white bass, crappie, channel
catfish and bluegill.

Smaller lakes such as Richmond, Langdon and Limpp lakes

are in northwest Missouri, while Lake Shelbina, Vandalia Lake or Tri-City Lake dot the northeast.

The Conservation Commission operates many small lakes as trout-management ponds. Here an angler pays $1.00 and fishes all day for trout. The limit is 5 a day, and the best bait is a small piece of cheese on a tiny hook. The ponds are stocked almost daily, and the best fishing is immediately after a stocking.

The construction of the many new dams in Missouri has given a big boost to fishing, and the state is on the way to becoming a Midwest fishing center.

Montana

Tourist information from:

Montana State Highway Commission
Advertising Department
Helena, Montana

Fishing information from:

Montana Fish and Game Department
Helena, Montana

Fish in Montana: rainbow trout, native black-spotted cutthroat trout, cutthroat trout, brown trout, Mackinaw trout, Dolly Varden trout, Kokanee salmon, landlocked silver salmon, whitefish, grayling, walleye pike, sauger, bass, drum, channel catfish and rough fish.

The big northwest state of Montana (147,138 square miles) has some of America's best fishing in its 11 national forests, 2 national parks and 20 state parks.

The famous Glacier National Park offers the best trout fishing of any national park, with its 250 icy lakes and miles of cold streams. Many of the best fishing waters in the park can only be reached by foot or on horseback. Some of the fishing streams are within sight of the glaciers of the park, where waters in the streams are cold and invigorating for trout.

Guests can stay at the Swiss chalet Many Glacier Hotel, which is but one of 7 lodges in the park, or they may stay at motels, motor inns or the provided camping areas. At the M.G. Ranch, Pablo arranges fishing trips into the back country of the park; and Hidden Meadow Ranch, Polebridge, Montana, is a dude ranch where sports-minded guests of the park may stay.

Some well-known fishing lakes in the park include St. Mary's Lake, Lake McDonald and Waterton Lake, all of which have big Mackinaws. The park streams and smaller lakes can be counted on to produce cutthroat, brook, rainbow and Dolly Varden trout. No fishing license is required.

South of Glacier National Park along the Continental Divide there is the 990,000-acre Bob Marshall Wilderness. Here the Flathead National Forest is on the east side of the Divide, and the Lewis and Clark National Forest on the east. The area has back-country trout fishing for all species, including the exotic black-spotted native cutthroat.

Flathead National Forest has fishing for cutthroat and Dolly Varden trout in the three forks of the Upper Flathead River. The Lower Flathead River can be boated and has cutthroat, Dolly Varden, rainbow and brown trout.

This area has Flathead Lake (189 square miles) near Polson, with good fishing for rainbows, cutthroat, Dolly Varden trout and whitefish. There is some bass fishing in the lake and Ko-kanee-salmon fishing is extremely good here every fall when the fully matured fish come into spawn. Whitefish Lake near White-fish and Columbia Falls is also known for its sockeye salmon.

The Lewis and Clark National Forest has fishing in the Sun River, which flows into the Missouri. The Sun River is a rainbow-and brook-trout stream which is accessible near Augusta. The Judith River has the same fish and also brown trout. Still another trout stream of the forest is the Teton River. Lewiston and Great Falls are the towns for lodging, and the South Paradise Ranch at Lewiston caters to sportsmen.

Located in northwest Montana on the Canadian-Idaho borders is the Kootenai National Forest. The Yaak, Fisher and Kootenai rivers offer wilderness fishing in this park. Fish caught here are generally Dolly Varden, cutthroat and rainbow trout. Basis of operation could be Libby, Troy or Eureka.

Coming southeast through the Cabinet Mountains, there is the Lolo National Forest and the Thompson River State Forest. There is stream and lake fishing in this section of the state, and Georgetown Lake has native black-spotted trout, rainbow trout, brook trout, silver salmon and grayling. Many campgrounds and dude ranches are in the area. One ranch is the Diamond L Ranch, Seeley Lake, Montana, which is just 75 miles from Missoula.

A second national park partially in Montana is Yellowstone Park on the southern border. A description of the facilities of Yellowstone are listed for Wyoming.

The Yellowstone River has its headwaters in the park and then flows northeasterly. There is cutthroat-trout fishing in the headwaters, and the river changes to a rainbow- and brown-trout stream as it nears Livingston. Finally in the east of Montana the water of the Yellowstone River warms up, and the sports fishing is for walleye pike, sauger, channel catfish and fresh-water drum. The tributaries of the Yellowstone include the Stillwater River, Clarks Fork of the Yellowstone, Shields River, Hellroaring Creek or Slough Creek, which can be expected to yield rainbows and brown in their lower portions and cutthroat in the headwaters.

The Madison River, which starts in Yellowstone Park, flows northward to the Missouri. This river ranks as one of the best trout streams in the country and provides excellent opportunities to dry-fly fish for hard-striking rainbows and brown trout. Also taken are grayling, whitefish and cutthroat trout. Two impoundments of the river, Hebgen Lake and Madison Reservoir, offer good fishing. Much of the Madison River can be waded, and in spite of its fame it is lightly fished, because it flows through a sparsely populated area, running through the Absaroka Wilderness.

Some of the areas outside of Yellowstone that are worth fishing include Hidden, Cliff, Elk and Wade lakes. All these have boats, and fish caught are landlocked silver salmon, cutthroat trout, brown trout and rainbow trout. This is the area of the Beaverhead National Forest, where moose, elk, goats, bear and a few wild buffalo can still be found. Packers from Jackson Hole, Wyoming, Virginia City or Dillon, Montana, will take sportsmen into the area for hunting and fishing. Some of the back-country lakes in this location have golden trout.

The Missouri River has its headwaters in Montana, and from the beginning the Great Falls is a rainbow- and brown-trout river. There are impoundments near its inception where the fishing is for trout and sockeye salmon. Hauser Lake is reserved for trout fishing. Down river below Fort Peck Dam there are rainbow trout, sauger and walleye pike, and from there until the river flows into North Dakota the fishing is primarily for walleye pike and sauger. Catches of channel catfish, fresh-water drum and carp are common here. The Missouri tributaries hold the same fish as the big river.

Fort Peck Lake (383 square miles) near Fort Peck is an impoundment of the Missouri. In addition to walleye pike, sauger and goldeye, the big lake has paddlefish or polyodon, which go up to 6 feet in length. Facilities are in Fort Peck.

Only the western third of Montana is in the Rocky Mountains, where cold-water trout fishing predominates. The remainder of the state consists of prairie and badlands and has warmer-water fishing. One advantage for fishermen in Montana is plenty of elbow room, for the state is very sparsely populated.

A sports-minded visitor to Montana would do well to remember that there are over 70 dude ranches throughout the state that cater to sportsmen. A letter to the Highway Commission will bring a list of the ranches and of the packers for wilderness trips—the best fishing Montana has to offer, ranking with the best there is.

Nebraska

Tourist Information from:

State of Nebraska
Division of Resources
Room 1107
State Capital
Lincoln 9, Nebraska

Specific fishing information from:

Game, Forestation and Parks Commission
State House
Lincoln 9, Nebraska

Fish in Nebraska: rainbow trout, brown trout, largemouth and smallmouth bass, walleye pike, sauger, northern pike, crappie, white bass, channel catfish, bluegill, gar, perch, sturgeon and rough fish.

Fishing America's "Great Plains State" means fishing in the waters of the 77,237 square miles of Nebraska.

Three major rivers flow from west to east across Nebraska, and they make up most of the state's fishing. The Niobrara in the north is a good rainbow- and brown-trout stream in its western portion, but from about the middle of the state east it is a catfish stream. The northwest of Nebraska has trout in the White River and Monroe Creek and also in the headwaters of the Snake River and Boardsman's Creek. South from where the Niobrara flows into the Missouri, and in the tailwaters of the Missouri River at Gavin Point, there are catfish, sauger and sturgeon.

Crystal Lake, a 1,000-acre lake near Dakota City, has northern pike, walleye and largemouth bass. A state park at the lake provides cabins, camping and boat rentals.

The second big river running across the state is the Platte. The North Platte has the state's biggest lake, 35,200-acre McConaughy Reservoir Lake, near Ogallala. A variety of fish can be caught here, including rainbow trout, walleye pike, largemouth bass, white bass, crappie and catfish. Accommodations at the lake include a state park which has camping and boat rentals.

East of Maloney on the Platte River there are a series of reservoirs connected by canals which have the same fish as the big reservoir. Jeffrey Reservoir, south of Brady, is known for its walleye and northern pike.

The Republican River running across much of southern Nebraska has flood-control reservoirs that have walleye pike, largemouth bass, bluegill, crappie and catfish. The reservoirs include

Swanson, Enders (actually on Frenchman River) and Harlan County near Alma. Each of the reservoirs has a state park with camping and boat rentals.

Nebraska has trout in the northwest near the South Dakota–Wyoming border and other game fishing throughout the state.

Nevada

Tourist information from:

Department of Economic Development
Carson City, Nevada

Specific fishing information from:

Nevada Fish and Game Department
Box 678
Reno, Nevada

Fish in Nevada: Largemouth bass, crappie, bluegill, Sacramento perch, rainbow trout, cutthroat trout, lake trout, brook trout, Kokanee salmon, channel catfish and other fish.

The visitor to the state of Nevada (110,540 square miles) will find there is good gambling as well as excellent warm- and cold-water fishing.

Located less than 20 miles east of fabulous Las Vegas is 246-square-mile Lake Mead. This is one of the recognized largemouth bass hot-spots of the country. Other catches are crappie, bluegill and channel catfish. Boulder Beach, 6 miles from Boulder City, has a tackle shop, boat rentals, a trailer camp and a campground. Las Vegas Bay near Henderson has a campground, boat and motor rentals. Echo Bay near Overton has boat rentals, cabins and a trailer village.

Lake Mohave, 67 miles downstream, is another reservoir of the Colorado River. A narrow lake within Black Canyon, it has facilities at Eldorado Cover, 30 miles south of Boulder City, that include camping areas, cabins, a trailer camp and boats. Cotton Wood Cover is 15 miles east of Searchlight, Nevada, and has camping, a trailer village, boats, motor rentals and a tackle shop. Fish caught are warm-water game fish: bass, crappie and bluegill, with rainbow trout in the headwaters of the lake.

An Arizona or Nevada license may be used to fish both Lake Mead and Lake Mohave; however, a special stamp from the opposite state must be affixed to the license.

Far across the deserts of Nevada on the western borders there are high mountains and cool lakes which have record-sized cutthroat trout in them.

Lake Walker (64,000 acres) near Hawthorne in Mineral County has cutthroat trout as well as brook trout and Sacramento perch (which are locally referred to as bass). Cutthroat fishing in the lake starts in November and lasts until May, but April and May are the top months. Walker Lake boat harbor has boat rentals and motors, while nearby Hawthorne has complete accommodations, plus gambling and night spots. Guides are available here, and charter-boat captain J. Johnson, Hawthorne, Nevada, takes parties out on the lake. The country around the lake is an amateur geologist's delight, for there are gold, silver and uranium in the mountains. The Walker River has the same fish as the lake.

Further north is Pyramid Lake, located 30 miles northeast of Reno in the Pyramid Paiute Indian Reservation. The lake is 170 square miles and has an island which is a pyramid-shaped rock for which the lake was named. The world-record cutthroat trout came from this lake—a 41-pounder. Other fish that can be taken are rainbows, brookies, brown trout, Kokanee salmon, Sacramento perch and rough fish, including one called cui-ui. Sutcliff on the lake has a dude ranch, cabins and a private air strip. On the Truckee River just above the lake is located the town of Nixon, where Indian fishing guides are available. The town has everything for the fisherman, including air strip, lodging and tackle shop.

Reno is the center of Nevada trout fishing, and only 20 miles southwest of the city on the California-Nevada border is Lake Tahoe, a clear lake going to a depth of 1,645 feet. The lake once possessed black-spotted cutthroat trout in such number they were commercially taken, but through waste, neglect, bad conservation and pollution these fish died out. This lake, like many others, went through the conservation evolution with white men first doing everything possible to destroy nature and, when it was almost destroyed, suddenly waking up and trying to save what was left. Today fishing is good, and the lake has Mackinaw trout, rainbow trout, brown trout, brook trout and Kokanee salmon. Accommodations are all around the lake, for this is a big resort area, and Reno and Carson City are a short distance away.

Rye Patch Reservoir Lake near Lovelock has largemouth bass, rainbow and cutthroat trout, with boats and lodging hired at the lake.

The visitor will do well to remember that Las Vegas in eastern Nevada has gambling and warm-water game fishing, while Reno in the west has gambling and cold-water game fishing.

New Hampshire

Tourist information from:

State Planning and Development Commission
629 Capitol Street
Concord, New Hampshire

Fishing information from:

Fish and Game Department
Concord, New Hampshire

Fish in New Hampshire: brook trout, brown trout, golden trout, splake trout, rainbow trout, lake trout, landlocked salmon, smallmouth bass, largemouth bass, pickerel, white perch, northern pike, walleye pike and others.

The beautiful "White Mountain State," of New Hampshire is 9,304 square miles in area and has within its borders 1,300 lakes and rivers for excellent fishing. The Connecticut River makes up the western border of the state. In its northern headwaters the Connecticut is a fine trout stream with rainbows, browns and brookies, while further south pike, pickerel, bass and walleye are the principal fish.

In the northern reaches there are Indian Stream and Perry Stream, which are full of brook trout. Both of these are accessible from Pittsburg on Route 3. The undeveloped Crystal Mountain area has good fishing and is noted for the swift Diamond River and the Dead Diamond River, which are brook-trout streams.

The Androscoggin River, a brookie and rainbow stream, flows past Berlin in northeast New Hampshire. Lakes in the far north include the First Connecticut Lake (2,800 acres), the Second Connecticut Lake (1,300 acres), both of which are famous for landlocked salmon, lake trout and brook trout. Lake Francis, a little further south near Pittsburg, is a fine pickerel lake and produces salmon and rainbows, too. Umbagog Lake borders New Hampshire and Maine and is a well-known salmon lake, and has lake trout and pickerel as well.

The waters of the White Mountain National Forest make up the fishing in the middle of the state. Some streams found in the forest are Pemigewasset River, (brookies), the Swift River (brookies and rainbows) and Wildcat Brook (brook trout). Conway and North Conway are the resorts near these streams. Mount Washington (6,288 feet) is a few miles north of North Conway on Route 16, and the area is full of mountains rising 3,000 feet and up, with swift streams on their sides.

The 20-mile-long Lake Winnepesaukee (44,600 acres) is south of the White Mountain National Forest, and it centers the best-known resort area in New Hampshire. The lake is known for its pickerel, bass, salmon and lake trout. Other lakes in the area include Squam Lake (6,800 acres) with bass and pickerel; New-found Lake (4,100 acres) with salmon and lake trout; Ossipee Lake (3,100 acres) with bass salmon and lake trout; and Lake Wentworth (150 acres) with smallmouth bass and pickerel.

Further south near Sunapee is Sunapee Lake (4,100 acres), famous as the original home of the Sunapee golden trout. Unfortunately the goldens in this lake have crossed with lake trout and are no longer pure, but in Tewksbury Pond near Grafton, Sunapee trout (goldens) are still available. Lake Sunapee has lake trout, bass, salmon and pickerel. Long Pond near Lempster has splake trout, which are a cross between brook trout and lake trout. The world-record Sunapee trout—11 pounds 8 ounces—was caught in Lake Sunapee.

Other lakes in the south of New Hampshire include Massabesic, near Manchester, with brown trout and bass; Spofford near Chesterfield with bass; and Contoocook, near Contoocook, with bass.

Streams here include the Merrimack River, which flows through Manchester and has bass, pickerel, and pike, and the Ashuelot River, another bass stream.

New Hampshire realizes good fishing is one of its precious natural resources, and it has set up a very aggressive fish-management program. In the last ten years it has reclaimed more than 100 lakes and ponds for trout and salmon. Today, there are over 100,000 acres of lakes and ponds stocked annually with trout and salmon.

New Hampshire is constantly trying to plant sports fish in new areas. In the coming years anglers should be well rewarded by these good conservation practices.

New Jersey

Tourist information from:

New Jersey State Promotion Section
Department of Conservation and Economic Development
520 East State Street
Trenton 25, New Jersey

Fishing information from:

New Jersey Division of Fish and Game
State House Annex
Trenton, New Jersey

Fish in New Jersey: brook trout, brown trout, rainbow trout, smallmouth bass, largemouth bass, bluegill sunfish, calico bass, yellow perch, white perch, pickerel, and rough fish.

New Jersey (7,836 square miles) is a heavily populated eastern seaboard industrial state. In days gone by it sported excellent trout fishing and salmon streams, but now salmon are only a memory and very few native trout are left. Trout caught today in New Jersey are for the most part stocked fish, resulting from the aggressive program carried on by the conservation department, which stocks 1,400 miles of stream annually. The Pompton Lakes are located in the north of the state and are only an hour's drive from New York City. Largemouth bass, white perch and calico bass are caught here. The Pompton River has brook trout, rainbow trout and brown trout in the spring.

Greenwood Lake (1,900 acres) near Hewitt is another resort for New York refugees. This lake has some surprising largemouth bass, as well as white perch, calico bass, sunfish and other rough fish.

A few miles further west the Jersey angler has his best chance to get native trout. The trout streams that run into the Delaware River are Big Flat Brook (Upper and Lower) and the Paulins Kill and Musconetcong rivers. New Jersey's three species of trout run in these rivers, which are among the state's favorite streams.

Some largemouth-bass lakes in the northwest include Cranberry Lake near Cranberry, Culvers Lake, Swartswood Lake near Newton, Lackawanna Lake near Andover, and Musconetcong Lake near Stanhope. The last two lakes also have a sizable pickerel population. Lake Hopatcong, which has Hopatcong State Park on its shores near Netcong, has white perch, largemouth bass and calico bass.

The Delaware River borders the west of New Jersey and has some very good bass and pickerel fishing. Pleasant canoe trips where some white water is encountered can be taken anywhere in the area from Port Jervis, New York, south to Delaware Water Gap.

The Raritan River is stocked with trout in its upper reaches. The Medford Lakes produced a 9-pound 3-ounce chain pickerel in 1957, which is still the world's record. South of Camden near Clayton is Wilson Lake, and near Swedesboro is Swedesboro Lake, both largemouth-bass lakes. There are many small lakes and ponds throughout New Jersey, and most of them have bass. Any one is worth a try.

Along the coast of New Jersey the accent is on some very fine ocean fishing at the many coastal resorts there. However, fresh-water bass fishing is also possible from Ludlam's Lake near Dennisville, Bargaintown Lake near Bargaintown, Barnegat Lake near Forked River, Carasaljo Lake near Lakewood, and Shadow Lake near Red Bank.

Places to stay should never concern the visitor, for tourist accommodations are plentiful and good. Also the major lakes of the state can be counted on to have boats available for rental.

The world-record yellow perch—a 4-pound 3-ounce fish—was taken at Bordentown, New Jersey. The pickerel record also comes from New Jersey, which clearly indicates the productivity of the state's lake waters.

New Mexico

Tourist information from:

New Mexico Department of Development
State Capitol
Santa Fe, New Mexico

Fishing information from:

Department of Game and Fish
Box 2060
Santa Fe, New Mexico

Fish in New Mexico: rainbow trout, brown trout, brook trout, cutthroat trout, largemouth bass, smallmouth bass, walleye, blue-gill, crappie, channel catfish, perch and rough fish.

New Mexico (121,666 square miles) has some fine fishing, although Hollywood has pictured it as the state of the parched cowboy. Certainly there is much dry desert land in the state, but there are also mountains with cold-water trout fishing.

The state's trout fishing takes place in three mountainous areas. The first and largest is the northern area along the Colorado border, encompassing a triangle from Cedar Hill and Raton on the border running down close to Bernalillo, which is just above Albuquerque. These mountains offer winter sports, with elevations as high as 13,000 feet. In the area the Rio Grande has good-sized trout, as do the Rio Brazos and the Rio Chama. Elk Horn Lodge, 8,000 feet above sea level, near Chama provides guides for trout fishing for the Chama River and other streams and lakes.

There is camping in the area at Hyde State Park, north of Santa Fe. Fenton Lake, 20 miles north of Jemez Springs, has a 34-acre lake for fishing which does not permit boats, but there is camping on the lake. Pecos Recreation area, 13 miles north of Pecos, offers stream fishing and camping.

Northeast New Mexico has the headwaters for the Red, Pecos, Cimarron and Canadian rivers, all of which are trout streams.

The second trout area is a quadrangle on the Arizona border running approximately from Red Hill east to Magdalena, then south to Kingston and finally west to Mule Creek on the Arizona border. This area takes in much of the rugged Gila National Forest. The Continental Divide runs through the area, and these mountains of the Sierra Madre rise to elevations of 10,000 feet. The Gila River, San Francisco River, Willow Creek and many smaller streams have trout. Bear Canyon Lake just north of San Lorenzo has trout, bass and facilities for camping. Guides for trips into this rugged country are available at Silver City. To give an example of the ruggedness and remoteness of some of this area, Willow Creek Ranch (P.O. Box 325, Reserve, New Mexico) is at an 8,200-foot elevation in the wilderness. Fine fishing, hunting, horseback riding and pack trips are to be had here, but the ranch suggests guests bring their own towels and main groceries, for there is only a small commissary on hand.

The third trout area covers the Lincoln National Forest and the Mescalero Indian Reservation. The area stretches north and south of Cloudcroft, about 30 miles each way. Cedar Creek just north of Ruidoso has fishing, hunting and camping facilities. Ruidoso is a fine resort in this area.

Throughout New Mexico cutthroat and rainbow trout are the favorites, with brown and brookies running close behind. The state has stopped stocking eastern brook trout because they were found to reproduce too rapidly in the cold, clear waters; and in many areas the lakes became overpopulated and the trout stunted.

Two trout lakes in New Mexico are Bluewater Lake near Gallup in the Cibola National Forest, where there are boats and camping; and Charette Lake near Springer. Bluewater Lake has rainbow trout in its 3,000 acres, and Charette Lake has rainbows and browns.

Outside of the trout areas, warm-water game fishing is available in several reservoir lakes. Conchas Reservoir Lake (10,000 acres) near Tucumcari was built as a watershed but is important as a water-sport lake. Fish here are walleye pike, channel catfish, largemouth bass, crappie and bluegill. There are cabins, a lodge, 2 trailer parks and camping facilities. Boats are available on the lake.

Near the town with the strange name of Truth or Consequences (formerly Hot Springs) is the state's biggest lake— 30,000-acre Elephant Butte Lake, which was the result of damming the Rio Grande River. Largemouth bass, walleye, channel catfish, bluegill and crappie can be caught here. Complete facilities are available on the lake. The Caballo Reservoir a few miles to the south has the same fish.

New Mexico is a big state, but it has a small population; and with cold, clear, fast-running streams, natural lakes and reservoir lakes, it offers fine fishing in many places.

New York

Tourist information from:

Vacation Information Center
342 Madison Avenue
New York 17, New York

Fishing information (camping) from:

State of New York
Conservation Department
Division of Conservation Education
Albany 1, New York

Fish in New York: largemouth bass, smallmouth bass, walleye pike, pickerel, northern pike, muskellunge, lake trout, brook trout, rainbow trout, brown trout, landlocked salmon, sunfish, crappie, white bass, carp and rough fish.

New York (49,576 square miles) has a population numbering well over 15 million, yet the state has fishing that in many places is equal to the best there is. The lower portion of New York near the crowded metropolitan area, of course, has fishing only to a limited degree, but in the north and the west of the state the fishing is superb.

On Long Island the accent is on excellent salt-water sport, but bass and pan fish may be taken at Lake Ronkonkoma or in some of the ponds that dot the island.

Within a few hours' drive the 8 million New York City residents can get some decent fresh-water fishing if they know where to go. Trout fishing in these lower reaches should be discounted; it is poor or at best spotty, for there are few native trout available. Some streams for trout are the Saw Mill River above Elmsford, the Croton River below Croton Dam, Hollowbrook Creek near Peekskill (this stream still has a few natives left) and the reservoir streams. The latter include the West Branch Croton River near Carmel, East Branch Croton River near Sodom, the Cross River in Ward Pound Ridge Reservation—all stocked streams.

Fishing in reservoir lakes or streams calls for a special reservoir permit, obtainable free from the New York City Water Department.

New York City fishermen know their best chance for local fresh-water fishing is in the lakes to the north of the city. The reservoir lakes include Kensico Reservoir near Valhalla, New

Croton Reservoir near Croton-on-the-Hudson, Cross River Reservoir near Katonah, Titicus Reservoir near Purdy's and the West Branch, Middle Branch and East Branch reservoirs accessible from Carmel. These lakes have bass and trout. Unfortunately no boats are rentable on any reservoir.

Nonreservoir lakes include Lake Mohansic at Mohansic State Park, which supplies boats for bass, pickerel, bluegill and crappie fishing. Lake Mahopac near Mahopac is a good bass, bluegill, pickerel and crappie lake. Peach Lake near North Salem has bass and pickerel. Fahnestock State Park has 2 small lakes, one a bass lake, and the other a trout-stocked lake with boats available.

Across the Hudson River in Palisades Interstate Park along Seven Lakes Parkway, there are boats at Hessian Lake (trout and bass), Silvermine Lake (smallmouth bass), Lake Tiorati (bass and pickerel), Lake Kanawauke (bass and pickerel), Lake Sebago (bass) and Lake Askoti (trout). Trout streams here include Queensboro Brook, Tiorati Brook, the Ramapo River and Stony Brook.

The Catskill Mountains region finds a rapid improvement in trout fishing. Here waters run colder and faster, and with a drop-off in population concentration, Catskill waters are better able to support trout. Such famous streams as Esopus Creek, near Phoenicia, Rondout Creek, near Kingston, and Schoharie Creek, which empties into the Mohawk River, are all trout streams. Also, the Beaver Kill, which has brook, brown and rainbow trout, is productive. State camp sites for the public are at Beaver Kill near Livingston Manor, Devils Tombstone near Hunter, North Lake near Haines Falls, Toe Path Mountain near Middleburg and Woodland Valley near Phoenicia. For the less hardy there are excellent accommodations for tourists and sportsmen throughout this whole area.

Natural lakes in the Catskills are few, and only small ponds exist; but no matter how small the pond is, it generally can be counted on to have bass. The Ashokan Reservoir (12 miles long and 2 miles wide) is a big body of water in the area. Fish here include trout, smallmouth bass, and walleye pike. A New York City reservoir permit is necessary to fish here.

Further west, the Delaware River has smallmouth bass, pickerel and walleye pike in the main body. Trout can be caught in the upper reaches of the river and in the West Branch. Pleasant and interesting canoe trips can be taken from Narrowsburg to Port Jervis.

The Adirondack region is a fisherman's paradise, with fine, cold lakes and streams. There are built-up resort areas along historic Route 9 and unspoiled rustic land in the western Adirondacks. The state annually stocks almost 300 Adirondack ponds by plane, because these ponds are inaccessible by land.

Lake George on Route 9 is a 30-mile-long lake and is the best-known fishing lake in New York. Landlocked salmon, lake trout, smallmouth and largemouth bass can be caught here. The New York State record salmon—a 16-pound 14-ounce fish—came from this water. The state owns 47 islands in the lake which can be used as public campsites, and complete camping outfits and canoes may be rented at Bolton Landing. Lake Luzerne nearby has redeye and sockeye salmon, as well as northern pike.

Lake Champlain to the north is twice as large as Lake George and offers fishing for largemouth bass, smallmouth bass, northern pike, walleye pike and pickerel.

Further west there are the resort centers of Lake Placid and Saranac Lake. Then there are trout and lake trout in Lake Placid, and the same fish are in the upper and lower Saranac Lakes, with boats available. Nearby there are trout at Spitfire Lake and St. Regis Pond. Mount Marcy, the highest peak in the state (5,344 feet), is a few miles to the south. The West Branch of the Ausable River, which is the best-known trout stream in New York, is just north of Lake Placid.

The Tupper Lake Resort area is noted for Tupper Lake, containing trout and smallmouth bass, northern pike and walleye. Splake trout may be taken at Panther Pond and Green Pond. Further south is Long Lake, with smallmouth bass. Then Indian Lake (4,500 acres), located north of Speculator, is a rustic spot with good lake trout and northern pike. The Indian River is a good trout river. West in the Adirondacks there is Old Forge in the Fulton Chain of Lakes, which have trout and lake trout.

The most famous trout stream here is the West Branch of the Ausable, and almost equally as good is the East Branch of that river. The Black River from Carthage south, or west Canada Creek near West Canada Mountain, are fine trout producers. There are hundreds of miles of streams and almost all of them have trout.

Fishing canoe trips are a specialty of the Adirondack region, and canoes may be rented at Old Forge, Raquette Lake, Blue Mountain Lake, Saranac Lake and Long Lake. An 8- to 16-day trip will make anyone forget all his troubles. It is a real chance for communion with nature. Those contemplating such a trip should write to the Conservation Department for Recreation Circular 7—a free guide to the Adirondacks, including complete maps of the canoe routes.

Lake Otsego and Canadarago Lake are located near Cooperstown, home of the baseball Hall of Fame. Trout and smallmouth bass can be caught here.

The northwest of the state is bordered by the St. Lawrence River, and here in the Thousand Islands region (actually about 1,800 islands) there is some fine fishing. Guides and boats are available at Clayton, Cape Vincent and Alexandria Bay. Walleye pike, pickerel, northern pike and muskie are the chief sports fish. A world-record 69-pound 15-ounce muskie has already come out of this water.

New York state also has the world-record northern pike taken from its waters—a 46-pound 2-ounce monster from Sacandaga Reservoir.

Oneida Lake, a 20-mile lake north of Syracuse, has largemouth bass, smallmouth bass and pikeperch.

The Finger Lakes region includes Skaneateles, Owasco, Cayuga, Seneca and Canandaigua lakes. Finger Lakes run north and south, because during prehistoric times glaciers cut deep gorges in the land. Later these gorges filled with water as the glaciers melted. Seneca Lake is 40 miles long and Cayuga over 30 miles long. Moravia, Ithaca and Watkins Glen are the chief resorts where boats are available. Fish include lake trout, trout, smallmouth bass, salmon (Cayuga Lake) and walleye pike (Canandaigua Lake).

Catherine Creek near Watkins Glen is a famous spot for a run of early-season trout, and fishermen stand elbow to elbow working the water for one of the big 20-pound trout from Seneca Lake.

Western New York is noted for smallmouth-bass fishing in two Great Lakes, Lake Ontario (7,540 square miles) and Lake Erie (9,940 square miles). Lake Erie also has walleye pike. The Niagara River, which connects the two Great Lakes, has muskellunge fishing. Spectacular Niagara Falls is located here, which is always worth a trip to see.

In the far southwestern corner of the state near Jamestown is Chautauqua Lake, which is known for its muskie and also has smallmouth bass. Chautauqua Creek is a trout stream.

New York state fishing is varied and interesting. Away from the great population centers it equals the best there is.

Magazines dealing with New York outdoors:

The Conservationist   Cost: $2.00 a year
New York State Conservation Department
Albany 1, New York

Sportsmen's Life
Roosevelt, Long Island
(Primarily Long Island fishing)

North Carolina

Tourist information from:

North Carolina State Travel Bureau
Department of Conservation and Development
Raleigh, North Carolina

Wildlife refuge fishing and rules from:

Wildlife Resources Commission
Box 2919
Raleigh, North Carolina

Fish in North Carolina: brown trout, brook trout, rainbow trout, smallmouth bass, largemouth bass, bluegill, crappie, walleye pike, yellow perch, white perch, white bass, landlocked striped bass and rough fish.

North Carolina (52,712 square miles), like many other eastern seaboard states, has fishing within its borders that varies with the topography of the land.

The western part of North Carolina is mountainous, with elevations running as high as 6,684-foot Mount Mitchell, a few miles above Asheville. In the west is Great Smoky Mountains National Park, with 6,642-foot Clingmans Dome and Fontana Lake (10,670 acres of water), created by 480-foot Fontana Dam on the south of the big park. There is superb bass fishing in the lake, and boats may be rented at Fontana Village, a year-round resort. The trout streams north of the lake—Forney Creek, Eagle Creek, Hazel Creek and Noland Creek—can only be reached by boat.

Lake Chatuge (7,150 acres) on the Georgia border is well known for its huge crappie and bass. Boats can be hired at Hayesville.

Reservoir Lake, Hiwassee, near Murphy is 6,240 acres of water in the southwestern tip of the state. This is another famous bass lake, which also has excellent pan fishing. Boats are available at Murphy or Hiwassee Village near the dam.

Lake Santeetlah (2,850 acres) near Robbinsville, and Lake Nantahala (1,160 acres) in the Nantahala National Forest near Andrews are bass lakes. Other lakes in the Appalachian Mountains of the west include Lake Lure near Chimney Rock, Thorpe Lake near Glenville, Lake Cheoah near Tapoco Resort and Lake Calderwood—all of which are bass and crappie lakes.

A drive southwest along the dramatic Blue Ridge Parkway brings an angler right into this area of North Carolina. Many reservoirs have been built here, due to an annual rainfall of over 50 inches.

There are thousands of miles of trout streams in the Adirondacks, and further east in the Blue Ridge section there are many miles of smallmouth-bass streams, which later become largemouth-bass streams and other warm-water game-fish streams in the middle-valley section of the state.

Some trout streams are the Linville River near Linville Gorge, Valley River near Andrews, Shooting Creek near Shooting Creek, Tuckaseigee River above Cullowhee, Big Rock Creek near Red Hill, Davidson River near Brevard and Howard Creek near Todd. Generally the more rugged the country, the better the trout fishing.

Smallmouth-bass streams include the New River, both the North and South forks, Elk Creek and the Johns River. Recommended canoeing-fishing trips for the skilled white-water canoe man are the Little Tennessee, Hiwassee and the Green rivers. Less experienced canoe men will find all the excitement they crave on the Tugaloo.

The middle of the state has wider, softer rivers, and, on the Yadkin River above Albemarle, is Lake Catawba (325 shore-line miles of the Georgia border near Gastonia), and further north Lookout Shoals Lake, Lake Hickory and Lake Rhodhiss. Largemouth bass, bluegill and crappie are the fish. Lake James just to the west also has walleye pike.

The Yadkin River group of reservoir lakes include High Rock (15,750 acres), Badin (5,973 acres), Tillery (5,000 acres) and Blewett Falls lakes (2,500 acres). Largemouth bass, bluegill and crappie are the fish. Boats are available on Tillery Reservoir at Morrow Mountain State Park and other places.

Kerr Reservoir (or Buggs Island Lake, as it is sometimes called) on the Virginia border near Henderson is 50,000 acres of fishing water that has excellent bass fishing. A new excitement is landlocked striped bass, the best fishing for which is below Kerr Dam. Boats have been made available at Townsville Landing and other places by the North Carolina Wildlife Resources Commission.

The most productive fishing throughout the center of the state is in the spring and fall, for hot summer weather tends to drive the fish down.

The eastern part of the state is known for its coastal fishing, but such places as Currituck Sound and Back Bay have fine bass fishing in the bays. Water from the rivers comes down to the coast and cannot mix with the salt water fast enough, so the water remains sufficiently fresh to support bass, pickerel, bluegill and white perch. Further south on the coast the bays are completely salty and have fine salt-water fishing.

The east has some natural large lakes, such as Mattamuskeet near Fairfield (30,000 acres). Lake Phelps near Pettigrew State Park and Lake Waccamaw near Whiteville are bass and panfish lakes.

North Carolina boasts open-season fishing for all fish except trout, and although the fishing in different parts of the state takes on different characteristics it can be said to be productive everywhere.

Magazine dealing with North Carolina outdoors:

Wildlife in North Carolina   Cost: 50 cents a year
P.O. Box 2919
Raleigh, North Carolina

North Dakota

Tourist information from:

Greater North Dakota Association
Box 1781
Fargo, North Dakota

Fishing information from:

North Dakota Game and Fish Department
Bismarck, North Dakota

Nonresident 7-day license costs only $1.00.

Fish in North Dakota: northern pike, walleye, sauger, yellow perch, brown trout, rainbow trout, brook trout, largemouth bass, bluegill, crappie, channel catfish, blue catfish, sturgeon and rough fish.

The 70,665-square-mile state of North Dakota has my vote as the most overlooked fishing area in the United States. It has good fishing, but because it has the misfortune to lie between Minnesota, with its thousands of lakes, and Montana, with its spectacular mountain fishing, North Dakota fishing is neglected.

North Dakota has some fine northern pike, walleye and sauger, in thoroughly uncrowded waters that in many instances are hardly fished at all.

The biggest body of water is Garrison Dam Reservoir, which is a monstrous 610-square-mile lake formed by the Missouri River. The Fort Berthold Indian Reservation covers much of the surrounding area. Facilities for lodging can be found at Garrison, Riverdale or New Town. Snake Creek National Wildlife Refuge is near the dam, and there is good fishing at Riverdale. Fish in the reservoir are northern pike, walleye, sauger, yellow perch, sturgeon, rainbow trout and rough fish. The world-record sauger—a beautiful 8-pound 3-ounce fish—came out of the lake in 1959. This expansive lake has wonderful possibilities for developing into a resort area of importance.

Another reservoir lake that adds to the state's fishing is 4,500-acre Heart Butte Reservoir, located south of Glen Ullin. This reservoir has walleye and sauger, but facilities are scarce.

Hamman Lake near Amidon has rainbow and brook trout, as does Spring Lake near Rhame down at the Montana–South Dakota border. There are also rainbow trout in Jensen Lake further north near Killdeer, and in Dawson Pond near St. Anthony.

Reservoir Lake Ashtabula (6,000 acres) near Valley City offers northern pike, walleye and sauger. Boats are available. Below the lake the Sheyenne River has good fishing for the same fish.

The Jamestown Reservoir near Jamestown has northern pike, bluegill and bullhead. Historic Fort Seward is located here.

Located in the middle of the state near the Canadian border is Lake Metigoshe, north of Bottineau. Fishing is for northern pike, walleye, sauger and yellow perch. Boats and cabins are available in Lake Metigoshe State Park, one of the few places in the state that does have lakeside facilities.

A visiting angler to North Dakota should always be prepared to stay in a nearby city because of the scarcity of facilities. However, all lakes have unimproved camping places available.

The northern border has small, 16-acre Lake Darling near Foxholm, where walleye, sauger, northern pike and yellow perch are caught. The perch is the favorite species. Below the lake the Mouse River has good sport for these fish, too.

A short distance east there is Gordon Lake near Belcourt, where brook trout and rainbow trout can be caught. Trout have done amazingly well in the state considering they were introduced only a few years ago.

The rivers of the state are, of course, headed by the Missouri, which has good walleye fishing, where it is not part of the Garrison Reservoir, and has brown trout in places. Then the Red River, which borders much of the east of the state, is known for its walleye fishing and also has northern pike and crappie.

North Dakota is a cold state, and fishing is for cold-water species. Here is the northern rim of bass fishing, but the bass are neither large nor plentiful. However, northern pike, walleye, sauger and yellow perch are excellent. Muskellunge have been introduced to the larger waters and hold promise for the future, as does the stocking and planting of trout.

Ice fishing is popular in the winter when it's not too cold, for the water gets covered with a really thick layer of ice. Sometimes heavy ice and snow kill large sections of the fish population by cutting off the oxygen from the lake.

The new reservoir lakes, especially Garrison Reservoir, have added much to the state's fishing potential, and with plenty of room there is ample opportunity for good fishing.

Magazine dealing with North Dakota outdoors:

North Dakota Outdoors   Cost: $1.00 a year
State Game and Fish Commission
Bismarck, North Dakota

Ohio

Tourist information from:

Department of Industrial and Economic Development
700 Bryden Road
Columbus 15, Ohio

Fishing information from:

Ohio Division of Wildlife
1500 Dublin Road
Columbus, Ohio

Fish in Ohio: largemouth bass, smallmouth bass, bluegill, bullhead, carp, channel catfish, crappie, muskellunge, white bass, sunfish, northern pike and walleye.

The state of Ohio (41,222 square miles) has few fishing restrictions, and unlike other states there are no size or bag limits for the fisherman to worry about.

The northern border of Ohio is on the 9,940-square-mile Lake Erie. Here the land is flat and sloping toward the lake. The northern rivers that flow into the lake include the Ashtabula, Black, Cayahoga, Grand, Maumee, Sandusky and Vermilion. Most of the sports fishing in the north is done in Lake Erie, where Sandusky Bay, the Bass Islands and Put-in-Bay are popular. Fish taken in this region include white bass, walleye, perch and black bass. Ice fishing for walleye and perch is also popular.

The southern part of the state is hilly, and the rivers flow into the Ohio. These include the Scioto, Miami and Muskingum rivers. Once, over 100 years ago, fishing in the Ohio and its tributaries was sport supreme; but with the increase in industrialization pollution, the river became a running sewer and fishing decreased severely. Sportsmen banded together for the tough job of forcing through legislation restricting dumping, and consequently fish life is on the increase. There is still a long way to go, but things are getting better. Fish here include channel catfish, carp, crappie and sunfish. Altogether the Ohio has 12,000 miles of running water.

The state claims there are 500 lakes available for fishing and lists 186 of them open to the public. Actually many of these lakes are nothing but small ponds and one of them has an area of only 1 acre of water. Some of the more sizable lakes and reservoirs in the state follow.

In the northeastern section of Ohio, a short drive from Akron, are Atwood, Leesville, and Mill reservoirs, and Pleasant Hill Lake. Crappie fishing is the highlight of these lakes, but bluegill, carp and channel catfish are also taken. Cabin rates at Atwood and Pleasant Hill can be secured from:

Park Superintendent	Park Superintendent
Atwood Lake Park	Pleasant Hill Lake Park
Route No. 1	Route No. 2
Mineral City, Ohio	Perrysville, Ohio

The 12 Portage Lakes south of Akron have bass, carp and walleye pike.

Other sizable lakes include Pymatuning Reservoir (15,000 acres) in the northeast corner of the state. It has bass, walleye, pike, channel catfish and crappie. Also in this area are Berlin Reservoir (3,650 acres) and Mosquito Creek Reservoir (7,850 acres). Bass, bluegill and crappie are the chief fish here.

Near Ulrichsville is the Clendening Reservoir (1,800 acres), where bass and bluegill and occasional muskie are taken. Buckeye Lake (3,300 acres) near Millerport has bass, largemouth bass, bluegill, crappie and channel catfish.

Lake St. Mary's (11,000 acres) and Indian Lake (5,800 acres) are in the northwest. Indian Lake is 1,500 feet above sea level and is located near Bellefontaine. Fish caught here include largemouth bass, channel catfish, crappie, sunfish and walleye pike. Indian Lake also has smallmouth bass.

The southeastern section of the state has Jackson Lake (250 acres) near Jackson, with bass and crappie. Grant Lake further west is 268 acres of water with bass and sunfish. Also Rocky

Fork Lake (2,100 acres) near Bainbridge has bass, bluegill and crappie.

Accommodations are generally plentiful and good throughout the state.

Oklahoma

Tourist information from:

Oklahoma Planning and Resources Board
533 State Capitol
Oklahoma City, Oklahoma

Fishing information from:

Department of Wildlife and Conservation
Oklahoma City, Oklahoma

No closed season for fishing in Oklahoma.

Fish in Oklahoma: largemouth bass, smallmouth bass, white bass, crappie, bluegill, rainbow trout, channel catfish, flathead catfish, bullhead, carp and rough fish.

Oklahoma (69,919 square miles) is often thought of as a dry state, but it actually has 450,000 square acres of water, including 30 rivers and over 300 lakes for fresh-water fishing.

The northeast of the state near Ketchum, where the state reaches into the Ozark Mountains, holds popular 46,300-acre reservoir Grand Lake, called the Grand Lake of the Cherokees. There are many tourist accommodations around it, and camping facilities are in the Cherokee and Honey Creek recreational areas. The fish caught are smallmouth, largemouth, and white bass, crappie, channel catfish and rough fish.

The Spavinaw Lakes are close to the base of Grand Lake and have the same fish as the big lake. Walleye pike have been stocked here, and there is every indication they will take.

Fort Gibson Lake (19,000 square surface acres) on the Grand River is located less than 30 miles due east from Tulsa. Sequoyah State Park, with cottages and the 250-room Western Hills Lodge, is on the lake. There are boats and heated fishing docks for those preferring the rocking-chair variety of crappie fishing. Fishing on the docks is done outside or inside, for each dock has a hollow, pool-like opening in its center. Many docks throughout the state are air-cooled in the summer, and since the area surrounding them is chummed, fishing for crappie is generally good. Fort Gibson Lake's most popular fishing is for crappie, with bass, walleye and channel catfish behind the little scrapper.

Tenkiller Lake, a 12,500-acre reservoir of the Illinois River is located 20 miles southeast of Fort Gibson Lake. The Illinois River is a fine bass stream that runs through the hills of eastern Oklahoma. The river filled this lake up with a fine assortment of smallmouth, largemouth, white bass, bluegill, crappie, channel catfish and flathead catfish. Trout also have been stocked in the lake. The facilities include boats, enclosed fishing docks and overnight lodging places.

Float trips can be arranged on the Illinois River through Paradise Valley Fishing Floats, Tahlequah. The river is a pleasant place to float, for it is bounded by high bluffs and green forests. Other floats in Oklahoma can be taken on the Mountain Fork River.

The southern border of Oklahoma has Lake Texoma (95,000 acres), the largest lake in Oklahoma or Texas and one of the 10 largest reservoir lakes in the world. There are many facilities of all types around this resort lake, including the super-luxurious Lake Texoma Lodge in Texoma State Park. Heated and air-cooled fishing barges, boats, cabins, motels, hotels and a paved air strip are on the lake. Fish caught are largemouth bass, white bass, bluegill, crappie and channel catfish.

Scenic Murray State Park surrounds 5,700-acre Murray Reservoir Lake, a popular fishing center with lodge and camping areas. All the warm-water game fish are in this lake.

A group of small lakes located near Lawton include Lake Lawtonka (1,900 acres), Elmer Thomas Lake, Rush Lake and others. Boats are available for good bass and crappie fishing.

Quartz Mountain State Park is on the shores of 7,000-acre Altus-Lugert Reservoir in the Wichita Mountains. This lake, one

of the few in southwest Oklahoma, is like an oasis in this dry land
and is a popular resort. There are a fine lodge, a fishing dock,
boats and camping facilities. Fish caught are warm-water game
fish, including largemouth bass, bluegill, crappie and channel
catfish.

The Great Salt Plains Reservoir Lake (10,000 acres) is located
in the northwest of Oklahoma near Cherokee, by the Great Salt
Plains National Wildlife Refuge. This was once a well-known
catfish lake but droughts have cut off too much of the sweet
water, and fishing has diminished. There is good geese and duck
hunting in the area.

Fort Supply Lake in northwest Oklahoma near Fort Supply is
1,800 acres, one of the few lakes of the northwestern plains.
Largemouth bass, crappie, white bass and channel catfish are
caught in its water. It also has boats and camping facilities.

The rivers of Oklahoma flow across the state from west to east.
They include the Arkansas, Cimarron, Canadian and Red rivers.
The best fishing rivers are those in the northeast, including the
Black Ford, Grand, Illinois, Mountain Fork and Kiamichi rivers.
Black bass, crappie, bluegill and big catfish are the usual catches.

Oklahomans are extremely enthusiastic about the state's fishing
future, for there are 6 new reservoirs being planned or under
construction. These thousands of acres of new water will greatly
improve what is already fine fishing.

Additional local information:

Brill's Outdoor Guide to Oklahoma and Texoma Cost: $1.00
1630 South Main   Published
Tulsa, Oklahoma   annually

Oregon

Tourist information from:

Oregon State Highway Department
101 State Highway Building
Salem, Oregon

Fishing information from:

Oregon State Fish and Game Commission
1634 S.W. Alder Street
Portland, Oregon

Fish in Oregon: king salmon, silver salmon, cutthroat trout, steelhead, rainbow trout, brown trout, brook trout, Kokanee salmon, largemouth bass, crappie and other fish.

When an angler's thoughts turn to the Pacific Coast state of Oregon (96,981 square miles), his thoughts turn to steelhead and salmon fishing.

The best-known fishing stream in the state, of course, is the world-famous Rogue River located in southern Oregon. This is one of the few rivers of the coast that cuts through the coastal mountains and into the Cascade Mountains. The lower sections of the Rogue have fine silver-salmon fishing in September and king-salmon fishing in April, May and June. Steelhead fishing begins at Gold Beach in August and September; upstream at Grants Pass it extends from September to November. The summer months offer upstream fishing for rainbows and brookies, and the North and South forks are both good producers. Facilities are plentiful, and two national forests with over 50 camp sites border the Rogue River. Rogue River National Forest is east of Grants Pass and Siskiyou National Forest west of the pass. Guides for fishing are available at Gold Beach and Grants Pass. Check local laws for boat fishing, for it is restricted certain times of the year. A Rogue River float trip can be arranged through:

The Sierra Club River Touring Committee
1050 Mills Tower
San Francisco 4, California

Crater Lake National Park is located near the headwaters of the Rogue River. The monstrous crater that is partially water-filled gives the park its name.

Klamath Falls with Upper Klamath Lake (48,000 acres) is a short distance south, and fishing here is for rainbow trout. The Klamath River has been dammed in California so that salmon runs have been cut off from the area.

Other coastal rivers of importance include the Umpqua River, which empties into the Pacific at Reedsport, having come from the northwest area above Diamond Lake (Diamond Lake is a rainbow-trout lake). Salmon fishing in the Umpqua River is as far upstream as the dam at Winchester. The fish seasons are the same as in the Rogue. The North Fork of the river lies in the Umpqua National Forest, and this fork has the best fishing. Thirteen camp sites in the forest can be used as jump-off places for steelhead or rainbow fishing. Brown trout are in the headwaters. Reedsport and Winchester offer the best accommodations along the river—in some sections of the river accommodations are scarce. Smaller salmon rivers in Oregon include the Willamette, Nehalem, Nestucca, Siletz, Yaquina, Alsea, Siuslaw, Coquille and Chetco rivers, and Ten Mile Creek.

The Columbia River, of course, makes up the northern border of Oregon and is the most important salmon stream in the country (*see* Washington). The Columbia River's tributary, the Willamette River, runs from south to north paralleling the Cascade Mountains, flowing through the Willamette Valley and emptying into the Columbia River near Portland.

The river offers salmon, steelhead, rainbow, cutthroat trout and shad. King-salmon season is March to June, and the fall season is from August to October. TheMcKenzie River is a Willamette River tributary that has some fine, fast water and some good rainbow fishing. Also taken are salmon, cutthroat trout and steelhead. Facilities are plentiful along Route 126, which parallels the river.

The Mount Hood National Forest has renowned Timberline Lodge as well as lakes, glaciers and cold-running trout streams. There are over 60 camp sites in the forest.

Another Columbia River tributary is the Deschutes River. Fish include spring Chinook, summer steelhead, resident rainbows, brook trout, brown trout, Kokanee salmon and Mackinaw trout. Salmon fishing centers from Maupin to the mouth of the river, and generally the rainbows, brown and brook trout are taken in the upper reaches. The land along the Deschutes has many lakes with trout (lake trout in Odell and Summit lakes in Deschutes National Forest), and Kokanee salmon can be expected to be taken in Seattle Lake in Jefferson County and Blue Lake in Wasco County. The Deschutes National Forest covers much of the area and offers almost 60 improved camp sites.

Northeastern Oregon has the Wallowa Mountains, which include the Wallowa-Whitman National Forest. Thirty improved camp sites, resorts and dude ranches are in the forest, making facilities plentiful. One Ranch—the Bar M Ranch, Gibbon, Oregon—is on the Umatila River, where steelhead and rainbows can be fished. The Grande Ronde, the Minam and Imnaha rivers are here, as well as the Snake River, which makes up the eastern border of this section of the state. Chinook salmon, steelhead, rainbows, brookies, Kokanee salmon and cutthroat trout are the important game fish of this area. Wallowa Lake near Enterprise is a resort center with good fishing for rainbow and Kokanee salmon. Two fine trout streams in Baker County are Eagle Creek and Pine Creek.

Southeastern Oregon offers fishing in the Owyhee Reservoir, which is located in undeveloped country. Travel to the reservoir is by jeep or other rugged vehicles, for roads are very poor. Fish caught are rainbow trout, bass and crappie. The Owyhee River has rainbow trout below the reservoir dam. The Oregon camper should write for maps and the free booklet *Forest Camping in Oregon* to:

U.S. Forest Service
P. O. Box 4137
Portland, Oregon

Oregon offers rod-breaking salmon and big hard-fighting, stubborn steelhead, besides other varieties of trout. It has 13 national forests, mountains, lakes and 15,000 miles of streams. No wonder men like Zane Grey fall in love with the state.

Pennsylvania

Tourist information from:

Department of Commerce
Vacation and Travel Bureau
Harrisburg, Pennsylvania

Fishing information from:

Pennsylvania Fish Commission
Harrisburg, Pennsylvania

Fish in Pennsylvania: brook trout, brown trout, rainbow trout, lake trout, walleye, crappie, perch, largemouth bass, smallmouth bass, bluegill, pike, pickerel, muskellunge and rough fish.

The "Quaker State" of Pennsylvania is 45,333 square miles in area. Its fishing varies, like its topography, from good to spotty.

The best fishing and some of the prettiest country in the state are in the northeastern section. Canoe fishing trips are fine sport for almost the whole length of the Delaware River. Fish caught are rainbow and brook trout in the upper reaches and brookies in the feeder streams. Below Damascus, which is a good starting point for canoeing, there are chain pickerel, walleye pike and, of course, smallmouth bass.

Seventy miles west and running a somewhat parallel course to the south is the Susquehanna River. Smallmouth and largemouth bass are the top sports fish, with chain pickerel, pike, walleye, bluegill and crappie also giving the angler excitement.

Certain sections of the Delaware are in rugged country, and access to water may be difficult; but it is just in these spots that fishing is best. Sunbury, where the West Branch of the Susquehanna meets the main stream, is a good fishing spot and a good take-off point for canoeing.

A few lakes in northeastern Pennsylvania have lake-trout fishing. They include 685-acre Harvey's Lake, 10 miles northwest of Wilkes-Barre, which also has rainbow trout, brook trout, bass and pickerel. Lake trout run in Crystal Lake just above Carbondale.

There are hundreds of lakes and ponds in this area, including Lake Wallenpaupack (5,700 acres) near Hawley, with rainbows, brown trout, bass and pickerel. Upper Wilcox Pond with trout, bass and pickerel and Upper Woods Pond in the same area have virtually the same fish, while Pecks Pond has primarily smallmouth bass and pickerel. Generally the vacationer and visiting angler would find fishing good and lodging plentiful throughout the Pocono Mountains area.

Lake Ontelaunee is just north of Reading near Moselem Springs.

Further southeast, the huge metropolis of Philadelphia has very little fishing to offer, for the Delaware River is brackish and polluted here, and fresh-water fish are gone. The Schuylkill River offers little more, and there are only a few ponds in the area. The best fishing is across the river in one of the fresh-water lakes near Trenton, New Jersey.

In the northwest section of Pennsylvania are the First Fork of the Sinnemahoning Creek and the Driftwood Branch of this creek, fine trout streams with rainbow and brook trout the specialties. The lake above the George B. Stevenson Dam, which has Sinnemahoning State Park on its shores, is also a fine fishing spot. This lake is considered by many to be the best smallmouth-bass lake in Pennsylvania, with catches of walleye and pickerel also good.

Further south near Bellefonte there are other fine trout streams, including Spring and Bald Eagle creeks.

Throughout the Allegheny National Forest are 300 miles of trout streams, and trout can be taken in Tionesta Creek, Salmon Hickory Creek, Clarion River and Sugar Run. The Beaver Meadows Waterfowl Refuge is in the Allegheny National Forest. There are facilities at Clarendon, Sheffield, Kane and Ridgway for hotels, motels and cabins, while the forest has 8 camp sites for the more rugged.

The northwest section of Pennsylvania borders on Lake Erie, and here the fishing is for black bass, white bass, perch, walleye and rough fish.

South of the big lake is the 15,000-acre Pymatuning Reservoir on the Ohio border. Fish in this large body of water include bass, crappie, walleye, pickerel, channel catfish, some muskie and trout. Boats and facilities are available at Linesville. Less than 5 miles east is 900-acre Lake Conneaut, which has bass, bluegill, crappie and muskie. Lake Conneaut is one of the best muskellunge lakes of Pennsylvania, giving up some real monsters from time to time.

Land throughout the mining area of the state is often scarred, while acid drainage into the water kills fish life, and the rivers and streams run dirty.

The Allegheny River and the Ohio River meet within the city of Pittsburgh. The Allegheny River has bass, walleye and muskie in its upper reaches, but around the metropolis there are only rough fish. The Ohio is much the same story.

The lake above Conemaugh Dam near Blairsville is contaminated with acid mine drainage and does not support fish.

The southern border of the state has fishing in Youghiogheny Reservoir. Several years ago it looked as if this lake would be lost for fishing because of acid mine drainage, but northern-pike stocking in 1958, 1959 and 1960 has shown fine results. There is good largemouth-bass fishing here, and walleye were introduced in 1960. Fishing should get steadily better with good conservation practices.

Pennsylvania is a fish-loving state, and to keep up its production the Fish Commission stocks over 4,000 miles of stream annually. The natives' quest for fishing information is partially satisfied by the Fish Commission's magazine, the *Pennsylvania Angler*, which is published monthly in Harrisburg. This magazine features articles about Pennsylvania fishing by authors who know the state. I always feel very nostalgic about the *Pennsylvania Angler*, for it published the first article I ever wrote. The cost of the *Angler* is $1.00 per year.

Rhode Island

Tourist information from:

> State Development Council
> Information Division
> State House
> Providence 2, Rhode Island

A permit is required to fish all state-management waters.

Write to:

> Division of Game and Fish
> 83 Park Street
> Providence, Rhode Island

Note: No fishing license is required for ladies in the state.

Fish in Rhode Island: largemouth and smallmouth bass, black crappie, pickerel, yellow perch, white perch, channel catfish, bluegill and trout (rainbow, brown and brook, through stocking).

Rhode Island is the smallest of the 50 states, only 1,214 square miles in area. Although the accent here is on salt-water fishing, there is ample fresh-water sport.

An active program of stocking trout throughout Rhode Island gives anglers brook, brown and rainbow trout in almost 200 miles of streams. Brookies, the stocked variety, are in Chickasheen and Perry Healey brooks in Burlingame State Park. Brown and rainbow trout are in Brickyard Pond, Watchaugh Pond (934 acres) in Burlingame State Park, Stafford Pond (476 acres) and the Ponagansett River.

Warm-water game fish, including bass, pickerel and bluegill, can be taken at Watchaugh Pond, Herring Pond (96 acres) in the Harrisville State Management Area, and Olney Pond in Lincoln Woods State Park.

Worden Pond (1,043 acres) and Pawcatuk in the Great Swamp State Management Area (no smallmouth here) also have these fish.

All together there are 44 state-management areas for fishing in Rhode Island, and 27 streams, lakes and rivers are stocked with trout.

South Carolina

Tourist information from:

State Development Board
Box 927
Columbia, South Carolina

Fishing information from:

Wildlife Resources Department
Department of Game
Columbia, South Carolina

Fish in South Carolina: landlocked striped bass, largemouth bass, bluegill, crappie, yellow perch, trout (few), carp, channel catfish, white bass and rough fish.

In South Carolina, a southeastern seaboard state 31,055 square miles in area, there are some exciting developments that the whole fishing world is watching with anxious eyes. The state seems to have ocean striped bass that have become landlocked in Lakes Moultrie and Marion, where they are reproducing and thriving.

This is extremely encouraging to fishermen, because they know it took only one barrel of stripers dumped into San Francisco Bay to get the whole West Coast started on this terrific sports fish. Now if a strain of striper has been successfully transplanted to other sweet water, there is the thrilling possibility of 30- to 50-pounders being pulled out of every TVA lake or from the Great Lakes. Stripers have been transplanted in Buggs Island Lake, North Carolina–Virginia, successfully, and now biologists are busily at work elsewhere.

Lake Moultrie (60,000 acres) and Lake Marion (110,000 acres) together make up the Santee-Cooper Wildlife Area that is located between Charleston and Columbia. These are TVA reservoirs. There are over 40 fishing camps in the area, some of which are located at Moncks Corner, Manning, Eutawville, Summerton and at the mouth of the Diversion Canal. Fish caught here are, of course, headed by the stripers sometimes called Santee-Cooper bass or rock bass. Also caught are largemouth bass, white bass, bluegill, crappie, catfish and rough fish. The catfish grow to monstrous size in these lakes; in fact, the world-record channel catfish—a 57-pounder—was hauled out of these waters in 1960. Then to add to the luster of Santee-Cooper is the fact that the world's biggest black crappie—a 5-pounder—was taken here.

In the center of the state just west of Columbia is located 50,000-acre Lake Murray. Largemouth bass, bluegill, crappie and yellow perch are the chief fish. Lake Greenwood (12,000 acres) a little northwest of Lake Murray is another TVA reservoir that is the result of damming the Saluda River. This lake has the same fish as Lake Murray, and both lakes have boats, tourist accommodations and camping facilities.

North of Columbia is the Wateree Reservoir, where there is a good supply of warm-water game fish.

On the North Carolina border a few miles south of Charlotte there is Lake Catawba, again with largemouth bass, bluegill and crappie.

The northwest section of the state has Tugaloo Lake, a reservoir on the Georgia border near Westminster. Facilities for the warm-water fishing of the lake are at Tallulah Lodge.

The big reservoir on the Georgia border is Clark Hill Reservoir (78,000 acres), a few miles northwest of Augusta, Georgia. There are boats at Clarks Hill, Parksville and Bordeaux for bass, bluegill, crappie and catfish.

The waters of the state—including the Asheopoo, Cooper, Edisto, Combahee, Pee Dee, Santee, and Waccamaw rivers—can be counted on to produce largemouth bass, crappie, bluegill and catfish.

South Carolina has productive warm-water fishing; and in spite of the fact that the state has two world records tucked away, I still feel the most exciting prospects are those striped bass, for they virtually guarantee a third record: What other state can claim 40-pound landlocked striped bass?

South Dakota

Tourist information from:

Publicity Director
Department of Highways
Pierre, South Dakota

Fishing information from:

South Dakota Department of Game, Fish and Parks
Pierre, South Dakota

Fish in South Dakota: brown trout, rainbow trout, brook trout, largemouth bass, northern pike, sauger, blue catfish, channel catfish, bluegill, crappie, yellow perch and rough fish.

South Dakota (77,047 square miles) in area has the absolute geographical center of the Continental United States in its northwest section, just above the Belle Fourche Reservoir.

Below this spot and extending into Wyoming are the Black Hills of Dakota. There are brown and rainbow trout in such streams as Spearfish Creek near Hill City, and Spring Creek located south of Rapid City. The leading lake fishing in this part of the state is that done in the 15,500-acre Angostura Reservoir Lake near Hot Springs. Fish include rainbow trout, largemouth bass, walleye, crappie and channel catfish. There are complete facilities at Hot Springs, and camping and boats at the lake. Other smaller lakes in the Black Hills include Sheridan Lake near Hill City, and Stockade Lake near Custer. Both have rainbows and brown trout. The Belle Fouche Reservoir is a bass–pan-fish lake.

A trip to this section of the country is incomplete without a visit to the awesome sight of the four Presidents carved out of Mount Rushmore. The Black Hills National Forest covers much of the area, and there are over 50 camp sites distributed throughout the forest.

A short distance east but still in the southwest of the state are the Badlands of South Dakota and Badlands National Park. Here barren rocks and dryness paint a dramatic picture.

Running north to south through the middle of South Dakota

is the Missouri River. In 1959 this stretch of water gave up the biggest catfish ever taken—a 97-pound blue catfish. The river has now been dammed for flood-control purposes, and gigantic Reservoir Lake Oahe (466 square miles) has been formed. In the south central part of the state is Fort Randall Reservoir. These two reservoirs can be fished for largemouth bass, walleye pike, northern pike, sturgeon, sauger, channel catfish and, of course, blue catfish. River Island Park is at the north of Fort Randall Reservoir.

Northeastern South Dakota has a group of lakes which boast the same good fishing found throughout neighboring Minnesota. Among these are the 12,000-acre reservoir Lake Traverse near Sisseton, and slightly larger and deeper Big Stone Lake south of it on the Minnesota border. These lakes have largemouth bass, northern pike, walleye pike, bluegill, crappie and bullhead. Both have ample boat rentals, camping areas and lodging facilities. The nearby towns of Sisseton or Milbank can be used as bases.

Other lakes in the east are 1½-mile Clear Lake near Lake City, and 2½-mile Roy Lake, accessible from the same town. Lakes 5 square miles or larger include Lake Kampeska near Watertown, Lake Poinsett near Arlington and Lake Madison near Madison. These have the same fish as the border lakes.

South Dakota now has 3 major fishing areas a visitor may look to: the Black Hills in the west, the two reservoir lakes in the center, and the Minnesota-type lakes in the east. Together they offer fine opportunities for fishing in what was once considered an arid state.

Tennessee

Tourist information from:

> Division of State Information
> Department of Conservation
> 233 Cordell Hull Building
> Nashville 3, Tennessee

Also

Knoxville Tourist Bureau
P. O. Box 237
Knoxville, Tennessee

Fishing information from:

Tennessee Game and Fish Commission
Cordell Hull Building
Nashville 3, Tennessee

Fish in Tennessee: rainbow trout, brown trout, brook trout, largemouth bass, smallmouth bass, white bass, yellow bass, walleye pike, muskellunge, crappie, blue catfish, bullhead, channel catfish, flathead catfish, carp and rough fish.

The advent of the Tennessee Valley Authority brought 600,000 acres of fishing water to Tennessee's 42,246 square miles of land, and this new water makes the state one of the fresh-water fishing centers of the country. There are 22 major lakes and reservoirs here that hold the biggest bass anywhere. There are also rivers and streams throughout the state, and fishing is everywhere.

The Tennessee River was dammed and formed into Kentucky Lake, which is 184 miles long with 2,380 miles of shore line, covering 261,000 acres in Tennessee and Kentucky. There are almost 100 places for boat rentals on this resort lake; some are at Model, Fort Henry, Buchanan, Springville, Big Sandy, Waverly and Camden. This, the biggest lake in Tennessee, is a bass lake, with smallmouth, largemouth and white bass, along with crappie and bluegill. Sizable catfish also come out of this lake.

Pickwick Lake, a 53-mile-long lake, is directly south of Kentucky Lake. Boats for fishing here may be obtained at Pickwick Dam and Iuka, Mississippi. Largemouth bass, white bass, walleye pike, crappie and catfish are the fish caught. The city of Savannah sponsors an annual catfish derby below the dam, and if he wants any prizes, an angler had better come up with 30-pounders.

The far northwest corner of the state has Reelfoot Lake, 14,500 acres of warm semi-tropical water that is a cypress garden. The lake came into existence as the result of an earthquake at the turn of the century. Fish caught here are largemouth bass, yellow bass, Kentucky bass and crappie. Boats and lodging are available at Tiptonville.

Almost directly in the center of the state there is Old Hickory Lake, a reservoir covering 22,000 acres, which boasts fine bass fishing. Boats are at Old Hickory, Lebanon and Hendersonville, and the visitor should be aware that facilities are somewhat scarce around this lake.

Dale Hollow Lake, a 40,000-acre reservoir which came about through the damming of the Cumberland River, is located on the Kentucky-Tennessee border. Boats are at Celina and Byrdston. Fish caught are largemouth and smallmouth bass, white bass, walleye pike and crappie. The world-record smallmouth bass came out of Dale Hollow—an 11-pound 15-ounce terror. It was caught in the Kentucky section of the lake, but natives swear it was born and raised in Tennessee and only wandered north accidentally. There are some really monstrous brown trout below Dale Hollow Dam, and a 26-pounder has already been taken there. This water is easily accessible from Gainesboro.

Center Hill Lake, south of Dale Hollow near Smithville, is 20,000 acres and is famous for walleye pike, with the fish going up to 21 pounds there. Also largemouth and smallmouth bass as well as crappie are in the lake. Boats are at Smithville, Alexandria and Walling.

The eastern part of Tennessee has many reservoirs created from the waters of the Tennessee River and its feeder streams. Bass, bass and more bass are the prize fish, with crappie and walleye pike also taken regularly. The lakes include Fort Patrick Henry, South Holston, Boone, Wilbur, Watauga, Davy Crockett, Cherokee (30,000-acre bass lake with boats at Rutledge), Douglas, Fort Loudoun (14,500-acre bass lake with boats at Knoxville), Watts Bar (12 docks and boats at Spring City and Rockwood) and Chickamauga Lake above Chattanooga. Norris Lake is close to Knoxville, Tennessee, and is the oldest TVA lake having been completed in 1936. Guides and boats are available at such places as Norris Dock in Lake City and Stiner's Fishing Camp, Sharps Chapel, Tennessee. Fishing specialties are walleye and sauger, and the catches are phenomenal.

Knoxville is at the center of these eastern lakes and is an excellent jump-off place for the trout fishing in the Great Smoky Mountain National Park. The Little Tennessee, the West Prong Little Pigeon, Middle Prong Little Pigeon and the Little rivers are trout streams. Near Newport there are trout streams such as Gulf Fork, Wolf, Trail Fork, Cosby, Indian Camp, Dry Fork, Little, and Big Creeks, all located in or near the Cherokee National Forest. There are 13 public camp sites in the forest and hotels at nearby Etowah and Mountain City. The Tellico River is noted for its trout fishing. Chilhowee Lake, which is stocked with rainbow trout, is within 40 miles of Knoxville.

The major rivers in the state, the Tennessee and Cumberland, have already been mentioned; with the TVA these rivers are now actually a chain of lakes for hydroelectric power and lake fishing. The west border of Tennessee is the Mississippi River. Here rough fish are taken both by rod and reel and by commercial methods.

Fishing in Tennessee lakes, which the state considers the "Great Lakes of the South," is excellent for warm-water game fish, especially smallmouth bass. There is no closed season on these fish, and they grow exceptionally large because food is plentiful. The water is clean and never freezes up. The bass here are on feed all year long, which makes them exceptionally big offering.

Texas

Tourist information from:

The State of Texas
Texas Highway Department
Information and Statistics Division
Austin 14, Texas

Fishing information from:

Texas Game and Fish Commission
Walton Building
Austin, Texas

Specific state park information:

Write managers of individual parks

Fish in Texas: largemouth bass, smallmouth bass, white bass, bluegill, crappie, channel catfish, alligator gar, longnose gar, sunfish and rough fish.

Texas is a gigantic 267,339 square miles in area, of which 3,395 are very fishable water. The western part is arid and has less than 10 inches annual rainfall, while the Gulf Coast has over 50 inches of rain annually. Throughout the state there are lakes, reservoirs, and fast- and slow-running streams and rivers for fresh-water sport.

The biggest body of water is the 95,000-acre reservoir Lake Texoma, which has 1,250 miles of shore line on the Texas-Oklahoma border. The lake came about with the storing of the waters of the Red River when Denison Dam was completed. The area around the lake quickly grew into a resort center of fishing camps, hotels, motels and boat liveries. Eisenhower State Park is now under construction near Denison, the center of this resort area.

One interesting development on the lake is the big fishing barges where anglers pay a fee to fish from soft chairs. Those not caring to weather the sun can go inside the air-cooled barge and fish in the pool-like openings to the lake. The water around the barge is chummed to attract the fish, so that catches are quite good.

Fish caught in Lake Texoma are black bass, white bass, crappie, bluegill and channel catfish.

Near the Arkansas border Lake Texarkana is close to the city of Texarkana. Atlanta State Park has camping facilities. Kickapoo Lodge above Douglassville has a complete line of all facilities, including a light-plane air strip for those who don't care to drive. Fish in the lake are bass, bream, crappie and channel catfish.

Lake Ferry and Caddo Lake are near Marshal and are south of Lake Texarkana. Caddo Lake State Park is near Karnack, and has cabins, camping facilities and boats. The lakes have the same fish as Lake Texarkana, and Caddo is a renowned bass lake.

Whitney Lake is located near Hillsboro. This 16,000-acre lake is the result of damming the Brazos River in 1951. Many lodging places and camps surround it. Lake Whitney State Park has Fisherman's Inn and camp, boat and trailer-camp facilities. There is good trout-line fishing for yellow and channel catfish in the lake, as well as bass, crappie and bream fishing.

Eighty miles upstream on the Brazos River there is Possum Kingdom Lake near Graham. Possum Kingdom State Park near Caddo has cabins, camping and boats for the visiting fisherman. Fish are the same as in the lower lake.

Lake Tawakoni, 50 miles east of Dallas near Quinlan, is a 36,700-acre reservoir under construction, which the Sabine River will fill in a few years. When it is filled, Texas will have another sportsland of importance.

Above Austin the Colorado River has the famous Highland Lakes, an 150-mile stairway encompassing 76,000 acres of sports-fishing water. The lakes are Lake Buchanan (23,000 acres of water at the top), Lake Inks (900 acres), Lake Granite (6,300 acres), Lake Marble Falls (900 acres), Lake Travis (42,000 acres) and Lake Austin (3,000 acres).

The first two lakes, Lake Buchanan and Lake Inks, are convenient to Burnet. There are fishing lodges on Lake Buchanan, and Inks State Park has camping and boats to service Inks Lake. One of the Texas hatcheries (which all together release a total of 15 million fish a year) is located on Inks Lake.

Granite Shoals Lake has a free fishing pier at Wirtz Park. Lake Marble Falls has Fred Wood's Fishing Camp at Kingsland and Sportsman Lodge at Marble Falls. Lake Marble Falls is a dramatic spot, surrounded as it is by sheer limestone and marble bluffs.

Lake Travis, the biggest lake, has dude ranches, fishing camps and lodges for fishermen. Finally, Lake Austin, located in the state's capital, has many tourist accommodations. Fish caught in these highland lakes are largemouth bass, smallmouth bass, white bass, bream, crappie and catfish. The white-bass population is astronomical.

Reservoir Lake Corpus Christi is 25 miles west of that city, near Mathis. Corpus Christi has all tourist facilities, and Lake Corpus Christi State Park has camping and boat rentals. Fish are largemouth and smallmouth bass, crappie and catfish.

The Rio Grande River on the Mexican border has Falcon Dam, which has formed the 50,000-acre Falcon Reservoir Lake near Falcon Heights. Falcon State Park has boat-launching facilities, but it is basically undeveloped, as is much of the area around this lake. Fish caught here are primarily largemouth bass and catfish.

Further west, Devils Lake above Del Rio has boats and motels for the fisherman. Fish are warm-water fish.

Big Bend National Park in the far southwest is 707,000 acres of arid land rising as high as 7,835-foot Emory Peak. Fishing here is restricted to the Rio Grande, but nonetheless the park is an interesting place to visit, with its wildlife in the deep canyons and on the Sheep Mountains. Cabins are available at the Ranger station in the Chisos Mountains.

The rivers of Texas have two world's records to their credit. The Rio Grande had a gigantic 279-pound alligator gar pulled from it in 1951, while the Trinity River holds the record for longnose gar—a 50-pound 5-ouncer. Some people may consider these records dubious; but actually gar fishing is wild, and it often takes a pistol shot to finally subdue one of the monsters. Gars make interesting sport spearing, bow-and-arrow shooting or by standard fishing.

The Rio Grande River borders Texas and Mexico and flows for 1,210 miles in Texas. It has some bass fishing and rough fish. The Colorado River runs 890 miles through Texas, and has largemouth and smallmouth bass, bluegill, crappie and catfish. The Brazos River runs through the state for 659 miles and has warm-water game fish. Finally the Red River borders Texas and Oklahoma for almost 760 miles, and also has warm-water game fish.

Other long rivers are the Sabine, the Trinity, the Nueces, the Neches and the Pecos.

Texas can be said generally to have warm-water fishing that is varied and interesting and that gets better with each new reservoir that is constructed.

Magazine dealing with Texas outdoors: Cost: $2.00 a year

Texas Game and Fish
Texas Game and Fish Commission
Walton Building
Austin, Texas

Utah

Tourist information from:

Tourist and Publicity Council
State Capitol Building
Salt Lake City, Utah

Fishing information from:

Utah State Fish and Game Department
1956 West North Temple
Salt Lake City, Utah

Fish in Utah: rainbow trout, brown trout, cutthroat trout, brook trout, Mackinaw trout, golden trout, grayling, bass, walleye pike and bluegill, whitefish, Kokanee salmon and rough fish.

Utah (84,916 square miles in area)—primitive northeast Utah especially—has some of the wildest, most rugged and best fishing waters anywhere in the country. This Rocky Mountain state has over 2,000 lakes and hundreds of miles of streams in addition to 7 national forests and 2 national parks that make it a sportsman's dream. The state stays busy keeping up the good fishing, for it stocks approximately 9 million fish a year from its dozen hatcheries.

The Logan River in the north of Utah is renowned as a trout stream with excellent fly-fishing opportunities. There are brown trout, rainbow trout, cutthroat trout, brook trout, bass and blue-gill taken in the stream. One monstrous brown weighing 37 pounds 4 ounces came out of the Logan. Cache National Forest has much of the famous stream running through it, and there are 7 camping areas in Logan Canyon. The city of Logan has all facilities for the visitor.

Bear Lake on the Idaho border heads the list of lakes in the north of the state, and it is 21 miles long and 7 miles wide in parts. It has rainbow trout, lake trout and whitefish in its clean, cold waters. The resorts of Garden City and Laketown make this a pleasant place to stay for fishermen. There are also camping facilities, cabins and trailer parks for more budget-minded sportsmen.

Northeastern Utah has mountains rising as high as 13,498-foot Kings Peak. Swift, clear streams run down these Uinta Mountain slopes, while cold, clear lakes make up the valleys. Trout streams are everywhere, including the Duchesne River, Whiterocks River, Brush Cliff Creek, Uinta River, Lake Fork River, Rock River and countless unnamed rivers. These streams are heavy with rainbows, cutthroats, browns, brookies, goldens and grayling. Camping in the area can be found on the Uinta River in Uinta Canyon.

The same fish that frequent the streams can be found in the cold lakes such as Fork Lake, Red Lake, Mirror Lake (a resort lake of the Grandaddy Lakes), Moon Lake or Kidney Lake. The Wasatch National Forest and the Ashley National Forest cover the area. Mirror Lake, east of Kamas, has a lodge, cabins, a trailer camp and boats as do the Green Lakes north of Vernal, and Spirit Lake south of Manila. Then Moon Lake at the base of Uintah and Ouray Indian Reservation near Duchesne has camping, cottages and boats for trout fishermen.

Central Utah has Utah Lake (8,000 acres) near Provo for bass, walleye pike and catfish. Accommodations are at Provo. Trout fishing in the vicinity can be done over almost 70 miles of the Provo River.

The 4,000-acre Strawberry Reservoir, in the shadow of 8,000-

foot mountains, is near Heber. Fish in this reservoir are rainbow trout, cutthroat trout and perch.

A distance south there is 2,500-acre Fish Lake near Richfield. Forty-pound battling Mackinaw trout have already been taken from this lake, as well as sizable rainbows, cutthroats, brookies and bass. There is camping in many areas of the Fish Lake National Forest. Richfield, located northwest of the lake, has all facilities for a visitor.

A visit to Zion National Park with its spectacular canyons of the Virgin River is a must when in southwest Utah. The park has a lodge and camping facilities. Trout fishing in the area is in such places as the Navajo Lakes, Panguitch Lake, Mammoth Creek and Assay Creek.

Some long rivers flow through Utah that are fine for boating, floating and fishing. Float trips for the Colorado or Salmon rivers can be arranged through:

Hatch River Expedition Company
411 East 2nd North
Vernal, Utah

These trips offer exciting days in truly spectacular country, where civilization is almost nonexistent and nature is king.

Private boat trips on the Green River are fun, and periodically large groups of boatmen get together for a 225-mile trip starting at Green River, Utah, then going down the Green River 168 miles and up the Colorado River 68 miles to Moab. On these trips sportsmen pass through dramatic canyons and spectacular scenery. In the river are catfish. Further information from: Moab Chamber of Commerce, Moab, Utah.

If any angler is thinking about fishing 2,570-square-mile Great Salt Lake, he had better forget it, for, while the lake is fine for floating and swimming, it is not a fish lake. Western Utah is generally as dry as a Prohibition meeting on a Sunday morning, and the Great Salt Lake Desert takes up much of the area.

The best fishing in Utah is the fine mountain fishing for trout and grayling. Warm-water fishing should improve considerably when Glen Canyon Dam is completed, for the Colorado will then make another really monstrous reservoir lake, most of which will be in southeastern Utah. Even so, these mountain trout will always look good to me.

Vermont

Tourist fishing information from:

> Development Commission
> Publicity Director
> 300 State Office Building
> Montpelier 22, Vermont

Fishing information from:

> Fish and Game Service
> State Office Building
> Montpelier 22, Vermont

Fish in Vermont: brook trout, brown trout, rainbow trout, lake trout, landlocked salmon, smallmouth bass, largemouth bass, perch, pike, perch, walleye pike, catfish, pickerel and northern pike.

The "Green Mountain State" of Vermont is relatively small—only 9,608 square miles—but has some fine, fast-running trout streams and over 400 lakes for fishing. The Connecticut River borders the east of the state, and it's good for walleye and northern pike in the south and trout in the north. A drive along the Connecticut River valley north of White River Junction on Route 5 will show some of the beauty of this state.

Lake Champlain borders much of the western portion of Vermont, and it offers smallmouth bass, northern pike, walleye, pickerel, perch and catfish. Burlington is the major resort center of this area. Other fishing in the Champlain area is in the river that feeds the lake—the Missisquoi River, which has largemouth and smallmouth bass from Swanton to the lake, while to the east there are only smallmouth bass. In the northern reaches of this river there are trout.

The Lamoille River has smallmouth bass, pike and perch from

the lake to Jeffersonville and trout—rainbows and browns—
above there. Other trout rivers are the Big and Little Otter,
the New Haven and the Middlebury, which has rainbows below
Bristol.

Ponds and lakes in the area include Lake Carmi, Fairfield
Pond and Lake Dunmore, with lake trout and salmon heading
the list. Shelburne and Hinesburg ponds have northern pike
and bass.

Northern Vermont has a remote section of land at the headwaters of the Nulhegan River, and this stream and its tributaries
are excellent for brook-trout fishing. Headwaters for the Missisquoi River are good for brook trout, and the Barton River is a
rainbow stream. The Clyde River is a spawning stream for landlocked salmon of Lake Memphremagog. The Nulhegan River,
which flows into the Connecticut, has rainbows in its lower
regions; Paul Stream has them to the Passumpsic River; and in
the Moose River the accent is on brook trout.

Lakes in the northeast include Lake Memphremagog on the
Canadian border, which has salmon, brown and rainbow trout.
Lake Willoughby near Barton has landlocked salmon and trout,
and Long Pond close by is a trout lake. Maidstone Lake near
Maidstone is a trout lake, and other spots include the Averill
Lakes, Crystal Lake and Parker Pond.

Southern Vermont has the famous Batten Kill River, which
consistently yields rainbow, brook and brown trout. The West
River has bass near its mouth, while rainbows and brown trout
take over north of Dummerston. The Saxtons River flows into the
Connecticut River at Bellows Falls and has brown trout in the
slower, big stream while brookies are upstream and in the feeder
streams. The White River is stocked with rainbows and browns.
In the west of the state near Castleton, Lakes Bomoseen, Hortonia
and St. Catherine have bass, pickerel and northern pike. The
power reservoirs, the Whitingham and Somerset, have bass,
pickerel and yellow perch.

Good fishing is the rule in almost any part of the state, and
the fishing gets even better the further north one ventures. Lodging is not a serious problem in the state, for motels are common

and many big New England homes welcome tourists. Write for the free booklet that is published annually by the State Development Commission: *Vermont Visitor's Handbook to Lodging and Eating Places.*

Virginia

Tourist information from:

> Department of Conservation and Development
> 820 State Office Building
> Richmond 19, Virginia

Fishing information from:

> Commonwealth of Virginia
> Commission of Game and Inland Fisheries
> P. O. Box 1642
> Richmond 13, Virginia

Fish in Virginia: largemouth bass, smallmouth bass, rock bass, landlocked striped bass, sunfish, crappie, walleye pike, pickerel, brook trout, rainbow trout, bluegill and rough fish.

The state of Virginia is 40,815 square miles in area and has fresh-water fishing that varies from average to very good. The quality of fishing, as in many other eastern seaboard states, differs throughout Virginia.

Two centers for fishing are the national parks, the George Washington National Forest and the Thomas Jefferson National Forest, in the western Appalachian Mountain section of the state. The George Washington Forest is in the Shenandoah section of the Blue Ridge Mountains where the sky-line drive runs along the crest. There are 68 stocked trout streams here and over 225 miles of fishing waters in the area. The resorts of Warm Springs, Hot Springs, Harrisburg and Woodstock are fine places to stay. Lakes with trout and other game fish are near Greenville and Harrisburg.

The Thomas Jefferson National Forest located further south has 45 stocked trout streams with 141 miles of fishing water.

There are fishing lakes with trout near Natural Bridge and Tacoma. The main centers of population are Roanoke, New Castle, Fincastle and Pulaski. Camping facilities are available throughout both forests. There is $1.00 charge in addition to the regular license for fishing in the parks.

Trout fishing in Virginia is restricted to the western mountain streams which include Big Stony Creek, Cedar Creek, Little Stony Passage Creek and Mountain Run—all of which are near Woodstock just north of Harrisburg. Near Hot Springs the Jackson River, Bull Pasture River and Smith Creek can be fished for trout, while bass can be fished in the Cow Pasture River. Near Rocky Mountain there are trout in Green Creek, and Maggodee Creek. Radford has trout in Tom's Creek, which also has small-mouth bass. The headwaters of the Roanoke River have bass; and the James River, which runs through the state, is a bass river.

Other rivers of the west are the Shenandoah, the Middle and the Jackson, all of which are trout-stocked wherever possible.

The John H. Kerr Reservoir bordering North Carolina is a 50,000-acre reservoir noted for its fine bass fishing. This reservoir has an open season for fishing, and a visitor is never further than a short drive away from boats and other lake facilities. Besides bass, catches include walleye and sunfish, and now landlocked striped bass or rockfish seem to have taken in the lake.

Clayton Lake near Pulaski is 5,000 acres of water, having large-mouth and smallmouth bass, crappie and walleye.

The Philpott Reservoir near Philpott provides boats and facilities. Largemouth, smallmouth bass, sunfish and crappie are the fish in good supply.

Lake Drummond (5,000 acres) near Norfolk has largemouth bass, crappie and bream.

Back Bay on the southeastern tip of Virginia is famed for its brackish-water fishing. The water here is fresh enough to support fresh-water fish, including largemouth bass, bluegill and crappie. There are some 25,000 acres of this water available for fishing a few miles southeast of Norfolk.

The state controls and vigorously stocks certain small lakes throughout Virginia. They include Lake Shenandoah (39 acres) near Harrisburg, and Scott-Wise Pond (68 acres) on Little Stony Creek near Coburn, which are trout-stocked lakes that have boats. Powhatan Lake near Powhatan is 75 acres of warm water. Silver Lake near Dayton is heavily populated with carp, and bow-and-arrow shooting of these fish is popular. Boats are available.

The visiting fisherman in Virginia should be aware that the state has blue laws, so before hook dunking on a Sunday, check the game laws.

Washington

Tourist information from:

State Advertising Commission
Olympia, Washington

Fishing information from:

Washington State Department of Game
600 North Capital Way
Olympia, Washington

Fish in Washington: king salmon, silver salmon, cutthroat trout, rainbow or steelhead trout, Dolly Varden, brown trout, brook trout, largemouth and smallmouth bass, whitefish, crappie and other fish.

Bordering the Pacific Ocean and Canada in our northwest is the 68,192-square-mile state of Washington. The Columbia River, the nation's second largest river and the nation's most important salmon stream, runs for 700 miles through the state and makes up its southern border on 300 miles of its route.

The Columbia River is the major drainage of the Northwest, including Idaho, Oregon and Washington, and it offers the angler fishing for king salmon, cohoe, cutthroat trout, steelhead, giant white sturgeon and shad. Steelhead fishing is best during the winter months but runs from January to June. Seasons are: Chinook runs, March, June and August to October; silver salmon,

October to December; shad, June to July; and sturgeon, March and April. One section of the river is the Grand Coulee Dam, the world's largest dam, which has formed the Columbia into 151-mile-long, 82,000-acre Franklin D. Roosevelt Lake. The Grand Coulee Recreation Area is on the lake, and there is fine fishing for the species of the river in the lake. Colville National Forest has a developed camp site here. The towns of Coulee City, Hunters and Kettle Falls are along the lake. There is good bass and crappie fishing below the dam.

Another famous river, the Snake, joins the Columbia near Pasco. This river offers the same fine salmon and trout as the Columbia. The Snake is stocked annually with trout and sturgeon. Other Columbia tributaries which have the same good fishing are the Cowlitz River and Kalama River near Longview, and the Naches River near Yakima. Fishing here is best in the late spring and summer months.

The Tieton River and Tieton Reservoir are near Tieton and are fine rainbow waters during the summer months.

Mount Rainier National Park, with the 14,410-foot, snow-topped Mount Rainier, is an awesome sight, well worth visiting. There are fishing camps throughout the parks and the 26 glaciers provide cold, clear water for vigorous trout. Paradise Inn is in the park, and one dude ranch in the area is just 6 miles from Mount Rainier—Double K Mountain Ranch, Goose Prairie, Washington.

Mount Rainier is one of the peaks of the Cascade Mountains, which run north and south in the state and divide it into two separate land and climate areas. Other high peaks of these mountains are Mount Adams (12,307 feet) above Trout Lake (much good fishing in the wilderness area surrounding this mountain) and Mount Saint Helens. Mount Baker located near the Canadian border is a 10,750-foot, snow-capped peak. National forests running from north to south through the Cascade Mountains are the Mount Baker National Forest, the Wenatchee National Forest, the Snoqualmie National Forest, and the Gifford Pinchot National Forest; they all offer fine lake and stream fishing for trout. Many highland lakes here are seldom if ever fished, and most of them now have trout because of the extensive stocking that has been done by airplane through these mountains. There are almost 200 camp sites through the forests. Their exact locations can be secured from the:

U.S. Forest Service
Regional Office
P. O. Box 4137
Portland 8, Oregon

Lake Chelan near Chelan is 55 miles long and 1,500 feet deep. Two state parks, Lake Chelan State Park and Alta Lake State Park, border this lake that has become a state resort. The Entiat River is a well-known rainbow stream in the area.

The Skagit River, the Skykomish River, the Tolt River, the Green River and the Puyallup River all flow into Puget Sound; and they have rainbow, cutthroat and steelhead fishing from late spring until early fall (no steelhead in the Skagit).

The Olympic National Park (1-million-acre park) and the Olympic National Forest are located on Olympic Peninsula. The area offers coastal fishing, salmon fishing, trout and steelhead fishing as well as other outdoor sports and camping in the dozen national forest camp sites. Lake Cushman has cutthroat-trout fishing. The Lazy "C" Dude Ranch, Brinnon, Washington, has good trout fishing in the Dosewallips River or other streams, besides offering Hood Canal salmon fishing.

Smaller lakes are located everywhere throughout the state and some with about 1,000 acres of water include Bumping Lake near Yakima (cutthroat trout), Sutherland Lake (cutthroats), Aldwell Lake (cutthroat, rainbow and brook trout) near Port Angeles, and Curlew Lake near Republic (cutthroats).

The state of Washington has thousands of miles of trout streams and salmon rivers and almost 10,000 lakes for fishing. Records show that approximately 90,000 trout are taken every opening day, which clearly indicates that Washington is a state with much fishing and many fish.

West Virginia

Tourist information from:

Industrial and Publicity Commission
State Capitol
Charleston 5, West Virginia

Fishing information from:

Conservation Commission of West Virginia
Charleston, West Virginia

Fish in West Virginia: rainbow trout, brown trout, brook trout, largemouth bass and smallmouth bass, white bass, bluegill, carp, crappie, channel catfish, walleye, flathead catfish, bullhead, pickerel, muskellunge and rough fish.

Note: An extra license is required for trout fishing in addition to the regular license.

The mountainous state of West Virginia (24,181 square miles) breaks off into two separate water-drainage systems. To the east the drain-off is into the Potomac River, which has its headwaters in this state. The western drainage is the Monongahela River system, including the Cheat and Buckhannon rivers, Middle Island Creek, Wheeling Creek, and the Little Kanawha and Great Kanawha system—all of which find their way to the big Ohio River.

Strangely there are few natural lakes in the state, but there are reservoirs. Lakes for trout fishing include Summit Lake near Richwood, Seneca Lake in Seneca State Forest near Forest Cabins, and Spruce Knob Lake in Monongahela National Forest near Petersburg. Other lakes for trout are Coopers Rock Lake near Morgantown, and Trout Pond in the George Washington National Forest near Wardensville.

Bass fishing is at Bear Rock Lakes near Wheeling, Bluestone Reservoir in Bluestone State Park near Hinton, and Lake Sherwood in Monongahela National Forest near White Sulphur Springs.

The pride and joy of the state's fishing is some good muskellunge water, which includes Middle Island Creek near St. Mary's, and Little Kanawha River near Grantsville, the best muskie water in the state. Also the Pocatalico River has recently been stocked with muskie, and everyone is keeping his fingers crossed that the fish take.

Smallmouth-bass fishing is at the South Branch of the Potomac River near Petersburg, the Elk River, the Big and Little Coal rivers near Charleston, the Greenbrier River near Sulphur Springs, and the Cacapon River near Berkeley Springs. Smallmouth and largemouth bass are in the Little Kanawha, the Hughes River and Wheeling Creek. Other warm-water fish also frequent these waters. Walleye are in the New, Elk and Greenbrier rivers.

Major trout streams in the state are the Williams River, Back Fork of the Elk River near Webster Springs, Seneca Creek, the North Fork of the South Branch of the Potomac River near Petersburg, the North Fork of the Cherry River near Richmond, and the East Fork of the Greenbrier River near Durbin. There are over 150 other recognized trout streams in the state and an active stocking program is in progress.

Facilities of hotels and motels are adequate in the towns and resorts mentioned, which are generally only a short drive to the fishing waters. The back-country area has poor facilities, so towns should be selected for lodging. Hook a 40-inch muskie, and you will taste the best of West Virginia fishing.

Magazine dealing with West Virginia outdoors:

West Virginia Conservation   Cost: $2.00 a year
Charleston, West Virginia

Wisconsin

Tourist information from:

Recreational Publicity Section
Wisconsin Conservation Department
Madison 1, Wisconsin

Fishing information from:

Wisconsin Conservation Department
Madison 1, Wisconsin

Fish in Wisconsin: muskellunge, northern pike, walleye pike, sauger, largemouth bass, smallmouth bass, brook, brown and rainbow trout, lake trout, cisco, catfish, sturgeon and other fish.

Wisconsin is 56,154 square miles of grassland that is known as "the state of cheese, milk and cherry pies;" but among fishermen it is also known as a state with over 8,600 lakes teeming with muskie, bass and walleye. Add to that 10,000 miles of running water of which 1,500 miles are trout streams, and it's not hard to understand why Wisconsin is a fisherman's favorite.

Many of the streams of Wisconsin are perfectly suited for canoeing and fishing, being neither too swift to be dangerous nor too slow to be dull. Canoe trips on waters surrounded by tall pines are memorable occasions. One trip can be taken on the Wolf River from Shawano, and fish caught here are brown, brook and rainbow trout. Another float could be on the Flambeau River near Park Falls, or further south in the Flambeau River State Forest (74,000 acres). Fishing here is for walleye, northern pike, largemouth and smallmouth bass and of course muskellunge.

Other well-known fishing rivers in Wisconsin include the Chippewa, which meets the Flambeau River near Ladysmith and flows southwest to the Mississippi River. Muskie, northern pike, walleye pike, largemouth and smallmouth bass, bluegill and crappie can be taken from the Chippewa.

The Brule River in the northwest section of the state has trout, rainbows, browns and brookies. This river runs through the Brule State Forest, where there are camping opportunities.

The famous St. Croix River makes up much of the northwestern Minnesota–Wisconsin border. There are walleye, northern pike, largemouth and smallmouth bass and catfish in this famous fishing river. Interstate Park on the St. Croix provides a camp base and some splendid scenery.

The St. Croix flows into the Mississippi at Prescott, and from here to the Illinois border almost 400 miles away, the Mississippi is the western border of Wisconsin. The old river of this northern section is a clear, young, vigorous river with huge bluffs along much of its shore. It offers good fishing for both largemouth and smallmouth bass, bluegill, crappie and catfish.

Another major river of Wisconsin is the Wisconsin, which flows south through the middle of the state and then west to Prairie du Chien, where it joins the Mississippi. Fishing in the Wisconsin is for northern pike, walleye pike, bass, bluegill, crappie and catfish. Many sections of the Wisconsin River are ideally suited for floats.

Wisconsin is primarily noted for its lake fishing, and there are so many lakes that a map of Wisconsin looks like a freckle-faced girl. The highest concentration of lakes is in the northeast and northwest.

The northeast section has good fishing for muskellunge, northern pike, and bass. Here in the Lac du Flambeau Indian Reservation on Lac du Flambeau, Indian guides are available to help anglers capture muskie and trout. Other lakes of the northeast include Fence Lake, White Sand Lake, Ike Walton Lake and the Flambeau Flowage Reservoir. Resort centers such as Land O'Lakes, Eagle River and Three Lakes are in the heart of the lake country. These resorts centers hold a special appeal to those fisherman who are gourmets, for the food of Wisconsin ranks with the best in the world.

Two state forests of the northeast section, Northern Highland State Forest and American Legion State Forest, are havens for sportsmen. They offer fishermen streams, lakes and camping facilities.

A short distance south is Rhinelander, an important paper-mill town of northeast Wisconsin. Within 10 miles of this city there are over 200 lakes, 9 trout streams and 2 rivers, all heavy with fish.

The Nicolet National Forest of northeastern Wisconsin is east of the general area already mentioned. This forest has 16 completed camp sites and offers lake and stream fishing for sportsmen, as well as ample opportunities for canoeing. The resorts in and surrounding the forests make accommodations plentiful and good.

Much of northwest Wisconsin is blanketed by the Chequamegon National Forest. The forest has streams and lakes of all sizes whose waters are noted for their muskie. Some of the lakes of the forest include Lake Namekagon near Cable and Moose Lake near Clam Lake.

The area surrounding Hayward on Highway 63 has Chippewa Lake (17,000 acres), Round Lake, Grindstone Lake, Lac Court Oreilles, Spider Lake, Windigo Lake and many others. Fish of this area include muskie, largemouth and smallmouth bass, walleye, bluegill, crappie and other fish. Fishing is everywhere, and catches can be counted on to be good.

Further south on Highway 63 in the town of Spooner Lake is located Spooner Lake, with Shell Lake nearby. These are clean, sandy lakes, well known for their swimming; fishing in them can bring a catch of the Wisconsin favorites.

Other major lakes throughout Wisconsin include the state's largest, Lake Winnebago (138,000 acres) near Oshkosh and Menasha. There are complete facilities including resorts, guides, camping and boats on the lake's shore, and fish caught are northern pike, walleye, largemouth and smallmouth bass, crappie and bluegill.

North of this lake near Shawano is 6,000-acre Lake Shawano. Shawano has good perch fishing as well as northern pike, walleye, bass, bluegill and crappie. It has complete facilities.

Near the town of Green Lake is Green Lake, which has typical Wisconsin fish, and Puckaway Lake just to the west has the same general species.

Lake Geneva (5,400 acres) is located in southern Wisconsin near the town of Lake Geneva. Complete with boats, guides and beaches, the lake offers largemouth and smallmouth bass, northern pike, walleye and rainbow trout. Other lakes of the south include Koshkonong, Sinissippi, and Lake Mendota near the capital, Madison.

Fishing is everywhere in Wisconsin, with really fine fishing accessible. No wonder Chicago fishermen say, "You haven't fished until you've fished Wisconsin."

Wyoming

Tourist information from:

Wyoming Travel Commission
Capitol Building
Cheyenne, Wyoming

Fishing information from:

Wyoming Game and Fish Commission
Box 378
Cheyenne, Wyoming

Fish in Wyoming: cutthroat trout, rainbow trout, golden trout, brown trout, brook trout, Mackinaw trout, Kokanee salmon, grayling, walleye pike, largemouth bass, crappie, catfish and rough fish.

Wyoming, a 97,914-square-mile northwestern state, is the state of Grand Teton and Yellowstone national parks, the state where the Snake River begins, and a state of spectacular trout fishing.

It is hard to think of Wyoming without thinking of Yellowstone Park, for the two go together like fish and chips. The park is located in northwest Wyoming on the Montana and Idaho borders. Here there are 10,000 geysers, including Old Faithful. There are boiling pools, a 308-foot waterfall, the grand canyon of Yellowstone, and a cold, clear lake at an elevation of 7,731 feet above sea level.

There is fine fishing throughout the park, and Yellowstone Lake (139 square miles and up to 300 feet in depth) has cold water that bristles with trout. Lake Lodge is on the lake; also cabins, motels and boats are there. No fishing license is required. Other lakes in the park include Shoshone, Lewis and Heart lakes. Stream fishing in the park is in Bechler, Madison, Firehole and

Gibbon rivers, and in the headwaters of the Snake River. The Firehole and Gibbon are fine streams for dry-fly fishing.

Just south of Yellowstone Park are the Jackson Hole area and Grand Teton National Park. The park has 11,257-acre Jackson Lake and beautiful Jenny Lake, which has four snow-capped mountains standing like bodyguards over the lake. The biggest is 13,766-foot Grand Teton Mountain. The Jackson Lodge on Jackson Lake accommodates 300 guests, and Colter Bay Marina on the lake has a tackle shop and boat rentals. There are other lodges and cabins in the park, and nearby Jackson Hole has a true western flavor that appeals to many visitors. Lake trout are the chief sports fish in Jackson and Jenny Lakes while cutthroat trout rank second. There is stream fishing in the Snake River and Gros Ventre Rivers in the park. Float trips on the Snake River are a specialty of Beaver Valley Guest Ranch, Box 489, Jackson, Wyoming.

Fishing in Wyoming is not exclusively in the parks but is everywhere. There are 5,000 lakes totaling over 130,000 acres of water, and 20,000 miles of running streams in the state.

The Snake River continues to have good fishing as it flows southwest out of the park area. There is good fishing in its tributaries, the Hoback, Little Greys, and the Greys rivers. The Greys River is a mineral-stained, reddish-colored river. Cutthroat trout are the top fish in these waters.

East from the Idaho border are the headwaters of the Green River, and across the Continental Divide the Wind River forms and flows eastward. Gannett Peak (elevation 13,785 feet and the highest point in Wyoming) is in this wilderness section. Trout fishing is everywhere, and Cooks Lake and Elbow Lake are known for their golden trout. The record golden trout came from Cooks Lake; it weighed 28 pounds 16 ounces. Pack trips arranged in Pinedale regularly head into the mountains to the lakes that have the goldens. Fremont Lake and Willow Lake near Pinedale have big rainbow trout. Bridger National Forest in the area has 25 camp sites and fishing throughout the wilderness area, and the Shoshone National Forest has winter sports' areas and camping.

Some of the finest places to stay in this section of Wyoming are the dude ranches. Circle S. Ranch, Cora, Wyoming, arranges fishing and floating trips on the Green River. Reservations are necessary here. If an angler doesn't bring home trout when he fishes this section of Wyoming, he just isn't made for fishing.

Located on Highway 20 near Cody is Buffalo Bill Reservoir, where fishing is for Mackinaw trout and rainbows. The Shoshone River has good brown and rainbow trout.

In the Bighorn Mountains in north central Wyoming is Big-horn National Forest, with 300 lakes and streams for fishing among the snow-capped peaks. There are camp sites, motels, cabins and dude ranches here. Fishing in the Tongue River and Goose Creek is for brown and rainbow trout.

Eastern Wyoming has part of the Black Hills in the north-eastern corner. Here there is fishing in 10,000-acre Keyhole Reservoir near Mooncraft. Fish are walleye and rainbow trout. There is stream fishing in Sand Creek.

The great plains of Wyoming cover much of the eastern por-tion of the state; they are the home of cattle ranches and have boating and fishing in new Lake Glendo. The North Platte River near Laramie has big, elusive brown trout.

South central Wyoming has fishing in Pathfinder Reservoir and 20,000-acre Seminoe Reservoir near Rawlins and Sinclair. Fish are brown trout and rainbow trout, and boats are available at the lakes. The Sweetwater River west of Pathfinder Reservoir is a brown-trout stream.

Wyoming's lowest elevation is 3,125 feet above sea level, and the highest is almost 14,000 feet. It is a mountainous state, sparsely populated with people but heavily populated with wild-life and trout; if this is your dish then Wyoming is your state.

Magazine dealing with Wyoming outdoors:

Wyoming Wildlife   Cost: $1.00 per year
Wyoming Game and Fish Commission
Box 378
Cheyenne, Wyoming

National Forests

National Forests are in 43 states and they offer almost 3 million acres of public lakes, 70,000 miles of streams for fishing, as well as other recreational and tourist facilities.

Information regarding tourist accommodations in forests can be secured from:

National Forest Recreation Association
2695 Greenwich Street
San Francisco 23, California

Specific information regarding a particular forest can be secured by writing the *forest supervisor* at the particular forest headquarters. All forests listed have fishing.

National Forest	*Headquarters*
ALABAMA	
William B. Bankhead	Montgomery
Conecuh	Montgomery
Talladega	Montgomery
ALASKA	
Chugach	Juneau
Tongass	Juneau
ARIZONA	
Apache	Springerville
Coconino	Flagstaff
Coronado	Tucson
Kaibab	Williams
Prescott	Prescott
Tonto	Phoenix
ARKANSAS	
Ouachita	Hot Springs
Ozark	Russellville

National Forest	*Headquarters*
CALIFORNIA	
Angeles	Los Angeles
Cleveland	San Diego
El Dorado	Placerville
Inyo	Bishop
Klamath	Yreka
Lassen	Susanville
Los Padres	Santa Barbara
Mendocino	Willows
Modoc	Alturas
Plumas	Quincy
San Bernadino	San Bernardino
Sequoia	Porterville
Shasta-Trinity	Redding
Sierra	Fresno
Six Rivers	Eureka
Stanislaus	Sonora
Tahoe	Nevada City
COLORADO	
Arapaho	Idaho Springs
Grand Mesa-Un-	
compahgre	Delta
Gunnison	Gunnison
Pike	Colorado Springs
Rio Grande	Monte Vista
Roosevelt	Fort Collins
Routt	Steamboat Springs
San Isabel	Pueblo
San Juan	Durango
White River	Glenwood Springs
FLORIDA	
Apalachicola	Tallahassee
Ocala	Tallahassee
Osceola	Lake City

National Forest	*Headquarters*

GEORGIA

| Chattahoochee | Gainesville |

IDAHO

Boise	Boise
Caribou	Pocatello
Challis	Challis
Clearwater	Orofino
Coeur d'Alene	Coeur d'Alene
Kaniksu	Sandpoint
Nezperce	Grangeville
Payette	McCall
St. Joe	St. Maries
Salmon	Salmon
Sawtooth	Twin Falls
Targhee	St. Anthony

ILLINOIS

| Shawnee | Harrisburg |

INDIANA

| Hoosier | Bedford |

KENTUCKY

| Cumberland | Winchester |

LOUISIANA

| Kisatchie | Alexandria |

MICHIGAN

Hiawatha	Escanaba
Huron	Cadillac
Manistee	Cadillac
Marquette	Escanaba
Ottawa	Ironwood

National Forest	*Headquarters*
MINNESOTA	
Chippewa	Cass Lake
Superior	Duluth
MISSISSIPPI	
Bienville	Jackson
Delta	Rolling Fork
De Soto	Jackson
Homochitto	Meadville
MISSOURI	
Clark	Harrisburg (Illinois)
Mark Twain	Rolla
MONTANA	
Beaverhead	Dillon
Bitterroot	Hamilton
Custer	Billings
Deerlodge	Butte
Flathead	Kalispell
Gallatin	Bozeman
Helena	Helena
Kootenai	Libby
Lewis and Clarke	Great Falls
Lolo	Missoula
NEBRASKA	
Nebraska	Halsey
NEVADA	
Humboldt	Elko
Nevada	Ely
Toiyabe	Reno
NEW HAMPSHIRE	
White Mountain	Laconia

National Forest *Headquarters*

NEW MEXICO

Carson	Taos
Cibola	Albuquerque
Gila	Silver City
Lincoln	Alamogordo
Santa Fe	Santa Fe

NORTH CAROLINA

Croatan	Asheville
Nantahala	Asheville
Pisgah	Asheville

OHIO

Wayne	Bedford (Indiana)

OREGON

Deschutes	Bend
Malheur	John Day
Mount Hood	Portland
Ochoco	Prineville
Rogue River	Medford
Siskiyou	Grants Pass
Siuslaw	Corvallis
Umatilla	Pendleton
Umpqua	Roseburg
Wallowa-Whitman	Baker
Willamette	Eugene

PENNSYLVANIA

Allegheny	Warren

SOUTH CAROLINA

Francis Marion	Columbia
Sumter	Columbia

National Forest	*Headquarters*
SOUTH DAKOTA	
Black Hills	Custer
TENNESSEE	
Cherokee	Cleveland
TEXAS	
Angelina	Lufkin
Davy Crockett	Crockett
Sabine	St. Augustine
Sam Houston	Lufkin
UTAH	
Ashley	Vernal
Cache	Logan
Dixie	Cedar City
Fishlake	Richfield
Manti-LaSal	Price
Uinta	Provo
Wasatch	Salt Lake City
VERMONT	
Green Mountain	Rutland
VIRGINIA	
George Washington	Harrisonburg
Jefferson	Roanoke
WASHINGTON	
Colville	Colville
Gifford Pinchot	Vancouver
Mount Baker	Bellingham
Okanogan	Okanogan
Olympic	Olympia
Snoqualmie	Seattle
Wenatchee	Wenatchee

National Forest	*Headquarters*
WEST VIRGINIA	
Monongahela	Elkins
WISCONSIN	
Chequamegon	Park Falls
Nicolet	Rhinelander
WYOMING	
Bighorn	Sheridan
Bridger	Kemmerer
Medicine Bow	Laramie
Shoshone	Cody
Teton	Jackson

Fundamentals

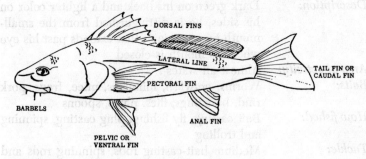

DORSAL FINS

LATERAL LINE

TAIL FIN OR
CAUDAL FIN

PECTORAL FIN

BARBELS

ANAL FIN

PELVIC OR
VENTRAL FIN

Parts of a fish.

Popular name:	Bass, Kentucky
Latin name:	Micropterus punctalatus
Other names:	Spotted bass, bass
Size:	Up to 15 inches in length and 4 lbs. in weight
Description:	Resembles a largemouth except for spotted, longitudinal lines on lower half of body
Area of activity:	TVA states and Ohio River valley
Baits:	Bugs, worms, crawfish, minnows, plugs, spoons
How fished:	Bait casting, trolling, spinning or fly fishing
Tackle:	Medium bait-casting rods, spinning rods and fly rods
Rig: Line	4-lb. test *Leader:* Monofilament
Hooks	No. 2 to 2/0
Edibility:	Good
Comments:	This is a fine sports fish who is often taken when one is angling for largemouth bass.

❋   ❋   ❋

Popular name:	Bass, Largemouth
Latin name:	Micropterus salmoides
Other names:	Black bass, bigmouth, lineside, green bass, straw bass, bass
Size:	Up to 25 lbs. in South and 15 lbs. in North; averages 1 to 3 lbs.

Description:	Dark green on his back and a lighter color on his sides, he is distinguished from the smallmouth by a jaw joint that extends past his eye when his mouth is closed
Area of activity:	Almost all states
Baits:	Worms, crawfish, minnows, mice, frogs, pork rind, bass bugs, flies, plugs, spoons
How fished:	Bait casting, fly fishing, plug casting, spinning and trolling
Tackle:	Medium bait-casting rods, spinning rods and fly rods
Rig: Line	4- to 8-lb. test *Leader:* Monofilament
Hooks	No. 2 to 4/0
Edibility:	Good
Comments:	This excellent sports fish is often found in surprisingly small lakes. He thrives in warm water. A largemouth bass's mean temper is often his undoing, for he hits viciously at anything in the water—fish, fly, plug, bird, or spoon.

* * *

Popular name:	Bass, Rock
Latin name:	Ambloplites rupestris
Other names:	Redeye, goggle-eye, northern rock bass, rock sunfish
Size:	Up to 2 lbs.; averages ½ lb.
Description:	A sunfish, generally greenish in color, who has a single dorsal fin and a black spot on the gill cover
Area of activity:	Entire United States
Baits:	Worms, minnows, crawfish, flies, plugs, spinners
How fished:	Trolled in daytime; evening fishing is done near shore with artificials or live bait

Tackle:	Ultralight or light tackle
Rig: Line	2-lb. test *Leader:* Monofilament
Hooks	No. 4 to 2/0
Edibility:	Edible
Comments:	The fish stays in deep holes during days and is near shore only in the evenings. He is generally taken in rocky areas of streams and lakes and is often taken by smallmouth-bass fishermen.

* * *

Popular name:	Bass, Smallmouth
Latin name:	Micropterus dolomieu
Other names:	Black bass, brown bass, swago bass, bronzeback, tiger bass, little bass, bass
Size:	Up to 12 lbs. in the South and 5 lbs. in the North; averages 1 to 2 lbs.
Description:	Color changes with water conditions, but he is usually bronze or greenish on back and sides. His color is usually darker than the largemouth's. His belly is white, and his mouth does not extend beyond the line of the eye
Area of activity:	Throughout the country except in the extreme Southern states
Baits:	Minnows, frogs, crawfish, worms, bait fish, pork rind, flies, bass bugs, spinners, plugs, spoons
How fished:	From shore or in boats, in rivers, streams or lakes; big lakes (over 100 acres of clear water) support him best
Tackle:	Medium or light spinning rods, bait-casting rods and fly rods
Rig: Line	2- to 6-lb. test *Leader:* Monofilament
Hooks	No. 4 to 2/0
Edibility:	Excellent

Comments:	A vicious fighter who is considered by many fishermen to be the hardest-fighting fish that swims. He prefers cooler water than the large-mouth, and thrives in large lakes, cool rivers and streams.

* * *

Popular name:	Bass, Striped (Landlocked)
Latin name:	Roccus saxatilis
Other names:	Santee-Cooper bass, rockfish, striper
Size:	Up to 30 lbs.
Description:	The ocean striped bass become landlocked, he is greenish-silver in color and has black stripes running the length of his body
Area of activity:	Lake Moultrie and Lake Marion, South Carolina; and Buggs Island Lake, North Carolina–Virginia
Baits:	Spoons, plugs, bait fish
How fished:	Casting or trolling from a boat
Tackle:	Medium to heavy-duty, fresh-water rods
Rig: Line	8- to 20-lb. test *Leader:* Monofilament
Hooks	No. 1/0 to 4/0
Edibility:	Excellent
Comments:	He has recently become landlocked in the TVA lakes. He has not as yet been identified as a subspecies of the ocean fish. If the striped bass should be successful in other fresh-water lakes it would make for a fantastic picture of future fresh-water fishing.

* * *

Popular name:	Bass, White
Latin name:	Roccus chrysops
Other names:	Silver bass, striped bass
Size:	Up to 5 lbs.; averages 1 lb.

Description:	Bass-shaped, silvery in color with gold tinges on sides. Thin lateral lines on his back and sides run from head to tail. He has 2 distinct dorsal fins
Area of activity:	From Great Lakes to the Gulf states
Baits:	Flies, spinners, spoons, plugs, minnows, worms, pork rind. Best bait: minnows
How fished:	Fly fishing, trolling or still-fishing
Tackle:	Ultralight or light fly rods, bait-casting rods and spinning rods
Rig: Line	2- to 6-lb. test *Leader:* Monofilament
Hooks	No. 4 to 1/0
Edibility:	Good
Comments:	He is among the largest pan fish available to anglers. He travels in large schools and is best taken along the shore line in the evenings. He will usually stay in water 20–40 feet deep during the day. He is a fast-growing fish who lives only 4 years.

❋   ❋   ❋

Popular name:	Bass, Yellow
Latin name:	Roccus mississippiensis
Other names:	Gold bass, bass, streaker
Size:	Averages less than 1 lb.
Description:	Bright golden-yellow sides over which run darker longitudinal lines. His back is olive-green, and his belly is white
Area of activity:	Mississippi and Ohio River valleys
Baits:	Worms, minnows, flies, spoons
How fished:	Still-fished or trolled
Tackle:	Any light tackle
Rig: Line	2-lb. test *Leader:* Monofilament
Hooks	No. 4 to 1/0
Edibility:	Edible
Comments:	He is a fine pan fish.

❋   ❋   ❋

Popular name: Bowfin
Latin name: Amia calva
Other names: Dogfish, mudfish, grindle, cypress trout, prairie bass
Size: Up to 24 inches in length, 12 lbs. in weight
Description: Primitive-looking, with a massive head, long dorsal fins and a body covered with thick scales. He is olive-green in color and has a dark yellow belly
Area of activity: East and Midwest
Baits: Dead minnows, crawfish, mollusks, worms, plugs
How fished: Bottom-fished with natural baits or very slow-moving plugs
Tackle: Sturdy spinning and bait-casting rods
Rig: Line 6- to 8-lb. test *Leader:* Monofilament
Hooks No. 6 to 2/0
Edibility: Edible
Comments: This is a prehistoric fish who stays in weedy, shallow lakes or muddy rivers, where he feeds extensively on bait and panfish. His meat is usually smoked, baked or marinated to make it tasty and edible. He is a hard striker and fighter, yet very little fishing is done directly for him—he is caught only incidentally.

* * *

Popular name: Buffalo Fish, Largemouth
Latin name: Ictiobus cyprinellus
Other names: Bigmouth buffalo fish, buffalo, redmouth buffalo
Size: Up to 80 lbs., with 20-pounders common
Description: Resembles a carp; however, he has no barbels. Also his fins are soft-rayed and not sharp like the carp's
Area of activity: The Midwest and Lake Erie

Baits:	Dough balls, worms, mollusks, insects
How fished:	Bottom-fished
Tackle:	Any tackle
Rig: Line	6- to 20-lb. test *Leader:* Monofilament
Hooks	No. 4 to No. 1
Edibility:	Edible
Comments:	He is a prolific spawner. The female lays up to 400,000 eggs a year. He grows fast and overcrowds lakes. He is a member of the sucker family. Another species of buffalo fish is the smallmouth buffalo (Ictiobus bubalus) which grows to 40 lbs. and is found in the Mississippi River valley.

●   ●   ●

Popular name:	Bullhead, Black
Latin name:	Ictalurus melas
Other names:	Horned pout, stinger, common bullhead, brown catfish
Size:	Up to 3 lbs.; averages less than 1 lb.
Description:	A bullhead with black chin barbels. He has a black to grayish body and a light underside. He can be distinguished from other bullhead by a light color band on the base of his tail fin
Area of activity:	Throughout the United States but most abundant in the central part of the country
Baits:	Dead fish, worms, crustaceans, pork rind, dough balls, sweet corn.
How fished:	Bottom-fished from shore or from a boat
Tackle:	Any light tackle
Rig: Line	2- to 4-lb. test *Leader:* Monofilament or gut
Hooks	No. 4 to 1/0
Edibility:	Good
Comments:	He is a small fish that is widely distributed.

●   ●   ●

Popular name:	Bullhead, Brown
Latin name:	Ictalurus nebulosus
Other names:	Horned pout, speckled bullhead, catfish, bull-head
Size:	Up to 5 lbs.; averages 1 lb.
Description:	His color varies with the water. He is mostly brownish-yellow to brownish-black, with a lighter color on its belly. Forward spines of pectoral and dorsal fins are sharp and can inflict cuts
Area of activity:	Throughout Midwest from the Canadian border to the Gulf. Also on Pacific Coast
Baits:	Worms, dough balls, bait fish, pork rind, crawfish
How fished:	Still-fished on the bottom
Tackle:	Any tackle
Rig: Line *Hooks*	2- to 5-lb. test *Leader:* Monofilament or gut No. 4 to 1/0
Edibility:	Good
Comments:	He is a pan fish who is a favorite with young fishermen, and the largest bullhead in the country.

❋   ❋   ❋

Popular name:	Bullhead, Flat
Latin name:	Ameirus platycephalus
Other names:	Bullhead
Size:	Up to 2 lbs.; averages less than 1 lb.
Description:	A bullhead with a dark-gray back and a lighter color on the belly. He has a black spot at the base of his dorsal fin, and has white chin barbels. He is distinguished by a very flat head
Area of activity:	Southeastern United States, throughout Dixie
Baits:	Dead fish, worms, crustaceans, pork rind, crawfish

How fished:	Bottom-fished in lakes, rivers and creeks
Tackle:	Any light tackle
Rig: Line	2- to 4-lb. test *Leader:* Monofilament or gut
Hooks	No. 4 to No. 1
Edibility:	Good if skinned
Comments:	The best spots for fishing him are over sand bottoms. The fisherman should be careful taking him off a hook, for his sharp spines can inflict painful cuts.

* * *

Popular name:	Bullhead, Yellow
Latin name:	Ictalurus natalis
Other names:	Bullhead, Mississippi bullhead, brown bullhead, white whiskered bullhead
Size:	Up to 4½ lbs.; averages 1 lb.
Description:	A brownish-yellow color with darker mottles over his body. He has white chin barbels
Area of activity:	The Great Lakes region, throughout the Midwest and the Gulf states
Baits:	Dead fish, worms, crustaceans, pork rind, crawfish
How fished:	Bottom-fished in lakes, rivers and ponds
Tackle:	Any tackle
Rig: Line	2- to 4-lb. test *Leader:* Not necessary
Hooks	No. 4 to 1/0
Edibility:	Good, but should be skinned
Comments:	He is a popular pan fish of the Midwest who prefers clear water and stays in or near vegetation.

* * *

Popular name:	Burbot
Latin name:	Lota lota
Other names:	Ling cod, ling, lawyer, fresh-water cod
Size:	Up to 2½ feet in length and 10 lbs. in weight

Description:	A member of the cod family who has a rounded tail fin and a single barbel. His shape is long and almost eel-like and he has a flattened, small head. He is generally olive in color, with darker or yellow lines running through the color
Area of activity:	East Coast, Great Lakes area, Pacific Coast and Alaska
Baits:	Bait fish
How fished:	Bottom-fished
Tackle:	Bait-casting rods or spinning rods
Rig: Line	4- to 10-lb. test *Leader:* Monofilament
Hooks	No. 4 to 2/0
Edibility:	Edible
Comments:	He is sometimes taken by ice fishermen on the Great Lakes. Best time for fishing is in spring, when he is in streams for spawning. A subspecies grows to 60 lbs. and is found in Alaska.

❂ ❂ ❂

Popular name:	Carp
Latin name:	Cyprinus carpio
Other names:	German carp, goldfish
Size:	Up to 85 lbs. with 20-pounders common
Description:	A suckerlike mouth and a single dorsal fin. He is generally silver in color, but in muddy water gets brownish. Sometimes he takes on a golden color
Area of activity:	All states
Baits:	Dough balls, corn kernels
How fished:	Still-fished and speared
Tackle:	Bait-casting rods and spinning rods of medium to sturdy construction. Any type of rod made can take him if it is strong enough
Rig: Line	10- to 25-lb. test *Leader:* Monofilament
Hooks	No. 4 to No. 1, or treble hooks

Edibility:	Good—considered a delicacy in Europe
Comments:	He was imported from Europe in the nineteenth century and spread throughout the country. He is very prolific and tends to take over lakes. The common goldfish (Carassius auratus) is a member of the carp family.

*   *   *

Popular name:	Catfish, Blue
Latin name:	Ictalurus furcatus
Other names:	Catfish, bullhead, blue bullhead, great blue catfish, Mississippi catfish, great fork-tail catfish
Size:	Up to 100 lbs.; the biggest catfish in the country
Description:	A catfish, dark-colored, bluish-gray on back and lighter gray on sides. He has no dark spots like the channel catfish, for which he is often taken. He has a deeply forked tail, which, as with all other catfish, has no scales
Area of activity:	From the Great Lakes to the Gulf, down through the center of the country
Baits:	Anything edible
How fished:	Slow-trolling or still-fishing in deep holes. Also taken on trotlines or by jigging
Tackle:	Sturdy 5- to 5½-foot bait-casting rods and stiff-action spinning rods
Rig: Line	10- to 50-lb. test *Leader:* Monofilament
Hooks	No. 1 to 4/0
Edibility:	Good to excellent
Comments:	Fishing for him must be done deep, at or near the bottom. He prefers slow-moving water but is occasionally taken in swifter rivers or streams.

*   *   *

Popular name: Catfish, Channel
Latin name: Ictalurus punctatus
Other names: Cat, catfish, fork-tail catfish, silver catfish, speckled catfish, white catfish
Size: Up to 60 lbs.
Description: Black spots sprinkled on his body. The spines of dorsal and pectoral fins are sharp. He has barbels and whiskers on his chin
Area of activity: Canadian border to the Gulf of Mexico
Baits: Anything edible. He is fond of ripe fish and meats; also lures, plugs, spoons, spinners, flies
How fished: Still-fished on bottom, mostly at night
Tackle: Medium- to heavy-duty bait-casting rods and spinning rods
Rig: Line   10- to 20-lb. test   *Leader:* Monofilament
    Hooks   No. 2 to 4/0
Edibility: Excellent
Comments: He is the best sports fish of the catfish and may be taken in clear, fast-moving water or off the bottom in slow-moving water.

*   *   *

Popular name: Catfish, Flathead
Latin name: Pylodictis olivaris
Other names: Yellow catfish, catfish
Size: Up to 100 lbs.
Description: Heavily-mottled body dark brown in color. He has a long head and a protruding lower jaw
Area of activity: Ohio, Missouri, and Mississippi River valleys
Baits: All catfish baits, dead fish, crawfish
How fished: Bottom-fished or trotlined
Tackle: Heavy-duty spinning and bait-casting rods
Rig: Line   10- to 50-lb. test   *Leader:* Monofilament
    Hooks   No. 1 to 4/0
Edibility: Good

Comments: He prefers slow-moving, sluggish rivers. He is taken commercially in some areas.

* * *

Popular name:	Catfish, White
Latin name:	Ictalurus catus
Other names:	Catfish, bullhead, white bullhead
Size:	1 to 2 lbs.
Description:	Greenish-colored, with gray or greenish back and lighter sides and belly. He has a deeply forked tail
Area of activity:	Pennsylvania south and west to Texas; also California
Baits:	Small fish, cut fish, worms
How fished:	Bottom-fished
Tackle:	Light spinning rods and bait-casting rods
Rig: Line	2- to 5-lb test *Leader:* Monofilament
Hooks	No. 4 to No. 1
Edibility:	Good
Comments:	He prefers muddy bottoms in sluggish water.

* * *

Popular name:	Char, Arctic
Latin name:	Salvelinus alpinus
Other names:	Arctic trout, alpine trout, char
Size:	Up to 20 lbs; averages 2 lbs.
Description:	A spotted trout who has pinkish spots on his sides and a deeply forked tail
Area of activity:	Alaska and Canada
Baits:	Flies, spinners, spoons, bait fish
How fished:	Fly fishing, spinning or trolling in lakes
Tackle:	Light tackle
Rig: Line	2- to 4-lb. test *Leader:* Monofilament
Hooks	No. 8 to No. 2
Edibility:	Excellent

Comments:	He is a trout of the char family with small scales. He is related to brook, lake and Dolly Varden trout. Some char are sea-run, but many are landlocked in cold lakes.

*   *   *

Popular name:	Chub
Latin name:	Semotilus corporalis
Other names:	Fallfish, white chub
Size:	Up to 3 lbs.
Description:	A small, silver-colored, herring-shaped fish
Area of activity:	New England, New York and Pennsylvania
Baits:	Worms, minnows, flies
How fished:	Trout-fished
Tackle:	Light or ultralight tackle
Rig: Line	2- to 4-lb. test *Leader:* Monofilament
Hooks	No. 8 to No. 4
Edibility:	Poor
Comments:	He is found in many trout streams and is considered a pest. He is scrappy. The young chub are important as bait fish.

*   *   *

Popular name:	Crappie, Black
Latin name:	Pomoxis nigromaculatus
Other names:	Crappie, calico bass
Size:	Up to 12 inches in length, 5 lbs. in weight; averages ½ to 1 lb.
Description:	A member of the sunfish family; olive-colored and dark-green- and black-spotted. Anal and dorsal fins are irregularly marked with green and black spots
Area of activity:	All states
Baits:	Worms, minnows, small plugs, spinners, weighted flies
How fished:	Trolling, plug casting, or spinning from bait or shore

Tackle:	Light bait-casting rods, spinning rods and fly rods
Rig: Line	2- to 4-lb. test *Leader:* Monofilament
Hooks	No. 4 to 2/0
Edibility:	Good
Comments:	He is a pan fish that is considered by many to be a sports fish. He travels in schools through lakes and streams.

* * *

Popular name:	Crappie, White
Latin name:	Pomoxis annularis
Other names:	Goggle-eye, bachelor, silver crappie, crappie, papermouth, sac-a-lait
Size:	Up to 5½ lbs.; averages ½ to 1 lb.
Description:	A member of the sunfish family with a light olive color on sides and darker color on back. Irregularly spotted and generally a lighter color than the black crappie
Area of activity:	All states
Baits:	Minnows, worms, crustaceans, spinner, spinner–bucktail-fly combinations
How fished:	Best fishing near shore in springtime with baits or flies
Tackle:	Light or ultralight spinning rods, bait-casting rods and fly rods
Rig: Line	2- to 4-lb. test *Leader:* Monofilament
Hooks	No. 4 to 2/0
Edibility:	Good
Comments:	He nests in shallow water in the springtime. He was originally a Midwest native but has since been introduced to all states.

* * *

Popular name:	Drum, Fresh-water
Latin name:	Aplodinotus grunniens
Other names:	Drum, fresh-water sheepshead, croaker

Size:	Up to 3 lbs.
Description:	A silver-colored fish with large scales; somewhat humpbacked, and will grunt when out of water
Area of activity:	Ohio River area and Lake Erie
Baits:	Crayfish, worms, dead fish
How fished:	Bottom-fished
Tackle:	Any fresh-water tackle, most commonly baitcasting rods
Rig: Line	2- to 5-lb. test *Leader:* Monofilament
Hooks	Number 6 to No. 1
Edibility:	Edible
Comments:	His large ear bones are considered lucky and are often saved.

* * *

Popular name:	Eel
Latin name:	Anguilla bostoniensis
Other names:	American eel
Size:	Up to 6 feet in length
Description:	Long, snakelike body
Area of activity:	East Coast and Gulf states
Baits:	Worms, dead bait fish
How fished:	Bottom-fished at night. Many times a fisherman thinks he has hooked a snake. Remove him from hook and handle with a rag, for he's very slippery
Tackle:	Any tackle
Rig: Line	4- to 6-lb. test *Leader:* Monofilament
Hooks	No. 2 to 3/0
Edibility:	Excellent
Comments:	The female eel spends her life in fresh water and returns to salt water when she is ready to mate, while the male remains in salt or brackish water all his life. Eels mate only once and may live to 30 years.

* * *

Popular name:	Eel, Lamprey
Latin name:	Petromyzon marinus
Other names:	Lamprey, sea lamprey, lamprey eel, eel
Size:	Up to 30 inches in length and 8 lbs. in weight
Description:	An eel-like fish with two dorsal fins and a suction-cup mouth with which to attach himself to other fish and suck their blood
Area of activity:	Great Lakes area and along the Atlantic Coast
Baits:	None
How fished:	Speared
Edibility:	Not eaten
Comments:	A real menace, for he already has destroyed much of the lake-trout fishing in the Great Lakes. He is being combated with chemicals.

*   *   *

Popular name:	Gar, Alligator
Latin name:	Lepisosteus spatula
Other names:	Garfish, gator fish, gar
Size:	Up to 300 lbs, 8 feet in length; 150-pounders not uncommon
Description:	A garfish with a face like an alligator, he has heavy scales and breathes air
Area of activity:	Gulf states
Baits:	Chunks of fish
How fished:	Still-fished, often at night
Tackle:	Salt-water rods
Rig: Line	50-lb. test *Leader:* Wire
Hooks	No. 8/0 to 10/0
Edibility:	Flesh is edible, sometimes sold smoked; roe is poisonous
Comments:	He is a sluggish, prehistoric fish who can be as dangerous out of water as in.

*   *   *

Popular name:	Gar, Longnose
Latin name:	Lepisosteus osseus
Other names:	Billy gar, billfish, gar, shovelnose
Size:	Up to 5 feet in length, 50 lbs. in weight
Description:	A gar with a long, tubelike body and a bill-like mouth; his snout is 20 times the length of his head
Area of activity:	Southeastern states and the Gulf states
Baits:	Small fish, dead or alive
How fished:	Bait fishing, or speared or snared
Tackle:	Bait-casting rods
Rig: Line	20-lb. monofilament *Leader:* Wire
Hooks	No. 4/0 to 8/0
Edibility:	Flesh is edible, but roe is poisonous
Comments:	He is a prehistoric fish who is often seen sunning himself near the top of the water

*   *   *

Popular name:	Gar, Shortnose
Latin name:	Lepisosteus platostomus
Other names:	Billy gar, stubnosed gar, shortbill
Size:	Smallest of the gars, up to 30 inches in length
Description:	A gar without spots on top of his head
Area of activity:	The Mississippi River valley
Baits:	Crawfish, small fish
How fished:	Still-fished deep
Tackle:	Medium spinning rods and bait-casting rods
Rig: Line	6-lb. test *Leader:* Wire
Hooks	No. 1/0 to 4/0
Edibility:	Edible
Comments:	Seldom taken by sportsfishermen, he is small and considered a nuisance. He is often seen in schools sunning himself.

*   *   *

Popular name:	Gar, Spotted
Latin name:	Lepisosteus productus

Other names:	Garfish
Size:	Up to 45 inches in length
Description:	A shortnose gar with large round spots on his head
Area of activity:	The Midwest, from the Great Lakes to the Gulf states
Baits:	Small fish, minnows, suckers
How fished:	Still-fished
Tackle:	Medium bait-casting rods
Rig: Line	10-lb. test *Leader:* Wire
Hooks	No. 2/0 to 6/0
Edibility:	Edible
Comments:	He is often found in glacial lakes in the weedy sections, and in rivers. The Florida spotted gar—similar to him but smaller and with a shorter snout—replaces him in southern Georgia and Florida.

*   *   *

Popular name:	Grayling
Latin name:	Thymallus signifer
Other names:	American grayling, Arctic grayling
Size:	Up to 4 lbs.; averages 1 lb.
Description:	A purplish-colored fish noted for his long, flowing dorsal fin
Area of activity:	Alaska, Wyoming and Montana
Baits:	Flies, small spoons
How fished:	Stream- and lake-fished
Tackle:	Light or ultralight tackle
Rig: Line	2- to 4-lb. test *Leader:* Monofilament
Hooks	No. 12 to No. 6
Edibility:	Good
Comments:	He is a cold-water fish whose only real stronghold is Alaska.

*   *   *

Popular name: Muskellunge
Latin name: Esox masquinongy
Other names: Muskie, musky, muskalonge, tiger
Size: Up to 100 lbs. However fish 50 lbs and over are considered monsters
Description: Torpedo-shaped, with dark, irregular vertical lines on a light background. Small muskie are often confused with pike but can be distinguished by the scales on the upper half of their cheeks
Area of activity: The Northeast and as far west as northern Michigan and Wisconsin. Also the Mississippi valley
Baits: Perch, suckers, minnows, other bait fish, frogs, snakes, mice, spoons, plugs—hits anything that moves
How fished: Still-fished, trolled and bait-cast
Tackle: Sturdy fresh-water bait-casting rods or spinning rods with stiff action. Fly rods also used
Rig: Line   15-lb. monofilament   *Leader:* Wire
    Hooks   No. 4/0 to 8/0 long-shank
Edibility: Edible. Mostly a trophy fish
Comments: He is a real fresh-water prize. Voracious from the day he is born and a cannibal, he is relatively rare and is mainly found in the cold, clear waters of the northern states. The top state for him is Wisconsin, which is successfully stocking the species.

❋   ❋   ❋

Popular name: Muskellunge, Ohio
Latin name: Esox masquinongy ohiensis
Other names: Chautauqua muskellunge
Size: Up to 50 lbs.
Description: A subspecies of muskellunge with irregular bands on his sides

Area of activity: Western New York, Pennsylvania and in the Ohio River area. Also taken in West Virginia and in the TVA area

Baits: Bait fish up to 12 inches in length. Frogs, mice, etc. Spoons, plugs, spinner-fish combinations

How fished: Trolled or still-fished in deep holes

Tackle: Sturdy fresh-water tackle

Rig: Line 10- to 20-lb. test   *Leader:* Wire
   Hooks No. 3/0 to 8/0

Edibility: Edible

Comments: A subspecies of the muskie. A popular spot is Chautauqua Lake, New York. Other muskellunge subspecies include: Great Lakes muskellunge (Esox masquinongy masquinongy): Taken in the Great Lakes area and said to go over 100 lbs. Tiger muskellunge (Esox masquinongy immaculatus): found in northern Michigan, Wisconsin, and Minnesota.

*   *   *

Popular name: Paddlefish

Latin name: Polyodon spathula

Other names: Spoonbill, cat, flatbill

Size: Up to 7 feet in length: averages 2 to 3 feet. He can weigh 200 lbs., and is commonly over 50 lbs.

Description: Primitive, scaleless with an elongated snout and a sharklike mouth. The adult is toothless, while the young fish has sharp, fine teeth

Area of activity: The Mississippi and Missouri River basins

Baits: Small minnows, worms

How fished: Mostly caught by commercial fishing; or by jigging or snagging

Tackle: Sturdy bait-casting rods

Rig: Line 10- to 25-lb. test   *Leader:* Monofilament
   Hooks Treble hooks for snagging

Edibility: Excellent. Eggs are used as caviar

Comments: A primitive fish once very abundant but greatly diminished in recent years, often seen below a dam, where schools congregate, to be taken by jigging or snagging. He often swims on top with his dorsal fin out of water. Smoked paddlefish tastes exactly like smoked sturgeon, for which it is sometimes sold by unethical dealers for as much as $7.00 per pound.

* * *

Popular name: Perch, Sacramento
Latin name: Archoplites interruptus
Other names: Perch
Size: Up to 12 inches long and 2 lbs. in weight
Description: A member of the sunfish family with blotchy, vertical bars on his sides. He is bluish-green in color, dark on the back and light on the belly
Area of activity: Nevada and California
Baits: Live baits, flies
How fished: Pan-fished
Tackle: Ultralight bait-casting rods and fly rods
Rig: Line 2- to 4-lb. test *Leader:* Monofilament
   Hooks No. 6 to No. 1
Edibility: Good
Comments: Found originally in Pyramid Lake, Nevada, he is the only sunfish native to California.

* * *

Popular name: Perch, White
Latin name: Morone americana
Other names: Silver bass, silver perch, perch
Size: Up to 14 inches, 3 lbs. in weight; averages 1 lb.
Description: Brilliant, silvery, and bass-shaped. He has a thin, lateral line on his sides and scales between his eyes

Area of activity: East of the Allegheny Mountains from Maine to South Carolina, and in the Great Lakes

Baits: Insects, worms, bait fish, crustaceans. Also takes flies, spinner-flies, streamer-flies

How fished: Casting, trolling or still-fishing

Tackle: Light spinning rods bait-casting rods and fly rods

Rig: Line 2- to 4-lb. test *Leader:* Monofilament
 Hooks No. 8 to No. 4

Edibility: Good

Comments: A large pan fish of the bass family (which includes striped bass and white bass) he is anadromous and can live his complete life in either fresh or salt water. He is a school fish; and if one is caught, more are about. An angler should keep all he catches, for white perch tend to overpopulate lakes and stunt other fish.

✿　✿　✿

Popular name: Perch, Yellow

Latin name: Perca flavescens

Other names: Perch, Humpback

Size: Up to 15 inches in length, 5 lbs. in weight; averages under 1 lb.

Description: Six to 8 vertical bars on his sides. He appears humpbacked and has a concave head

Area of activity: All states

Baits: Worms, spinners, flies, minnows

How fished: Still-fished or trolled

Tackle: Light and ultralight bait-casting rods, spinning rods and fly rods

Rig: Line 2- to 4-lb. test *Leader:* Monofilament
 Hooks No. 8 to No. 4

Edibility: Good

Comments: He is a popular pan fish who travels about lakes in schools; if one is caught, more are about. He remains active all winter and is an ice fisherman's favorite.

❀ ❀ ❀

Popular name: Pickerel, Bulldog
Latin name: Esox americanus
Other names: Shortnose pickerel, banded pickerel, redfin pickerel, barred pickerel
Size: Up to 15 inches in length and 1 lb. in weight
Description: A pigmy member of the pike family with a shorter snout than other pike. He has about 20 blackish bars on his sides
Area of activity: Eastern United States from Maine to Florida
Baits: Small plugs, spoons, flies, minnows, crawfish
How fished: Still-fished, spinned or trolled
Tackle: Ultralight and light bait-casting rods, spinning rods, and fly rods
Rig: Line 2- to 4-lb. test   *Leader:* Monofilament
     Hooks No. 2 to 1/0
Edibility: Edible
Comments: He is a small pickerel found in the quiet waters of streams and in swampy areas along the East Coast.

❀ ❀ ❀

Popular name: Pickerel, Chain
Latin name: Esox niger
Other names: Pickerel, eastern pickerel
Size: Up to 2 feet in length, and 8 pounds in weight
Description: Torpedo-shaped, with map-type lines on a dark-greenish to brownish body. His gill covers are scaled
Area of activity: Maine to Florida and as far west as the Mississippi valley

Baits:	Minnows and other bait fish, frogs, crawfish, insects, or spoons, plugs and spinner-fly or spinner-minnow combinations. Pork rind is the traditional bait
How fished:	Hot-spots are lily pads, weeds and sunken logs, where angler may still-fish, troll or cast for them
Tackle:	Bait-casting rods, fly rods, spinning rods and cane poles
Rig: Line	5-lb monofilament *Leader:* Wire
Hooks	No. 1/0 to 3/0
Edibility:	Edible but bony
Comments:	A voracious feeder that lays in ambush for prey, he enjoys killing live bait and should be given plenty of time to swallow the bait.

* * *

Popular name:	Pickerel, Grass
Latin name:	Esox vermiculatus
Other names:	Pickerel, mud pickerel
Size:	Up to 12 inches in length
Description:	A pigmy member of the pike family, he has alternating light and dark bars on his sides
Area of activity:	Ohio River basin and St. Lawrence River. Also as far south as Alabama and Texas
Baits:	Small plugs, spoons, flies, crawfish
How fished:	Fished from shore or from a boat
Tackle:	Ultralight or light bait-casting rods and fly rods
Rig: Line	2- to 4-lb. test *Leader:* Monofilament
Hooks	No. 2 to 1/0
Edibility:	Edible
Comments:	He is a very small pickerel who tends to stay in quiet swampy water of streams.

* * *

Popular name:	Pike, Northern
Latin name:	Esox lucius
Other names:	Northerns, great northern pike, pike, jackfish
Size:	Up to 4 feet in length, and 50 lbs. in weight
Description:	Torpedo-shaped, with white spots on an olive-gray body; or greenish body and a yellow or white belly. His cheeks are fully scaled
Area of activity:	Alaska, the Great Lakes area south into the Mississippi valley, and the Northeast
Baits:	If it moves, it's a bait. He will take snakes, mice, frogs, crawfish, worms, bait fish or almost any spoon, spinner or plug made. Can be taken on streamer flies
How fished:	Still-fished or worked in weed beds or lily pads. In deep holes during day
Tackle:	Spinning rods, bait-casting rods and fly rods
Rig: Line	15-lb. monofilament *Leader:* Wire
Hooks	4/0 to 8/0 long-shank flies tied on No. 1/0 bass hooks
Edibility:	Edible but bony
Comments:	A solitary fish that lays in ambush to attack a prey, the pike is taken mostly over soft bottoms such as mud or marshes. He is a legendary fish, and many European folktales tell of monster pikes.

❖   ❖   ❖

Popular name:	Pike, Walleye
Latin name:	Stizostedion vitreum
Other names:	Walleye, pike perch, Susquehanna salmon, jack salmon, yellow pike, perch, hornfish
Size:	Up to 3 feet in length, and 25 lbs. in weight; averages 3 to 5 lbs.
Description:	A perch-shaped fish with 2 dorsal fins. The fins have very sharp gill covers. He is greenish in color and has oblique bars

Area of activity:	Entire country except the West and extreme South
Baits:	Minnows and other bait fish, worms, frogs, crawfish or lures, including spinners and spoons
How fished:	Fished deep, either by trolling or still-fishing
Tackle:	Bait-casting rods and medium spinning rods
Rig: Line	6- to 12-lb test *Leader:* Wire
Hooks	No. 1 to 4/0
Edibility:	Excellent
Comments:	He tends to travel in schools and almost always stays on the bottom. Fishermen should work his bait into the holes.

*   *   *

Popular name:	Salmon, Atlantic
Latin name:	Salmo salar
Other names:	Maine salmon, New England salmon
Size:	Up to 75 lbs. Salmon return from the sea weighing 10 to 20 lbs.; 14 inches is the legal size
Description:	Silvery color in salt water, turning brownish in fresh water
Area of activity:	Maine
Baits:	Salmon flies
How fished:	Wading in salmon rivers and fly-fishing
Tackle:	6-oz. fly rods
Rig: Line	Tapered fly-rod line *Leader:* Monofilament
Hooks	Salmon hooks
Edibility:	Excellent
Comments:	In the United States he is found only in the Machias, East Machias, Narraguagus, Dennys, Sheepscot, Pleasant and Penobscot rivers.

*   *   *

Popular name:	Salmon, Chinook
Latin name:	Oncorhynchus tschawytscha

Other names: King salmon, king, spring salmon, quinnat salmon, Tyee, Tule, jack salmon, sockdolagers.

Size: Up to 4 feet and 100 lbs.; 10- to 45-lb. fish are common

Description: Greenish back fading to silvery on sides and belly. Many black spots on back. Spawning fish grow dark

Area of activity: Alaska, Washington, Idaho, Oregon and California

Baits: Herring, silver spoons, jigs, spinners

How fished: Fished from skiffs by trolling or mooching. Also fished from jetties and from shore

Tackle: Spinning rods and boat rods

Rig: Line   15- to 35-lb. test   *Leader:* Wire

Hooks   No. 2/0 to 6/0

Edibility: Excellent

Comments: On a spawning migration he does not feed, but can be coaxed to take a hook, for he never loses his urge to kill.

* * *

Popular name: Salmon, Kokanee

Latin name: Oncorhynchus nerka

Other names: Little redfish, little salmon, blueback. Seagoing fish are known as: sockeye salmon, red salmon, Alaska salmon or redfish

Size: Landlocked up to 4 lbs.; sea-going up to 15 lbs.

Description: Silvery until its fourth year of life, when he turns red. There are no black spots on his back or sides

Area of activity: Alaska, Washington, Oregon, California, Montana, Idaho and Wyoming

Baits: Flies or spoons

How fished: Trolled off the bottom with small spoons or fly-fished near shore. Also snagged when in close to shore.

Tackle: Light fly rods and spinning rods

Rig: Line	2- to 6-lb. monofilament *Leader:* Monofilament
Hooks	No. 8 to No. 2 for landlocked fish; No. 5 to 1/0 for sea-going fish
Edibility:	Excellent
Comments:	The landlocked fish lives in lakes and is basically a plankton feeder until the last year of life. He lives at medium depth in the lakes. The sea-run fish is seldom caught by sports anglers.

*   *   *

Popular name:	Salmon, Landlocked
Latin name:	Salmo salar sebago
Other names:	Salmon, trout, eastern landlocked salmon
Size:	Up to 20 lbs.; averages under 5 lbs.
Description:	A trout-shaped fish where the fins under the head are blackish. The young salmon has red spots which fade as the fish gets older
Area of activity:	Maine, Vermont, New Hampshire and New York
Baits:	Streamer flies, smelt, wobblers
How fished:	Fly-fished or spinned in spring and fall. Deep trolling in the summer
Tackle:	Fly rods, spinning rods or bait-casting rods
Rig: Line	5- to 10-lb. monofilament *Leader:* Monofilament
Hooks	No. 6 to No. 2
Edibility:	Excellent
Comments:	He can live only in clear, cold water. The best chance for catching him on light tackle is right after the ice is out, when he chases smelt upstream.

*   *   *

Popular name:	Salmon, Silver
Latin name:	Oncorhynchus kisutch
Other names:	Coho, cohoe, silversides, hookbill

Size:	Up to 35 lbs.; averages 8 to 15 lbs.
Description:	Metallic-blue back with silvery sides and an underneath that is reddish during breeding
Area of activity:	The Pacific Coast as far south as Monterey
Baits:	Herring, small fish, salmon eggs, streamer flies, spoons
How fished:	Fished from skiffs, bridges or jetties
Tackle:	Fly rods and medium spinning rods
Rig: Line	5- to 20-lb. monofilament *Leader:* Wire or monofilament
Hooks	No. 1/0 to 2/0
Edibility:	Excellent
Comments:	He spawns in his third year, and is flashy, a hard fighter and murderous striker. He is off feed in fresh water but can be coaxed to take a bait or lure.

*   *   *

Popular name:	Sauger
Latin name:	Stizostedion canadense
Other names:	Pike perch, jack salmon
Size:	Up to 8 lbs.; averages 1 lb.
Description:	Resembles a small walleye pike
Area of activity:	The Midwest
Baits:	Minnows or other bait fish, crawfish, spinner-minnow combinations
How fished:	Bottom-fished in lakes and rivers
Tackle:	Any light tackle
Rig: Line	2- to 4-lb. test *Leader:* Monofilament
Hooks	No. 1 to 3/0
Edibility:	Good
Comments:	Best fishing is in the spring, when the fish travels in schools close to shore. Other times of the year he tends to stay in water 20 feet or more in depth.

*   *   *

Popular name: Shad, American
Latin name: Alosa sapidissima
Other names: Shad, white shad
Size: Up to 12 lbs.; averages 2 to 5 lbs.
Description: A herring, silvery in color with a dark-colored shoulder
Area of activity: The Atlantic and Pacific coasts
Baits: Flies, spinners, spoons
How fished: Fished from small boats or from shore on rivers
Tackle: Fly rods and light spinning rods
Rig: Line 5- to 15-lb. monofilament *Leader:* Monofilament
    Hooks No. 8 to 3/0
Edibility: Good; shad roe is a delicacy
Comments: The shad was introduced to the West Coast in 1871 and now thrives there. The shad of the Hudson and Delaware rivers does not take a hook.

* * *

Popular name: Shad, Hickory
Latin name: Pomolobus mediocris
Other names: Shad
Size: 2 to 5 lbs.
Description: A herring, silvery in color
Area of activity: Atlantic seaboard
Baits: Flies, spinners, spoons
How fished: Fished from small boats and from shore in migrating rivers
Tackle: Fly rods and light spinning rods
Rig: Line 5- to 10-lb. monofilament *Leader:* Monofilament
    Hooks No. 8 to 2/0
Edibility: Good

Comments:	The shad is not feeding when he comes into fresh water; therefore he must be teased into taking a hook.

❋   ❋   ❋

Popular name:	Sheefish
Latin name:	Stenodus leucichthys
Other names:	Innonnu, Innonu, and Inconnu
Size:	Up to 80 lbs.; 20- to 40-pounders common in some areas
Description:	A large whitefish with teeth on his jaws. He has a long, prominent lower jaw
Area of activity:	Alaska
Baits:	Bait fish, strip-cut fish
How fished:	Fished from boats in the Arctic rivers such as the Yukon and Mackenzie
Tackle:	Heavy-duty tackle
Rig: Line	12- to 30-lb. test *Leader:* Not necessary
Hooks	No. 4 to 2/0
Edibility:	Good
Comments:	He is a large Arctic member of the whitefish family, and an important food fish for the Eskimos of western Alaska. He comes into fresh water on his spring spawning run, but sometimes is landlocked in Arctic lakes.

❋   ❋   ❋

Popular name:	Smelt
Latin name:	Osmerus mordax
Other names:	American smelt, frostfish
Size:	Up to 12 inches in length but under 1 lb. in weight
Description:	Small and silvery
Area of activity:	New England and Great Lakes area
Baits:	Occasionally small flies

How fished:	Mostly netted
Tackle:	Nets
Rig: Line	None *Leader:* None
Hooks	None
Edibility:	Excellent
Comments:	He makes fine bait for landlocked salmon, and is netted during his spring spawning runs.

* * *

Popular name:	Squawfish, Colorado River
Latin name:	Ptychocheilus iucius
Other names:	Squawfish
Size:	Up to 6 feet in length, 80 lbs. in weight
Description:	A large member of the minnow family, has only a single dorsal fin and is brownish-silverish in color
Area of activity:	The Colorado River
Baits:	Bait fish, spinners, spoons
How fished:	Trolled or still-fished
Tackle:	Medium bait-casting rods and spinning rods
Rig: Line	6- to 20-lb. test *Leader:* Monofilament
Hooks	No. 4 to 2/0
Edibility:	Edible but bony
Comments:	He is a hard fighter who attacks a bait with furor. Another variety is the Sacramento squawfish (Ptychocheilus grande) which is found in the Sacramento River valley of California.

* * *

Popular name:	Squawfish, Columbia River
Latin name:	Ptychocheilus oregonensis
Other names:	Squawfish
Size:	Up to 2 feet in length; averages 2 to 4 lbs.
Description:	A large member of the minnow family with a greenish back and silvery-yellow sides

Area of activity:	Oregon and Washington, the Columbia River basin
Baits:	Flies, small spoons, baitfish
How fished:	Caught while trout fishing
Tackle:	Regular Western trout tackle
Rig: Line	4- to 8-lb test *Leader:* Monofilament
Hooks	No. 4 to 2/0
Edibility:	Edible
Comments:	The Indians of the area use him for food.

* * *

Popular name:	Sturgeon, Lake
Latin name:	Acipenser fulvescens
Other names:	Shovelnose, rock sturgeon, rubbernose sturgeon, dogface sturgeon, red sturgeon
Size:	Up to 300 lbs.; averages 8 to 15 lbs.
Description:	Armorlike, bony plates cover his body. He has 2 spiracles (openings) in his head
Area of activity:	The Midwest to the Gulf
Baits:	Worms, crawfish, minnows, mollusks
How fished:	Bottom-fished. Also speared through the ice
Tackle:	Medium tackle
Rig: Line	10-lb. test *Leader:* Monofilament
Hooks	No. 2 to 2/0
Edibility:	Excellent
Comments:	He is well along the road to extinction, and 100-lb. species are extremely rare today, whereas in the nineteenth century they were common. He grows and matures very slowly.

* * *

Popular name:	Sturgeon, White
Latin name:	Acipenser transmotanus
Other names:	Gray sturgeon, western sturgeon, sturgeon

Size: Up to 12 feet in length and 1,200 lbs. The
                   record weighed 360 lbs. and was 9 feet 3
                   inches in length
Description: Long body and a sucker mouth with barbels
                   under the snout. He is grayish in color with a
                   white belly
Area of activity: Idaho, Washington, Oregon, California and
                   Alaska
Baits: Fish eggs, crustaceans, bait fish
How fished: Trolled or still-fished
Tackle: Heavy-duty salt-water tackle
Rig: Line   50-lb. test   *Leader:* Wire
  Hooks   No. 8/0 to 10/0
Edibility: Excellent
Comments: One of the best spots for taking him is in the
                   Snake River above Lewiston, Idaho.

* * *

Popular name: Sucker, white
Latin name: Catostomus commersonni
Other names: Common sucker, sucker, mullet, whitehorse,
                   black sucker
Size: Up to 2½ feet in length, 8 lbs. in weight;
                   averages 1 lb.
Description: Mouth under his head enables him to sift
                   through silt for food. He has a white body and
                   darker back, and has a lateral line on his sides
Area of activity: All states east of the Rockies except the Gulf
                   states
Baits: Mollusks, bits of worms
How fished: Often caught while trout fishing with worms
Tackle: Light fly rods, spinning rods and bait-casting
                   rods
Rig: Line   2- to 4-lb. test   *Leader:* Monofilament
  Hooks   No. 6 to No. 2
Edibility: Edible—good to smoke. Best eating in spring
                   while flesh is firm

Comments: He is found in fresh-water lakes, streams and
                   rivers. Other suckers include: Spotted sucker,
                   creek chub sucker, northern sturgeon sucker,
                   dwarf sturgeon sucker and eastern creek chub
                   sucker.

❖   ❖   ❖

Popular name: Sunfish, Banded
Latin name: Enneacanthus obesus
Other names: Sunfish
Size: Up to 6 inches in length; averages 3 inches
Description: Spot on his ear is almost half the size of his
                   eye
Area of activity: The southern states
Baits: Worms, insects
How fished: Still-fished
Tackle: Ultralight tackle
Rig: Line   2-lb test   *Leader:* Monofilament
  Hooks   No. 10 to No. 6
Edibility: Too small for eating
Comments: A pest, for he is too small for sport or eating

❖   ❖   ❖

Popular name: Sunfish, Bluegill
Latin name: Lepomis macrochirus
Other names: Bluegill, sunfish, bream, sun perch
Size: Up to 5 lbs.; averages under 1 lb.
Description: Velvet-black ear flap. His back is greenish
                   and sides orange. The male has bright orange
                   and yellow chests
Area of activity: Entire United States
Baits: Bass bugs, flies, small spinners, small min-
                   nows, worms, grasshoppers, small insects
How fished: Best fishing in spring along shore line in his
                   nest. Still-fished or fly-fished
Tackle: Any ultralight or light tackle

Rig: Line	2- to 4-lb. test *Leader:* Monofilament
Hooks	No. 8 to No. 4
Edibility:	Good
Comments:	He is an excellent fish to start children on, for he inhabits the shore line, is easy to catch, is scrappy and is fine eating. A favorite Southern dish is bream rolled in cracker crumbs and fried.

*   *   *

Popular name:	Sunfish, Common
Latin name:	Lepomis gibbosus
Other names:	Pumpkinseed, dwarf sunfish, redspotted sunfish, pigmy sunfish
Size:	Up to 8 inches in length and ½ lb. in weight; usually weighs only a few ounces
Description:	Usually olive- to grassy-green, with a golden belly. He has a red mark on his ear flap and long, pointed, pectoral fins. The male's stomach is bright orange during breeding seasons
Area of activity:	All states
Baits:	Worms, flies, spinners
How fished:	Pan-fished
Tackle:	Ultralight tackle
Rig: Line	2-lb test *Leader:* Monofilament
Hooks	No. 8 to No. 2
Edibility:	Good, but the fish is small and bony
Comments:	A very abundant fish who is scrappy on ultralight tackle, he is perpetually hungry; therefore many anglers will have fun with him during the hot part of day when other fish will not strike.

*   *   *

Popular name:	Sunfish, Redbreast
Latin name:	Lepomis auritus

Other names: Kivver, kibbee, red-bellied sunfish, bream, yellowbreast sunfish

Size: Up to 8 inches in length and 2 lbs. in weight

Description: Scales on his sides have reddish spots on a bluish background. He has an orange belly, and his ear flap is dark

Area of activity: The eastern seaboard states and the Gulf states

Baits: Worms, insects

How fished: Pan-fished

Tackle: Ultralight tackle

Rig: Line   2-lb. test   *Leader:* Monofilament
     Hooks   No. 8 to No. 2

Edibility: Edible

Comments: Another of the many species of sunfish in our country, he prefers clean running water and will take flies and other artificials.

*   *   *

Popular name: Trout, Brook

Latin name: Salvelinus fontinalis

Other names: Speckled trout, eastern brook trout, square-tail or brookie

Size: Up to 15 lbs.; averages 1 to 2 lbs.

Description: Wavy olive marks appear on his back and red spots on his sides. His lines are touched with black-and-white markings

Area of activity: The Canadian border south to Georgia and in the West south to New Mexico

Baits: Worms, minnows, insects, nymphs, mollusks, spinners, spoons, flies

How fished: Fly fished with dry or wet flies or nymphs. Spin-fished with spinners, plugs, worms and various combinations

Tackle: Light flyrods and spinning rods

Rig: Line   Tapered fly line   *Leader:* Monofilament
    Hooks   No. 10 to No. 4
Edibility: Excellent
Comments: Originally an eastern seaboard fish who has been successfully transplanted throughout the West, he thrives in clean, cold, swift-running brooks. He spawns in the fall.

*   *   *

Popular name: Trout, Brown
Latin name: Salmo trutta
Other names: German trout, German brown trout, Loch Leven trout
Size: Up to 40 lbs; averages under 5 lbs
Description: Brownish-yellow in color, with black and brown spots on his back; the spots on his sides are encircled by light rings
Area of activity: Entire northern region of the United States
Baits: Flies, worms, bait fish, spinners, plugs
How fished: Most enjoyable is dry-fly fishing. Also wet-fly and nymph fishing. Spinning with small spinners, spoons or plugs is also popular
Tackle: Fly rods and spinning rods
Rig: Line   Torpedo or 6-lb. monofilament *Leader:* Monofilament
    Hooks   No. 8 to No. 6
Edibility: Excellent
Comments: He was introduced from Europe during the nineteenth century, and can survive waters that cannot support other species of trout. He is a wary fish and gives the angler a real challenge.

*   *   *

Popular name: Trout, Cutthroat
Latin name: Salmo clarki

Other names: Speckled trout, black-spotted trout, harvest trout, blueback

Size: Up to 40 lbs.; averages under 2 lbs.

Description: He is named after the two red lines on the lower sides of his jaw. He is black-spotted on his back, sides, head and tail

Area of activity: Alaska, Washington, Oregon, California, Nevada, Colorado, Wyoming, Idaho and Montana

Baits: Flies, spinners, wobblers, salmon eggs, bait fish

How fished: Fly-fished or spin-fished in streams and trolled in lakes

Tackle: Light fly rods and spinning rods

Rig: Line   2- to 4-lb. monofilament or fly line   *Leader:* Monofilament

    Hooks   No. 8 to No. 4

Edibility: Excellent

Comments: A relatively small fish, he is always a spirited fighter. Many subspecies exist. Cutthroats are both sea-run and landlocked.

      ❋   ❋   ❋

Popular name: Trout, Dolly Varden

Latin name: Salvelinus malma

Other names: Dolly Varden, bull trout, salmon trout, Dolly

Size: Up to 35 lbs.; averages 10 lbs.

Description: Elongated in shape and colorful, he has pale yellow and white spots on a greenish back and often has bright-colored sides

Area of activity: Along the Pacific Coast and Rocky Mountain area as far south as California

Baits: Flies for the small Dolly and live bait, spoons, spinners and salmon eggs for the big ones

How fished: Trolled in lakes or fished in deep holes in streams or rivers

Tackle:	Regular trout or steelhead tackle
Rig: Line	Tapered fly or 6-lb. monofilament *Leader:* Monofilament
Hooks	No. 4 to 2/0
Edibility:	Good
Comments:	He is anadromous in his northern ranges but stays strictly to fresh water in his southern areas. He should be fished low, right near the bottom.

* * *

Popular name:	Trout, Golden
Latin name:	Salmo aguabonita
Other names:	California golden trout
Size:	Up to 11 lbs.
Description:	Colored a beautiful gold, with a red band on his side
Area of activity:	The mountains of California, Wyoming and Montana
Baits:	Flies, small spoons
How fished:	Fly-fished or spinned from shore
Tackle:	Light, portable fly rods and spinning rods
Rig: Line	Tapered fly line or monofilament *Leader:* Monofilament
Hooks	No. 12 to No. 8 flies
Edibility:	Good
Comments:	He is found in the Rocky Mountains, in lakes or streams over 9,000 feet in elevation.

* * *

Popular name:	Trout, Lake
Latin name:	Salvelinus namaycush
Other names:	Togue, Mackinaw trout, fork tail, salmon trout
Size:	Up to 100 lbs.; averages 3 to 5 lbs.

Description:	Deeply-forked tail and spotted white on a dark background. He lacks the traditional trout red spots
Area of activity:	New England, New York, Pennsylvania, Great Lakes region, Rocky Mountain region and Alaska
Baits:	Bait fish and spoons in deep water and insects or crustaceans in shallow water
How fished:	Fished in lakes, where it is trolled with spoons and plugs or live bait
Tackle:	Sturdy bait-casting rods
Rig: Line	10-lb. test monofilament Monel wire *Leader:* Wire
Hooks	No. 4 to No. 1
Edibility:	Excellent
Comments:	Where lake trout thrives, water must remain under 65°. He is usually taken at a depth of 40 feet or more.

* * *

Popular name:	Trout, Rainbow
Latin name:	Salmo gairdneri
Other names:	Steelhead, Kamloops, coast rainbow trout
Size:	Up to 40 lbs.; 20-pounders are common in some waters
Description:	Heavily black-spotted, with a pink stripe on both sides
Area of activity:	All states except the warm Gulf states
Baits:	Flies; wet, dry or streamers. Spoons, plugs, minnows, salmon eggs, bait fish
How fished:	Fly-fished or spinned
Tackle:	Fly rods and spinning rods. Also trolled with sturdy bait-casting rods
Rig: Line	Torpedo or monofilament *Leader:* Monofilament
Hooks	No. 8 to No. 4

Edibility:	Excellent
Comments:	A cold-water fish originally found on the Pacific Coast, he has been introduced to other waters successfully. Best fishing is in fast water. He spawns in winter.

* * *

Popular name:	Trout, Splake
Size:	Up to 20 lbs.
Description:	This is a hybrid—a cross between a female lake trout and a male brook trout. He has the coloring of a lake trout but is spotted
Area of activity:	Wherever stocked
Baits:	Flies, spoons, bait fish
How fished:	Trolled or still-fished
Tackle:	Medium spinning rods and bait-casting rods
Rig: Line	2- to 8-lb. test *Leader:* Monofilament
Hooks	No. 8 to No. 4
Edibility:	Excellent
Comments:	The splake was one of the first hybrid trout in the nineteenth century. The purpose of experimenting with hybrid fish is to produce strains superior to existing species. Hoped for are bigger fish, disease-resistant fish, or fish that can take warm water. Many hybrids have been tried with varying success.

* * *

Popular name:	Trout, Sunapee
Latin name:	Salvelinus aurelus
Other names:	Golden trout, Sunapee golden trout
Size:	Up to 10 lbs.
Description:	Olive-green in color with pale orange spots. Belly becomes orange during the spawning season
Area of activity:	New Hampshire

Baits:	Streamer flies, smelt, spoons
How fished:	Fly-fished or trolled
Tackle:	Spinning rods, fly rods, and bait-casting rods
Rig: Line	6-lb. test monofilament *Leader:* Wire
Hooks	No. 6 to No. 2
Edibility:	Good
Comments:	A rare, beautiful fish once found only in Lake Sunapee, New Hampshire

* * *

Popular name:	Warmouth
Latin name:	Chaenobryttus coronarius
Other names:	Warmouth perch, goggle-eye, warmouth bass, mud bass, weed bass, wood bass
Size:	Averages 1 lb.
Description:	A greenish-colored sunfish, with mottled markings on sides and back. He has teeth on his tongue.
Area of activity:	South of New Jersey and throughout Dixie
Baits:	Minnows, worms, flies, small spoons
How fished:	Pan-fished
Tackle:	Ultralight tackle
Rig: Line	2-lb. test *Leader:* Monofilament
Hooks	No. 4 to 2/0
Edibility:	Edible
Comments:	He likes slow-moving water and frequents vegetable forests, and is considered by many to be one of the scrappiest members of the sunfish family. Often misidentified as a rock bass, he can easily be told from the other fish by its 3 spines on the anal fin; the rock bass has 6 spines on his anal fin.

* * *

Popular name:	Whitefish
Latin name:	Coregonus clupeaformis

Size:	Up to 15 lbs.; averages 2 to 4 lbs.
Description:	Silvery, with the appearance of a herring, he has a faint lateral line on his sides
Area of activity:	New England and the Great Lakes area
Baits:	Small minnows, small spoons
How fished:	Fished deep, trolled
Tackle:	Medium bait-casting rods or spinning rods
Rig: Line	6- to 15-lb. test *Leader:* Monofilament
Hooks	No. 10 to No. 6
Edibility:	Excellent
Comments:	The whitefish is hard to catch because he tends to stay in deep water.

*   *   *

Popular name:	Whitefish, Great Lakes
Latin name:	Coregonus artedi
Other names:	Whitefish, lake herring, cisco
Size:	Up to 10 lbs.; averages 1 lb.
Description:	Silvery, with the appearance of a herring
Area of activity:	The Great Lakes area and northern part of the Mississippi valley
Baits:	Small minnows, spoons, and, on occasion, flies
How fished:	Usually fished in water over 25 feet deep. Some whitefish will go hundreds of feet deep
Tackle:	Medium bait-casting rods and spinning rods
Rig: Line	6- to 10-lb. test *Leader:* Monofilament
Hooks	No. 8 to No. 6
Edibility:	Good
Comments:	He comes to the top only in the evening and early morning; at all other times he will be deep.

*   *   *

Popular name:	Whitefish, Rocky Mountain
Latin name:	Prosopium williamsoni

Other names:	Whitefish (mistakenly called grayling), mountain whitefish
Size:	Up to 4 lbs.
Description:	Resembles a grayling except dorsal fin is not as large. Grayish-blue on back, with silvery sides
Area of activity:	Colorado, Utah, Idaho and Wyoming
Baits:	Small flies, spoons
How fished:	Stream-fished
Tackle:	Light and ultralight spinning rods and fly rods
Rig: Line	2- to 4-lb. test *Leader:* Monofilament
Hooks	No. 18 to No. 12
Edibility:	Good
Comments:	He is a fine small sports fish of the Rocky Mountains.

* * *

Popular name:	Whitefish, Round
Latin name:	Prosopium clindraceum
Other names:	Whitefish
Size:	Up to 5 lbs.; averages 1 lb.
Description:	Silvery, with the appearance of a herring
Area of activity:	New England, New York and the Great Lakes region
Baits:	Small spinners, minnows, crustaceans
How fished:	Trolled along shore line
Tackle:	Light spinning rods, bait-casting rods and fly rods
Rig: Line	2- to 4-lb. test *Leader:* Monofilament
Hooks	No. 10 to No. 6
Edibility:	Good
Comments:	He tends to stay along the shore lines of lakes and in adjacent streams. He does not enter very deep water, as do other whitefish.

The author takes a stubborn brookie from the stream that runs through his property.

A catch of brookies from that stream.

The author took this 4-lb. 5-oz. bass on a tiny spinning lure.

Here is a fine string of fish, topped by the author's 5-lb. 11-oz. bass.

This pickerel tried hard to chew up the small wooden plug he was taken on.

Photo: Florida Game and Freshwater Fish Commission

A pickerel that couldn't resist a flashy lure.

Boys love fishing, and Jimmy proudly displays a string of pumpkinseed, bluegill, and yellow perch.

The author checks the equipment on a canoe float on the Delaware River.

This fisherman admires a 4-lb. brown trout from Sandy River, Maine.

Photo: Maine Department of Economic Development

A landlocked salmon from East Grand Lake, Maine. Grand Lake was one of the original salmon lakes in the country.

A view of some Michigan smelt dippers. The tiny smelt are taken in nets during the spring, when the fish come into streams to spawn.

Photo: Michigan Tourist Council

A typical Michigan fishing
village built on the ice.

Photo: Michigan Tourist Council

Sunfish and yellow perch are
the favorites of many ice
fishermen.

Photo: Michigan Tourist Council

A trout comes out of some of Michigan's white water.

Fishing is a sport the whole family can enjoy.

"Got one!"—words that are music to a fisherman's ears.

A view of some largemouth bass taken from one of Florida's 30,000 lakes.

Although fishing is not permitted in Silver Springs, Florida, there are
some fine bass, sunfish, and catfish found there.

An 80-lb. channel catfish taken by Bill
Bellis in the annual Catfish Derby at
Pickwick Dam in Savannah, Tennessee.

Photo: V. B. Scheffer, U.S. Fish and Wildlife Service

Netting sockeye salmon at Attu, Alaska.

Photo: Ernie Day, Boise, Idaho

Here is a fine catch of steelhead and salmon taken in the Salmon River with the help of guide Don L. Smith from North Fork, Idaho.

A giant sturgeon, weighing over 400 lbs., from the Snake River in southwestern Idaho.

Photo: Idaho Department of Fish & Game

The author takes a brook trout from a mountain stream.

This 12-inch brook trout fell prey to the author's light cahill.

These 5 brook trout, measuring 10 to 14 inches, were taken by the author in a small stream. Many small streams give anglers their best opportunities for filling a creel with brookies.

The author displays a sturdy, hard-fighting 11-lb. carp, which took a doughball.

The author took this 14-in rainbow trout, which went for a spinner-fly combination.

THE ART
OF BAIT
CASTING

Point rod in the direction of the target and dip it forward about 30°. Hold reel with the handle facing up and place thumb on the spool. The lure should be 6 inches from the rod tip.

Lift rod straight back over the shoulder until it
points about 20° back. Then snap rod forward and
allow lure and line to fly out to the target.

Thumb line as the lure flies to the target and
gradually increase thumb pressure to stop reel and
prevent backlash. Then switch rod and hold it in
both hands and begin retrieve. With a minimum of
practice an angler will be able to cast 75 ft. and
more with accuracy.

The Fresh-Water Fish of America

Largemouth Bass

The name largemouth bass (Micropterus salmoides) is syn onymous with monstrous, hard-fighting sports fish. What remains to be written about the largemouth? Each year tons of published material tell how to catch them—yet still I feel I can add a few tricks to help the angler catch more and bigger battling beauties.

Ole Mr. Largemouth is an American native. He originally came from the Midwest throughout the Mississippi Valley, the Gulf States, Florida and along the coast as far north as North Carolina. Anglers then spread the fish throughout the country, and now it is found in all states, including Hawaii. We just couldn't keep our mouth shut about this popular battler, so requests came from foreign countries; and the fish has been introduced into Europe and Africa.

The largemouth is the biggest member of the sunfish family, and a whopping 22-pound 4-ounce monster from Georgia is the world's record. Other largemouth approaching this weight are taken in the South, where the fish get an opportunity to feed 12 months of the year and do not have to hibernate during the winter. Generally bass start hibernation when the water tempera ture dips below 45°.

This is as cannibalistic a fish as there is; it attacks bait fish any time and in any manner. Bass do not swim fast—their top speed is 12 miles an hour—but they are agile and strong. Some times the bass will lay in ambush to pounce on unsuspecting prey. Other times it prowls for food. Smaller bass often travel in schools, vigorously attacking bait. The fish will hit in deep water right near the bottom, in medium-depth water or in water only a few inches deep. Sometimes a bass will break suddenly through a weed bed to attack a prey, while other times he may blast up at the surface at some unsuspecting snake or bird. On occasion bass have been known to attack baby alligators, for they fear nothing.

Bass have a pugnacious nature and are insatiable. If they are stuffed to the gills with food they will still attack a nearby bait fish, because it's their nature to kill. There was a spot I could always pick up some bass by merely trolling a minnow. If they were on feed they'd take the minnow as though it were the only meal they'd seen in days. Other times they were so stuffed they'd want nothing more; still they would attack, if only to kill the bait fish. They never ate the bait but merely tore into it until they were satisfied that it was dead; then they'd leave it completely alone. Sometimes this was irritating for us, but we found that by adding an extra hook in the tail of the minnow we were able to take many of the executioners.

Once I witnessed a young crow sitting on the branches of a tree that had fallen into the water. Suddenly there was an explosion underneath the tree followed by a second explosion, and the bird disappeared. Two big bass had been sitting under that tree, and both had dinner ideas at almost the same time. I never did know which one got the bird, but from the boil on the water they seemed to be having a lengthy discussion as to who was to get the choice morsel. I quickly tried casting an assortment of lures to the area, but these boys had bird on their mind and wanted none of my offerings.

On one fishing trip a friend of mine hooked into a small pickerel which was giving him a good fight, when his line literally doubled over because a 5-pound bass had smashed into it, thinking the pickerel would make a good meal. Bass take on pike and muskie their own size, and I'd bet on bass against sharks of equal size. They will hit anything: small alligator gar, which have skins tougher than top-grade leather, are regularly gobbled up by Mr. Bigmouth. A hook dislodged in a bass's mouth is dissolved by its body acids in a few weeks' time; so whatever it swallows, it will eventually be digested. Some strange things indeed have been found in their stomachs: poisonous snakes as deadly as the coral and longer than the bass itself, as well as remains of baby alligators, chunks of metal, pieces of plastic lures, and everything else imaginable. It's pretty difficult to find anything—especially if it swims, flies, crawls or walks near water —that hasn't been taken by bass. The fact that they attack anything and are ready to fight it to the end makes them excellent sports fish.

When an angler fishes in some particular bass waters often, he comes to know the habits of the fish of that lake or river intimately. In some lakes I know almost exactly where fish will be at a particular time of day or season. One spot I knew could always be counted on for some bull bass on patrol for gizzard shad. It was just outside a large, shallow cove full of weeds, where the bass lazily swam back and forth like a string of sentries. They'd stay there and pounce on any shad that stuck its nose outside the weeds. We fishermen loved the spot because we could go there and fish a silver minnow, or other minnow-imitating spoon, for plenty of action. Top plugs were almost useless.

Generally a largemouth isn't a fish to go skipping about the top of the water. He can't be bothered going after small flies; but give him something that is worth a trip through the ozone, and I'll guarantee he will lose no time in blasting off. Many a young duckling has taken its last breath because it presented a topside meal to a bigmouth down below.

Bass will attack the biggest bullfrogs, toads and lizards. Small animals such as muskrats, squirrels, rats or mice are always fair game when they come close to the water. Occasionally a bass gets so excited he flies through the air and ends up on land instead of water. Then it's his turn to be devoured, for nothing is as helpless as a fish out of water. The prowling raccoons, muskrats, rats, bears or birds lose no time in coming to devour as choice a morsel as a landed fish. I once left a string of fish unattended when I portaged a canoe from one Minnesota lake to another. By the time I got back to my fish, birds had picked out their eyes, and some other animal had already started working on the carcass. Meat doesn't go to waste in the wilds. It's too precious.

Late springtime is breeding time for largemouths. They swim into shallow coves or stream inlets to build nests. Bass are gentlemen at heart and do not build fancy nests the way some of their relatives do; in fact, in many cases it is stretching a point even to use the word "nest." Nevertheless the male stakes out his territory and then lures a female into the boudoir, where she begins depositing eggs. Sometimes he uses caveman tactics to get the female interested, but he always manages to get her there. A female may deposit 2,000 to 26,000 eggs at intermittent periods during a nesting season. Males pour milt over the eggs and then set up shop caring for them.

While the fish are caring for eggs, their tempers are short. They attack anything at the slightest provocation. A 30-pound catfish, carp or walleye that may try to get at a nest for a dinner will be chased by old Daddy Bass, who will come charging out of his nest with intent to kill.

Bass are choirboys the rest of the year in comparison to their temper during nesting. They are too intent to eat during the period when they stand guard over their eggs. Nothing is too big or too small to provoke Mr. Bigmouth into action. His temper flares the whole week it takes the eggs to hatch and continues on as he takes care of the fry. When the fry are out of their sacs and are schooling, Mister Bass will decide he has had enough, and will begin gobbling up dozens of his own fry who are foolish enough to remain. But all in all, bass are fine parents, and through their diligence they manage to send 2,000 to 4,000 young bass a year out to life.

Many of the young fish quickly fall prey to predators, the worst of which are often bass. Possibly 10 per cent may survive 1 year of life. Under normal conditions the young fish will grow to a size of 3 to 5 inches before the next spring. The second year finds them 8 to 10 inches long and already mature. Under ideal conditions they can grow even faster.

A lake I fished regularly had to be drained because of damage to its dam. The draining took every last drop of water from it except for the small stream that was its feeder. Loud moans from the fishermen accompanied the draining, and we watched a conservation department truck haul loads of bass away, many of them better than 8 pounds—some of them with our names on them. The dam was repaired quickly, and within 3 weeks there was water in the lake again. We fishermen banded together and organized stocking committees, but then we noticed thousands of fry in the lake. The eggs from the nests had stayed damp in the mud and had hatched after the lake refilled itself. Conditions were so ideal for the fry that by fall there was a lake full of 8-inch bass. Next year fish as long as 15 inches were coming out. Lack of competition for food and no predators to kill off the young let these fry grow at a fantastic rate. We fishermen were back in business on that lake within a year, and fishing was better than ever, although it took a number of years before 10-pounders started showing up again.

When bass are nesting they are the simplest of fish to get on a hook. Every requirement for good catches is there—the fish are in shallow water, and they will strike anything that annoys them. The states that permit spring fishing give any bass fisher-man an opportunity for a bonanza, for all that is required of him is to throw a plug or spoon near a bass nest and wait for the strike. Any plug or spoon that can disturb the serenity of the bass's home will bring a strike. Surface and diving plugs will pro-duce vicious hits.

Even in states that do not open their bass seasons until June or July, anglers will do well to start off the season fishing the shallows. Sometimes, especially after a cold spring, the fish may be as much as a month behind in breeding schedules, so that in early summer they are still in the shallows guarding young. Even after nesting is over, bass tend to stay in the shallows where they know there is an abundance of all kinds of young fish.

It isn't until the weather gets hot that bass, along with all the other fish of the lake, begin sliding away from the shallows into the deep water. When this happens it is best to get a boat and locate the bass hot-spots. The angler who consistently fishes his own lakes will usually get far better results than one who skips around from lake to lake, because he will be familiar with the spots the bass habitually go to. In our lake, the one that was drained, the new generation of bass set up shop in all the old haunts.

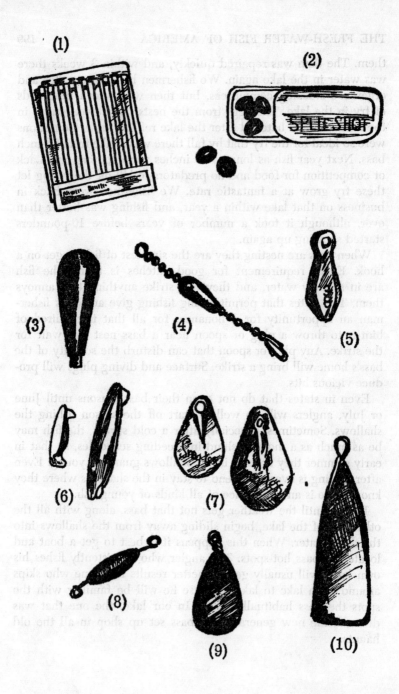

One of the biggest mistakes anglers repeatedly make at this time of the year is in fishing too shallow. Their offerings will be way over the heads of the fish. It may be hard to consider the largemouth, who is sometimes caught in 6 inches of water, as a deep-water fish, but he is. The big ones are usually 20 feet down, or more during hot weather, and their hideaways have to be found. A good spot to try is at the edge of the sudden drop-offs along the shore line. Right along the shelf where the lake drops off, or in a pocket below a drop-off is a good bet. Chances of catching a bass are better if there are weeds along the edges of the drop. These places harbor the big bulls; and if one 6-pounder-plus comes up, there are sure to be more waiting.

It pays to fish silently, for the bass are no longer in love and family responsibilities are behind them, so they are considerably more wary. If a noisy neighbor wants to come along on the trip, sneak out of the back door—and when you're fishing, don't make unnecessary noises or stomp around in the boat. If a fish is hit and can be led away from the hole quietly, there is always a good chance to go down and get his brother; but if the fish stirs up the bottom, chances are it's best to let the spot rest while you fish another place for half an hour.

Fishing deep for bass can be done with either artificial or natural baits. The natural baits to use are minnows, spinners or chubs and other small fish, including suckers and pumpkinseed. Crawfish are fine natural baits, too. Sometimes it helps to put a

---

Types of sinkers.

(1) *Strip Lead.* Strips of lead are twisted on a hook or line.
(2) *Split Shot.* Shot is squeezed on the line.
(3) *Adjustable.* For casting.
(4) *Bead Chain.*
(5) *Bank.* For bottom fishing in deep water.
(6) *Clincher.* Clamped on a line.
(7) *Non-twist trolling.*
(8) *Ringed.* Line twists on the ends of sinker.
(9) *Casting or trolling.*
(10) *Pyramid.* For bottom fishing.

spinner in front of a natural bait, for the spinner acts as a sinker and as an advertisement of the meal behind. For this kind of fishing I prefer to drift my boat, starting 50 to 60 feet away from a hot-spot and finally moving over it quietly. I feel that drifting helps give natural bait natural action down below. An occasional lifting of the rod tip will move the spinner and attract fish to the bait.

If drifting shows poor results in one spot, try other places or begin trolling. The motor of the boat should be set just above idling speed; leisurely rowing works just as well. The angler should have his lines out at least 40 feet behind the boat. Sometimes when several of us are fishing we set our lines at different distances and different depths; but in summer fishing, the bottom-running bait invariably gets the bass. Every effort should be made to get the bait low and keep it there, and the hotter the day the truer the rule. In some marginal low-oxygen lakes, fish cannot live too far down. Then they look for shadowy places and springs, stream inlets or any other places to rest.

Among the artificial lures that will hook bass while they are deep are the plastic variety. Plastic eels, frogs, crawfish, lizards, bugs, bait fish, hellgrammites or other insects are all proving to be real bass killers. The best way I've found to fish with these lines is to move them very slowly in pay-water. Fish often hit them again if they miss the first time, because they can't seem to believe that the things aren't real.

Deep-running plugs and spoons are old standard bass takers. The plugs are often fished with standard bait-casting rods or spinning rods. The plug or spoon is allowed to sink after it hits the water, and not until it is on the bottom is the retrieve begun. A good trick is to get offshore and cast right to the shore line, then retrieve the bait slowly toward the boat. This way the lure can be worked down into the holes at the lake's edge, and the plug looks like an injured fish searching for a place of cover. A plug which lends itself to this perfectly is the Wright-McGill Miracle Minnow, which is a deep-runner. Another deep-runner of the same type is the South Bend Li'l Rascal.

A good bet is to work deep plugs along weed beds or lily

pads. Cast in either direction along the bed, but cast over the area you think is a hot-spot and then work the lure in there on the retrieve. Be sure to give a lure plenty of time to get to the bottom. Lures like a Fish-Oreno or a Torpedo or spoons of the Silver Minnow or Daredevil variety will get plenty of strikes. Jigs are good, too, and red-and-white ones or yellow dollies do well for me. For best results, these must be jigged by moving the rod up and down. Small strips of pork rind behind a plug or jig will help it to take fish. Jigging also shows results during the winter months in the TVA lakes from Kentucky south.

The angler who likes to use bass bugs or top-water plugs should do his summer fishing early in the morning or in the evening. The hour before sunup and the two hours after sunup are excellent for top fishing. Then the time from an hour before sunset until about midnight is fine inshore again.

For bass bugging get a buddy to go out with you in a boat and take turns fishing. One rows and helps the other get into the shallows with the bugs. I suggest the rower drift a live bait behind the boat so he can remain in action. A bug can be thrown onto a lily pad or right in between the weeds. Some anglers use spinning tackle for this, but a fly rod is more fun and easier to use with bugs. After being thrown out, the bug is rested—sometimes I let it rest almost 30 seconds before I give the rod a slight rise to jump the bug a little. If there is a bass nearby he will be watching the bug carefully. He may swim about below but he will keep his eyes peeled on the bug and will gradually become convinced he has a meal. Just as the bug is twitched, the bass comes tearing up to make sure of the meal. The bug can be worked through the weeds or lilies by a slow retrieve of a jerk and a stop. It will appear like a tired bug trying to fight its way out of the water. Other times I jitter it, and after the first pause move it quickly through the water like a bug with plenty of strength. Try both methods, as they both have their days. My favorite bug is an old black popper which has some gold spots painted on it for eyes; other times a Gerbubble bug or a frog works wonders. Bright colored bugs work well on dark days while dark ones are good in broad daylight.

The bugs are nothing more than 1/0 or 2/0 long-shanked bass hooks with painted cork attached for body. Feathers are added to lend a more buggy appearance; and in the case of frogs, green bucktails look like legs in the water. Frogs are especially effective in the fall, when bass are bedding down in the mud for the winter.

Flies, of course, will take bass, and the best bets are streamers, which can be worked to imitate minnows. Wet flies in gaudy color patterns will get hits, too.

One of the most exciting ways to take a bass is to use top plugs. When the fish boils out of the water and hits a plug, it makes your heart skip a beat or two. There are fishermen that get a kind of buck fever and can't tighten up their line properly on man-sized smashes. Of the top plugs, a Creek Chub Injured Minnow thrown into the water and rested for 15 to 30 seconds before a retrieve is begun will catch the fish's eye. Then as the lure moves in, floating on its side, a bass could come up and smash the daylights out of it. Another good top bait is a Jitterbug. As it moves through the water it disturbs the surface, which attracts the fish. The popper plugs work on this same principle and a Creek Chub Plunker or a Hula Popper are both producers. Top-water plugs generally get the best results early mornings during the summer and in spring and fall fishing. Some fisherman feel that Louisiana, through which 41 per cent of the nation's drainage passes, harbors an equal percentage of the nation's largemouth population. Down here top-water lures are the superior producers in bayou and swamp fishing, where most fish are taken in less than 3 feet of water.

The No. 1 style of plug may well be the diving plug. It floats, but its motion makes it dive. The Flatfish is an internationally known plug that is said already to have sold over 20 million. It moves through the water, and because of its strange shape and wobbly action bass come close in order to see it better; and sometimes they just have to nudge it to see what is going on. This last action, of course, proves fatal, for the hooks are there to catch the curious visitor. The Bass-Oreno is another subsurface plug that attracts fish by its motion in the water. The Jointed

Pikie Minnow and the Pal-O-Mine-Jointed wiggle in the water
and resemble a fish. When being retrieved, lures like the Mustang
and the Pikie Minnow have snappy, wiggling action that attract
bass. Variations of speed attract fish. Rod-tip action is important
for almost all lures if best results are to be obtained.

Largemouth are found throughout the country, in the cold
waters of Maine, Minnesota and North Dakota, as well as in the
warm-bath waters of Florida, Louisiana and California.

These fish are the favorites for 1- or 2-acre farm ponds, because if they and bluegill can be started in a lake, there will be
plenty of fish for everyone. Sometimes farmers do not realize to
what size bass can grow in their ponds, for in ponds where there
are no suitable nesting areas, the bass do not reproduce, and the
few already in the lake grow large. Other times the bass take
over, and the pond becomes thick with the fish, so much so that
the angler catches one every few casts. In such a situation you
will be doing a farmer a favor by removing all the fish you can,
for the fish that remain will get much bigger if the population is
cut down.

Small lakes often bristle with bass, for the fish are perfectly
adaptable to lakes of 5 acres and up. In the states of Connecticut,
New York, New Jersey, Illinois, Indiana, Iowa and Ohio, bass
are the main game fish in almost every lake. Even small lakes
bring some big bass, for getting 10-pounders out of 5-acre
lakes isn't at all unusual.

The really big lakes of the country are, of course, the real
bass heavens. Here bass have ample food, and can grow and
swim freely. Some of the most famous largemouth lakes are Lake
Okeechobee in Florida; Lake Texoma in Texas and Oklahoma;
Kentucky Lake in Kentucky-Tennessee; Lake of the Ozarks in
Missouri; Lake Oahe in South Dakota; the John H. Kerr Reser-
voir of North Carolina-Virginia (sometimes called Buggs Island
Lake); the Santee Cooper Lakes, Moultrie and Marion, in South
Carolina; Pickwick Lake of Mississippi-Alabama; Lake Mead of
Arizona-Nevada, Elephant Butte Lake in New Mexico, and Clear
Lake in California.

They say to get bass over 10 pounds an angler has to go south, and the records seem to bear this out, for the biggest one ever taken in Iowa was under 10 pounds while the New York state record is 10 pounds 6 ounces. Compared to the southern records, these are just about half the size. Any location where bass do not have to hibernate in the winter will breed fish twice the size of those found in colder waters; but no matter what size a largemouth is, he is a terrific sports fish, and is welcome from any water.

Kentucky Bass

The Kentucky bass (Micropterus punctalatus) is taken in the same manner and in many of the same waters as the largemouth bass. This fish looks so much like a largemouth that he was for years misidentified as such.

The Kentucky bass is easily identified by the spotted longitudinal lines on its lower half. These lines are clearly defined and are opposed to the largemouth's blotches; and in many areas the fish is known as a spotted bass. Another identifying feature is a black spot on the tongue.

This bass ranges from Ohio south to the Gulf States, and some hot-spots are the Salt River of Kentucky and Norris Reservoir of Tennessee. Kentucky bass grow to a maximum of 15 inches, and all tackle and methods used for taking the fish are the same as for largemouth bass.

Smallmouth Bass

A smallmouth bass (Micropterus dolomieu) hits a line like a bolt of lightning and continues fighting in such a sensational manner that he is considered the king of sports fish. To dislodge a hook, he will jump, dance, dive, bulldog or go tail skipping across the top of the water. He will smash up out of the water after a bug or fly, or he will attack a low-running spoon like a Wild West marshal chasing a bank robber. It doesn't matter at all if he is taken on bait-casting rods, spinning rods or fly rods; he is a beautiful fighter against all equipment.

Too many fishing writers have treated the smallmouth as some kind of offshoot of the largemouth. The two are related, of course, but there are some important differences in their habits that will totally confuse the angler if he tries to apply largemouth knowledge to smallmouth.

First of all, a smallmouth bass does not have a small mouth. The difference in size of the fish's mouth is in the silhouette view, for if a line were drawn from the smallmouth's eye, it would pass behind the maxillary or upper jaw of the fish, while the largemouth's maxillary goes beyond the hind margin of the eye. Fishermen further distinguish between the fish by the vertical bars on the smallmouth as opposed to the blotches on the largemouth. Smallmouth are generally smaller fish. They can be identified as soon as hooked, for they are topside fighters.

Since both fish are members of the sunfish family, they have similar breeding habits. Both build nests and spawn in the spring. However, springtime breeding for the smallmouth is very intricate. The bass will start coming out of the lakes and into rivers and streams to find suitable breeding grounds. They will not breed anywhere, for they need either rock, sand or gravel bottoms. Many a lake has been stocked with smallmouth, and the fish have not taken simply because the lake lacked suitable breeding grounds.

The male of this species is the nest constructor. He builds a nest by constructing crater-type holes 1 to 3 feet wide. Then he goes out in search of a ripe female to lure her into the nest. Sometimes the female has to be coaxed, and the male will often bite the female to get her into the nest. When the fish pair off, they come back to the nest and lie side by side as the eggs are deposited and milted.

After the eggs are in the nest, the male wastes no time chasing the female out of there, for he alone takes care of the future fish. Other ripe females will be lured to a nest from time to time and more eggs are added to the cache. A female will deposit from 2,000 to 20,000 eggs in a year, with the amount being directly re-

lated to the size of the fish. When water temperatures are over
60° the eggs will hatch within a week, and the young fish begin
living off the sac of the egg. The male cares for the fish another
week until they swim away from the nest looking for minute
crustaceans. Young fish stay in schools the first year of life.

Males do not feed during nesting, but they readily attack anything near them. Sometimes if a stone is thrown into the water
near a nest, a bass will come up and belt it as it sinks. Deep-
running plugs or spoons run through a nesting area, which
makes smallmouths the easiest of pan fish to get onto a hook. If
a male is lost, generally a whole hatch is lost, for he is the
protector of the young. This is why so many states restrict early-
season bass fishing. In one year, the young smallmouth will
grow to a size of approximately 4 inches. The second year of life
they will double this size, and in the third year they will mature,
measuring about 10 inches. Fish in the TVA lakes find conditions
there so ideal that they manage to reach maturity and a size of
10 inches in 2 years' time. TVA's Dale Hollow Lake gave up the
world-record smallmouth—an 11-pound 15-inch monster, bigger
than ever dreamed existed. Through the northern perimeter of
the fish's activity a 5-pound fish will be about maximum size.
This fish could very well be 16 years old. Where fish are stunted
because the water is constantly too cold or food is sparse, they
may grow only to 7 or 8 inches in a lifetime.

The smallmouth bass is a North American native found in
all states east of the Rockies except Florida. The Gulf Coast area
is not noted for these fish; however, even these states have Ole
Razorback in their northern reaches. Smallmouth are a popular
fish in southern Canada, too. It always seemed strange to me that
the smallmouth, who is less adaptable to certain environments
than his relative the largemouth, was originally found through
a wider range of water.

Smallmouth have now been planted wherever the water seems
suitable for them. Perfect smallmouth water would be a cool
lake over 100 acres in size and more than 25 feet deep. The fish
do not take well in small, shallow lakes. They require lots of
clean water to move about in. Smallmouth bass also do well in

cool, clear rivers and streams and in many areas they live side by side with trout.

One likely reason why smallmouth bass were originally distributed over such a wide area is their habit of moving about. They swim far up and down rivers and into strange waters where, if conditions are right, they begin breeding.

To quote Dr. A. J. Henshall's oft-repeated words from his *Book of Black Basses,* the smallmouth is "inch for inch and pound for pound the gamest fish that swims." Once hooked, the fish will begin his fight with a burst into the ozone like a rocket out of Cape Canaveral. He may jump as many as 30 times during the course of a fight and may pull some other surprises that leave Mr. Fisherman with empty hooks or broken lines. Sometimes the fish pulls the cute trick of going through aerial acrobatics until suddenly after one jump, he dives right down to the bottom. I saw a good sportsman have his 4-pound leader snapped by a fish that weighed less than 2 pounds. Another trick of the smallmouth is to dive down to the bottom and appear to be slugging it out, suddenly to change direction and come rushing from the bottom straight up and out of the water in a spectacular leap.

One thing to remember with smallmouth bass is that you have to let them know who is boss right from the start. The timid angler is lost with these boys. A hook has to be set securely to hold smallmouth, because their mouths are made up of tough cartilage. Occasionally a fish will dive in under some underbrush or a log and try to get leverage to free himself, or he may actually stay there and have a tug of war with the angler. Handle this situation so that you are the boss. Give a twitch to the rod tip to let the fish know you're there, for this jars him and sometimes leads him out of the entanglement. Minnesota guides tell an angler to bang his rod butt on a boat, and the vibration will run down the line to the fish, getting him angry and jumping.

The angler who uses too heavy equipment or cane poles loses the fight of one of the country's sportiest fish. A smallmouth fights until he hasn't an ounce of strength left, and gives up only after he lies sickly on his side, completely exhausted. To get maximum sport, use the lightest tackle possible and never force a fish. Many times I've released smallmouth after a terrific battle simply because I admired their fight.

With sportsfishermen the fly rod still ranks as the No. 1 smallmouth rod, and it is especially good for fishing streams. Hollow glass fly rods are most popular, and 2-piece medium light rods 7½ to 8½ feet, 3½ to 4½ ounces would serve the average angler well. Floating line should be used. Nylon leader from 2- to 6-pound test measuring from 6 to 12 feet finishes the rig. The length of leader depends only upon water conditions, for in murky or turbulent water a 5-foot leader is all that is required. Very still- and clear-water fishing will require up to 12 feet of tapered leader so no shadows are cast. Top end leader is 6- to 8-pound test near the rod and then going down to 2-pound test near the fly or bug.

Method of fishing and skill at fishing are the most important items in consistent catches. Bass, like other fish in streams, face upstream, and the angler who fishes upstream does best. Downstream fishing is the natural instinct, but there are several distinct advantages to upstream fishing. The most important is that fish are less likely to see the angler, for they are facing away from the approaching man. Fish are wary in streams, and a shadow cast in front of them spooks them or puts them off feed. By working upstream the angler will in many cases be able to come to a spot practically on a level with the fish, and he will be able to see the fish in the water. However, if fishing that close, move very carefully, for it won't take much to scare them. Green or drab clothing helps conceal the angler, for fish can very definitely see color—especially the reds and yellows.

Move slowly and deliberately and cast above the fish, then let the fly float to them. If fishing a dry fly, start it in a rip and let it float back into a pool. Sometimes the fish will rise and just nick at a fly. Slack must be kept out of the line so on the slightest touch of the fish it can be struck. Tighten up immediately. Plenty of fish will be missed, but a fair share will be taken even on these slight hits. When smallmouths are blasting away at dry flies, there is absolutely no problem, for they hook themselves.

Wet flies are fished with sinking line, and in fast-moving water, pieces of shot are added. The fly should come into the pool just above the fish or at their level. The fly can be jerked or twitched by rod-tip movement. Vary the amount of rod action just as the kinds of flies are varied, and when successful stick with a successful combination. Sometimes Maribu flies will take potfuls of fish.

A small Indiana Spinner, June Bug or Elm Leaf Spinner added in front of the fly will be attractive if the water is murky. A spinner-streamer-fly combination is another taker during the murky-water periods. These combinations should be worked in the jerky underwater fashion.

Bass bugging for smallmouths starts in the spring and lasts until fall. It is an excellent way to take fish. The bass are especially fond of hairy bugs, and it seems the more hair on the package the harder and surer the hits. Try some like Weber's Whisker Bug, a Black and White Bass Hound or a Kade's Red and Yellow Ozark. If these bugs are not available, just remember—plenty of hair for plenty of bass.

Bugs for smallmouth are worked in the standard bugging manner in the inshore sections of lakes. They should be rested over sunken logs and obstructions or by drop-offs. Smallmouth are not likely to be in weed beds, for they prefer more open water. Good spots are over rocky or sandy bottoms. Cork-popping bugs may be popped along to create a disturbance. Sometimes they are productive fished very slowly like a half-dead bug. The fish will hit them hard, and when they start fighting there is a good chance that on the light tackle it will be an aerial battle.

Stream fishing with bugs calls for the bugs to be worked over the slow lazy holes, the area right after fast water or around and behind boulders that harbor fish. The principle is like working a dry fly, and the angler can do it by wading or by floating in a boat. Trips on rivers like the Susquehanna in Pennsylvania or the Green in Kentucky, with the angler pausing to work his bug in the big stretches of slow water, can turn up excellent results.

A long section of nylon leader is important with bugs or flies, and this, of course, becomes more important if the waters are low and clear. In low water, bass get shy, and heavy line or leader can cast shadows that put the fish on guard. Tapered leader is ideal fishing, but if this is not available, don't be alarmed, because many nice catches have been brought in on standard 6-pound leader. Even when bronze-back is put on guard, he won't stay that way long, providing he isn't frightened again. The angler who has spooked a fish should remain motionless for a few minutes, and chances are the fish will go right back to feeding.

One suggestion for increasing one's smallmouth catch is to fish with flies or bugs that have barbless hooks. Do not do this if your aim is a full creel, because with this kind of fishing even a hint of a mistake is a missed fish. The slightest slack or hesitation of the fisherman, and it's goodbye bass. However, this is a sure method to learn how to handle a fish properly. Everything must be done with the rod tip, and pressure must be kept constantly on the fish. Charges of the fish must be countered by the fast retreat of the rod tip and frantic reeling or hand-stripping of line. Jumps must be guarded by keeping pressure on the hooks. Sudden dives and rises are also war on slack line.

Many fish will be lost when an angler prepares to land them under ordinary conditions, but with barbless hooks the figure could rise close to 100 per cent. A fish landed on a barbless hook is a fish that has really been outskilled and outfought. If anyone can land even a third of the fish hooked on barbless hooks, he will find that by going back to regulation books he will have greatly improved his ability to handle fish.

A good time to practice barbless-hook fishing is a day when you have taken all the fish you want. It's exciting fishing because so many hits are missed, and each new strike adds to the tension of the angler trying to land fish under this difficult handicap. But when one day the angler hits into something really big, this practice can really pay off. Anyone who can handle smallmouth on barbless hooks can handle any fish swimming, big or small.

Spinning tackle and smallmouth bass go together like ham and eggs. The smallmouth is ideal for light spinning equipment. A rod of 6½ to 7 feet of medium-light action capable of casting

¼- to ½-ounce lures will do fine for smallmouths. Monofilament line—varying from 4- to 8-pound test, depending upon the skill of the angler—and a swivel snap make up the outfit.

The choice of lures depends upon the season. During the summer, top-water and diving plugs bring best results. It is best to fish in the early morning or evening, when the fish are topside. Sometimes in northern waters the bass may even be topside during the day, and they can be coaxed to a hook. Standard bass plugs or spoons will take the fish, but they should be kept down to ⅜- to ½-ounce weights when fishing with light spinning equipment. Garcia Corporation makes a complete line of spinning lures, including the Plunky, Eelet and the Abu Weeless and the Pecos series, which include the chub, shiner or dace—all of which can bring results. Many companies make thousands of lures to choose from, and gradually a collection can be built up; but as a start I'd have an Injured Minnow, Flatfish, Bass-Oreno, Miracle Minnow and Silver Minnow.

There will always remain an army of plug casters who do their work with bait-casting outfits. A good rod would be a hollow glass one 5 to 5½ feet in length with medium action. Reels should have 100 yards' capacity and be lightweight.

All the plugs that take largemouth can be used for smallmouths, too, and many local-area favorites will prove themselves to be killers. Never be afraid to ask a local fisherman or tackle-shop proprietor what is taking them. It is better to stick to somewhat lighter plugs for smallmouths than largemouths, and ¼- to ½-ounce weights are ample. Jigs will take fish when the smallmouths are low. The Pee Wee made by John C. Kremer Company is a typical productive jig.

Smallmouth bass take live baits just as will every other sports fish. The favorite bass food may well be soft-backed crawfish. Bass will tear into crawfish when they are in the soft-crow stage, just after they have molted their last hard shell. At these times the crawfish are all soft meat, and it takes awfully wary bass to pass one up. The way to fish with crawfish is with a No. 2 or No. 1 hook put into the back of the bait, which is fished near or on the bottom with or without a small float. When a fish

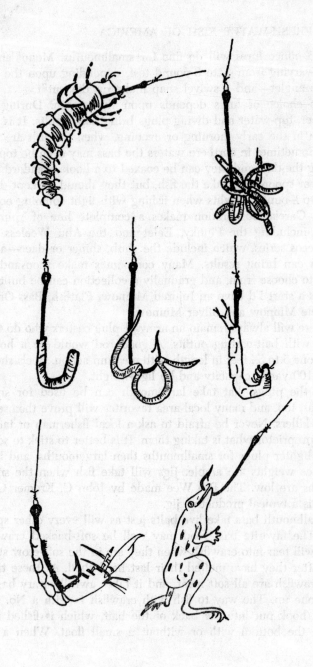

takes the bait, give him plenty of time, because the bait is live and tastes good to him. When he stops fooling and really takes it, you will know.

Other natural baits are grasshoppers, frogs and mice. A load of night crawlers floated into a bass hole can bring some fine action—especially if there has just been high water. Then the old reliable minnow should never be overlooked, because a minnow-spinner combination is more apt to take bass in the August doldrums than any other bait I know.

Some nationally famous lakes for smallmouth include Sebago Lake, Maine; Lake Champlain, Vermont-New York; Lake Winnipesaukee, New Hampshire; Quabbin Reservoir, Massachusetts; the Finger Lakes, New York; Black Lake, Michigan; Basswood Lake, Minnesota; Dale Hollow Lake, Kentucky and Tennessee; Grand Lake of the Cherokees, Oklahoma; Tah Kenitch Lake, Oregon; and Shasta Lake, California. Streams and rivers that are thick with smallmouth bass include the Delaware of New York and Pennsylvania; the Susquehanna of Pennsylvania; the St. Croix of Wisconsin; the Gasconade of Missouri; the Buffalo of Arkansas; the South Branch of the Potomac in West Virginia; the New River in North Carolina; and the Green River of Kentucky.

This fine sports fish is unpredictable, and at times even the best anglers come home with empty creels. One North Carolina angler will never disagree on this point, because he went fishing early one morning and almost immediately a smallmouth blasted

---

UPPER LEFT:	A hellgrammite on a hook.
UPPER RIGHT:	A multiworm hookup for bass.
MIDDLE LEFT:	A single worm hookup for (1) pan fish; (2) trout.
MIDDLE RIGHT:	A hookup of the larvae of a caddis fly makes excellent trout and pan fish bait.
BOTTOM LEFT:	A dead crawfish on a hook for bass or catfish. Live crawfish are often hooked only through the tail.
BOTTOM RIGHT:	A live frog hookup for casting or trolling.

out of the water, arched and fell back into his boat. He jumped on the fish and had himself a 3-pound bass. He knew this would be the day of days, and he fished a solid 8 hours. His catch, you guessed it, was one smallmouth—the one that jumped in his boat!

Many anglers rank the smallmouth bass as America's No 1 sports fish; and all anglers rank him right up there with the best, for he is every inch and every ounce a hard-fighting sports fish.

Bullhead

The popular little bullhead is a favorite of the rough-and-tumble school of fresh-water fishermen. No special tackle, no expensive lures and no long trips into the mountains are needed for these boys, because this favorite is in every lake, pond and slow river in almost all the continental states.

There are 4 species of bullhead: the brown bullhead (Ictalurus nebulosus), black bullhead (Ictalurus melas), yellow bullhead (Ictalurus natalis) and flat bullhead (Ameiurus platycephalus). The flat bullhead is found in the Southeast, the yellow bullhead throughout the Midwest and Great Lakes states, the brown bullhead through the same area and along the Atlantic and Pacific coasts, and the black bullhead, the most widely distributed of all, is taken almost everywhere in the country.

Bullhead are actually small members of the catfish family, and they have the same toughness, likes and dislikes as their bigger relatives. They stay in quiet ponds and slow-moving rivers and will not frequent turbulent trout streams because they do not like swift-running water. Their station in life is a soft, muddy bottom where they can grub around for food. Here the fish swim over the bottom searching with their barbels spread wide apart, for these barbels are sensitive and are used to locate food.

I have found bullhead fishing good right after storms and rains, when the bottom is riled up, because this is the time when food is coming down to the fish, which excites them into action. They will be all over the bottom, looking for bits of worms, crustaceans, dead fish, fish eggs, insect larvae or anything edible. They are scavengers and are likely to eat anything, and in this way they help keep the bottom of lakes clear.

The whole catfish family, including the bullhead, is a particularly hardy one, and able to survive where other fish die off. Bullhead can live in water of extremely low oxygen content where other fish have died months before. They can survive in polluted water much longer than other fish, and many ponds in cities can only support bullhead. When I was a young boy living in New Haven, Connecticut, the rugged bullhead gave me one of the first fishing bonanzas I can recall. We lived near some clay pits which supported perch, bass and bullhead. The company that owned the land needed the clay at the bottom of the pits for making brick, so they began draining the lakes. Bass and perch rapidly disappeared from sight, but as the lake kept getting lower and lower, it was evident that more and more bullhead were there. The small pools that remained literally crawled with the fish. This was all we boys needed to know, and we were off like a shot out of a cannon threading our way through the gook to advantageous fishing places.

Fish soon started coming in 2 or 3 at a time. We sent one boy back for pails and a small barrel, which filled up that afternoon. Deliriously happy, we hauled our catch up the clay pits and home, expecting full rewards for our catches. Somehow our mothers never quite understood, for all they saw were 4 mud-covered boys who they knew couldn't possibly be theirs. But I do remember those fish for they were some of the tastiest I ever had.

Bullhead are usually good fish to have about in any lake or river, with one possible exception. When they come into small ponds, they reproduce rapidly and overcrowd the area. The bullhead nest in the late springtime, and the parents care for the eggs and young; thus a high percentage of a hatch will survive. Unless there are checks on them, there will soon be a surplus. However, if there are pike, muskie, pickerel or bass about, the balance of the lake will keep, for the predatory fish find bullhead excellent eating. In those New Haven clay pits, bullhead were already overrunning the lakes, because in these particular lakes bass never made much headway.

In an average lake or river a good-sized bullhead will weigh 1 to 2 pounds and measure 10 to 12 inches. Black bullhead have been taken weighing as much as 8 pounds. However, I have seen some small ponds where stunting makes the biggest fish 6 inches long and weighing only a few ounces.

One of the prime rules of bullhead fishing is to fish on the bottom. Offerings more than 1 foot above the bottom will bring far fewer hits than those on the bottom. The perfect bait sits right on top of the soft bottom without sinking into the silt or mud. As the fish grubs about he soon sees the morsel, and it's not long before he takes it. Light sinkers are a must, for if an approaching fish feels a heavy sinker he tries to spit out the whole business and take off. An egg-type sinker or a piece of shot works fine, for neither disturbs a feeding fish. Heavy sinkers generally are not needed in this kind of fishing because, if currents are fast, the water is not good for bullhead.

These fish generally swallow a bait, but many times they will play with it until they make up their minds. Long-shanked hooks are best, because the chance of recovering a hook is better with this type than with a short one that can be swallowed. Best hook sizes are from No. 4 to 1/0, and nylon or gut leader helps if it is attached to the hook. Taking a bullhead off a hook can be painful because it has sharp dorsal fins or horns, which can cause cuts. If the angler grabs the fish behind the head when removing the hook, or if he holds it with a rag for dehooking, the difficulty is eliminated.

Rods for bullhead fishing should be light but sturdy. Cane poles are still used right alongside modern spinning rods and bait-casting rods. Line need only be 2-to 5-pound test, for it can handle the catches. During night fishing when the bullhead come closer to shore, cane poles and other equipment that will not backlash is recommended.

Baits for taking the bullhead can be pieces of dead fish, worm, crustaceans, bits of pork rind, and live or dead killies. Generally the angler will find that bullhead are not fussy eaters and are always willing to dig in handsomely.

The best seasons for bullhead fishing are late spring into early summer and very early in the fall. They are one of the last fish to get active in springtime, and cold water in the fall also slows them down. Summertime they head for the deep parts of a lake, and an angler should use a boat and fish near bottom, experimenting at different depths until he hits one. If one is about, there are usually more. Evening brings them into shore during spring, summer and fall, so that some anglers will swear good fishing begins at dusk.

When bullhead come from clean water they are excellent eating. They should be skinned and fried. There isn't too much meat on a 1- or 2-pounder though, so it's best to catch a mess of them. Follow the rules outlined, and fish in good bullhead water, and I can practically guarantee good catches.

Carp

The carp (Cyprinus carpio) is an Asiatic fish that emigrated from Europe to America in 1870. This fish spread itself through the country like a 98-cent bargain, and within 30 years' time it became so populous that many states began spending money to rid themselves of it. It is now found in all the continental states and Hawaii.

Many fishermen wish the carp had stayed in China, and it brings trout anglers to a slow boil if you even mention the word near them. But let's face it, carp are here to stay, for they have multiplied into the billions. So we might as well get used to them and take them for what they are—strong, sturdy fish that can survive in almost any kind of water.

Carp are good eating fish, too, and Americans eat tons of carp meat today. Here we don't go for the meat the way they do in Europe. Ever since the fish was first brought to the continent in the thirteenth century, Europeans have considered it a delicacy on a par with sturgeon.

Once I asked an old Czechoslovakian friend why carp meat was considered so wonderful in Europe and was so completely disregarded here. He explained that carp love to get in the mud and stay there, and in this way they get a muddy taste. He felt that in Europe the northern pike of the continent chase the carp out of the mud and generally give them a hard time. Here in America, he explained, carp get in the mud and nobody bothers chasing them, so they stay there and get an oily, muddy flavor.

There might be some truth in his explanation, but I feel that in America we still have an abundant supply of trout, salmon, grayling, walleye, perch and bass that come from clear water and taste fresh and clean. Since carp can and do live in water where few other fish survive, it only stands to reason that the fish will be flavored by the water it lives in. Thus, like all fish, carp from clean, clear water taste far different than those taken from polluted mudholes.

Carp are soft-fleshed fish and spoil quickly. Still, a young carp under 5 pounds skinned and fried tastes fine, just as does smoked carp. The dark meat of the fish should be cut off for best taste. Remember, too, that much carp goes into gefüllte fish, especially the cheaper grades.

Young carp make excellent live baits for bass, pickerel, or trout, and this fact alone has done more to spread the species than any organized planting of the fish could possibly do. Some fishermen have the habit of letting bait fish go free if they don't use it. Do this with a batch of young carp, and a trout lake can be spoiled in five years. Carp shouldn't be used as trout bait, and most certainly they should *never* be released after using. If this rule were followed, our country would have additional trout lakes that would take several pages to list.

Carp definitely take over a lake, for adult carp have a fondness for eating fish eggs; and a good-sized carp can devour a whole year's egg supply of trout for one meal. Fishermen must never release bait fish of unknown origin in a lake, for many times unwanted species will soon turn up in that lake. Because bass protect their eggs and their young, they fare much better in carp competition; in fact, they thrive on it, because bass find yearling carp an entree of supreme delectability. They go wild over them.

A carp fisherman is lucky in many respects, for he can live in the biggest cities, along the most polluted water of the country, and chances are that close by he will find his sport. Carp and catfish survive acid-polluted waters and low-oxygen waters much longer than other fish. They can be taken near New York, Philadelphia, Chicago, Los Angeles and most of the other major cities.

The fish are omnivorous, feeding on both vegetation and meat. They sift through mud for soft pieces of aquatic plants, insect larvae, mollusks, worms and, unfortunately, fish eggs. They eat continually and grow rapidly with some going over 50 pounds. The record fish came from Clearwater Lake, Minnesota, and weighed 55 pounds 5 ounces. Europeans and Asiatics swear they grow much bigger there. This is probably true, for in South Africa an 83-pound 8-ounce fish has already been taken, although not by sports fishing. Thirty-pounders are common, and even 40-pounders are never news.

Be ready for a tough battle when carp fishing, for they fight hard and mean. I refuse to make tackle recommendations, because every kind of tackle ever made and some kinds not even invented have been used to take the fish. I've seen broomsticks, branches, deep-sea tackle and fly rods used for them; but one thing is certain—if big ones are about, keep the tackle sturdy.

A number of years ago I was fishing with a cane pole on a friend's farm pond. There were plenty of carp there, but most of them were stunted. We were standing on the ledge of the bank having fun taking little ones, a pound or two. Suddenly my bobber went under, and I yanked, expecting the usual. This time, though, there was something really big on the end of it; and instead of its coming up as I planned, it just wouldn't budge. I was standing on a thin ledge and when my tug didn't lift anything I began losing my balance and couldn't regain it. The next thing I knew there was a big splash and I saw water all around me. Still holding on to the rod, I fought from there as my friend on the bank almost doubled over in hysterics. That was an instance where a carp almost caught a fisherman. The fish weighed in at just over 20 pounds—biggest that ever came out of there.

These fish take a hook gently, sifting it in and maybe giving it a gentle tug before releasing it. Don't strike. Let the fish play, because they will repeat this process several times before they really take it completely. Then strike gently but firmly and get ready for war. First they dive down into a hole and bull the line; or they will run into a current, or they may even charge a boat. They will try running along the bottom trying to tangle line, looking for leverage to rip the hook from their tender mouths. It's a fight all the way, lasting well over an hour at times. The angler is never sure of victory, because the last moments of boating or landing the fish are the most dangerous. More carp are lost then than at any other time.

It is strange that such a rough, coarse fish should have such a delicate approach to the hook. If a big sinker is used, the fish soon feels the drag of the sinker and makes off for another part of the lake. Therefore, fishfinder rigs or sliding sinkers are best if more than split shot is needed. Hooks, too, cannot be large because carp's mouths are small and delicate. Sizes ranging from No. 4 to No. 1 are best. Line, of course, depends on the kind of fishing, but 15-pound test is not too heavy for rugged fishing. If coarse lines are used it is best to use at least 3 to 5 feet of monofilament or gut leader.

To get one of these fish on a hook takes some strange baits. The dough ball or corn meal is the basic carp bait. Drop lumps of dough in boiling water for 5 minutes to make balls consistent. Dough balls with consistency stay on a hook better, thus resulting in fewer bare hooks and more strikes.

Other take-offs from the basic bait are concocted by many mad chefs, and include adding Worcestershire sauce or bitters to the mixture. Salt, molasses, vanilla, chocolate, oats and even tapioca are used, but the purpose is always the same: to get a mess of dough to stay on the hook. Successful baits should be put on the front of the hook and should not melt off. Simple flour-and-water paste works, as does fresh bread; but these come off hooks very easily and should be used only in emergencies.

Worms, sweet corn, boiled potatoes, marshmallows and occasionally even good old-fashioned spitballs will take them, too. If carp are about but are not hitting, don't be bashful about chumming, for they are rough fish and it's no holds barred. No one ever minds getting rid of a few carp in a lake. Bow-and-arrow fishing for them during spring breeding is even welcomed by fishermen; for the more people take them, the more room there is for other fish.

Many complaints are heard about carp, but no one ever complains of their fight, because they give their all every time—plus some. The only way to explain how a carp reacts on a hook is to imagine a wild bull on a lasso; and fishermen who hate them staunchly will admit, when pressed, that they fight hard.

Summing up carp: they are not a beautiful fish, but they are every inch a fighter. They are bad when they take over trout lakes or crowd other sports fish, but because they can live in water where other fish cannot survive they are sport to many fishermen who would otherwise get none. So if conservation departments can manage to keep these fighters in check and fishermen look at their plus side, then many more anglers will experience good sport from them.

Catfish

Down in Dixie they say there are 3 things necessary for good catfishing: (1) warm, muddy water, (2) darkness, and most important (3) mosquitoes.

If these 3 natural phenomena are found together, legend has it, good catfishing is guaranteed. It makes sense, for warm, muddy water means the slow-moving rivers or streams that catfish love. Darkness, of course, brings the fish out of the deep holes or brush piles where they hide during the days until they begin feeding in the evenings. Mosquitoes and catfish just go together like love and marriage; and if an angler is constantly annoyed by mosquitoes, the odds are that he is in productive waters. A good Dixieite would say, "If'n you ain't gitting bit, move 'til you gets stung. Y'll get cats."

There are hundreds of species of catfish in the world, and they vary all the way from the pigmy fish in home aquariums to some 700-pound monsters in Africa. Here in our country, four species are important to fishermen (not counting bullhead, which are discussed separately). They are channel catfish (Ictalurus punctatus), blue catfish (Ictalurus furcatus), white catfish (Ictalurus catus), and flathead catfish (Pylodictis olivaris), also known as yellow catfish. The channel catfish is the prize, the biggest having weighed an even 57 pounds and come from Lake Moultrie, South Carolina. A blue catfish weighing a whopping 97 pounds, from the Missouri River in South Dakota, is the record holder for the species.

The channel catfish likes somewhat swift and fast-moving water that is clean, whereas other catfish prefer slow-moving muddy waters. The channel catfish is found from the Gulf of Mexico north to the Canadian border and from the Rocky Mountains east to the coastal areas, with species being scarce in New York and New England. Down in Savannah, Tennessee, there is an annual catfish derby at Pickwick Dam, and you should see the monsters that win.

The blue catfish is known for his deep-forked tail, is found throughout the Mississippi River system and adjoining rivers, and may attain a weight of 100 pounds. The white catfish was once the eastern seaboard favorite but has been introduced into other rivers. The fish is abundant in California in the Sacramento River system. They are small fish, generally under the 4-pound mark.

The flathead catfish, yellow catfish, or mud cat as he is sometimes called, is found in most of the rivers that drain into the Gulf of Mexico, including the Mississippi River system, the Brazos and the Rio Grande. This species may also attain a size of 100 pounds.

Throughout the Deep South, catfish feed all year long, but in the northern reaches very few of them will do any feeding until water temperature is at least 40°. Up to a water temperature of 60° they feed irregularly and sluggishly, but once the water temperatures goes to 70° the boys are all over the bottom desperately searching for food.

Late spring is breeding time for these fish, and then males and females of the various species get busy preparing nests. Females deposit their eggs into the nests, and the males dutifully take care of them. A good-sized channel catfish may give 20,000 eggs in one springtime, while smaller fish give 8,000. The eggs are in a gelatin-like ball in the nest.

During the 7- or 8-day incubation period the male is an almost perfect parent, guarding and protecting the eggs. Occasionally though, he has been known to sample a few eggs, but for the most part he is a diligent parent who cares for the fry from the time they are born until finally he gets sick of all his responsibilities and begins gobbling up the young in carefree abandon. During mating season Mrs. Catfish goes over the bottom, eating anything that comes within her reach; and fishermen are thankful to her, for most catches taken during mating are females.

Sometimes during the hot summer season channel catfish will get very selective in their feeding, and an angler hasn't a chance unless he gives them exactly what they are after. During this time they may even pass up chicken entrails, which can generally be counted on to be productive. Sometimes they will feed purely on algae or vegetation of some sort, or they may be on a small-fish diet. It is often said they suffer from sore mouth in summer; but actually if the right bait is found, strikes will be endless.

September and October is a sign for the catfish to begin gorging themselves to get ready for winter hibernation. As temperatures drop the fish begin to get excited and take any kind of food and baits. Some of the biggest and best catches traditionally come in the fall. In warmer southern waters catfish feed well in the fall, too, but certainly not in the manner they do in the upper Missouri River in North Dakota.

During the winter, if the fish are caught in ice and become completely frozen in, they can survive, amazingly enough. Their ruggedness is further demonstrated during dry spells, when they can live in mud with no water, providing their gills are kept cool and wet. As the water returns to the rivers the catfish rise out of the mud and swim about, apparently healthy as ever. The channel catfish is remarkably healthy, being almost completely free of parasites regardless of the water he is found in.

Catfish foods are so varied that it would take pages just to list them; in short, catfish eat anything edible, plus many seemingly inedible items. They are carnivorous, feeding on dead or living things. At times they feed on algae, insect larvae, seeds from trees, frogs, crawfish, shrimp, hellgrammites or minnows, just to mention a few. A fish that takes such a variety of food in his natural diet can be taken on a great variety of baits. Among catfish baits are chicken entrails, soap, congealed blood, dough balls, stink or cheese.

Some catfish baits are prepared like the witches' brew in Shakespeare's *Macbeth*. Popular stink is made by decomposing minnows in a can or jar and then adding this ripe oil to cereal or flour which is congealed into a ball. Sometimes cheese is added for flavor. The congealed-blood bait is merely dried animal or chicken blood. The juice is drained off, and the hard blood is cut up for bait. Then the chicken-entrail bait has to be prepared to work right. This is done by taking the foregut of a chicken, cleaning it of fat and cutting it into 8-inch pieces. These are dropped in corn meal and finally soured for proper effect.

Any variation from the regular baits or any deviation in preparing a bait that proves it can take fish will be highly praised by other catfish fishermen. Some anglers have top-secret baits, and it is bad etiquette and a waste of time to try to find out a man's secret. Always remember to have 4 or 5 kinds of baits with you, so once the likes of the fish are discovered you will be supplied. Baits should be placed as close to the catfish as possible, for the whole body of a catfish is covered with taste buds; and he is probably the only fish that can be hit in the tail with a worm and can taste it.

Some catfish are taken by working a plug or spoon slow and deep, while others are taken by jigging; but for the most part catfish are taken on concoction baits. Big flathead catfish or blue catfish are often taken on natural baits, which may be chubs or big packages of night crawlers.

Almost as varied as the baits are the methods used for taking catfish. One popular kind is trotlining, which in many respects is very similar to the old New England way for taking codfish. Here fishermen string a line across a river or lake and hang from it many baited hooks. The hooks are baited with a variety of catfish favorites and left out all night. Some states have a maximum of 100 hooks or less allowed by law for trotlining, but others have no laws. The fisherman checks his lines during the night and morning, pulling each one up to see if there is a fish on it. Trotlining is the method by which many big blue catfish and flathead catfish are taken.

Getting a little bit further away from pure meat fishing and slightly more sporty is bottle or jug fishing. Here lines are tied to jugs, and the jugs are floated down a lazy, slow river or left to float in a lake. Hooks are baited, and when a fish hooks himself he begins fighting the jug. The fisherman watches for bouncing jugs and then swings into action, pulling in the hooked cat.

In some parts of the Midwest and South, great excitement will overcome a small group of fishermen whenever the water level in certain rivers and streams drops way down. When there are only a few shallow pools left, these men start dipping in and catching the big fish barehanded. I've never tried this, but one old-timer once put it, "They're tougher to hold onto than a greased pig in an olive oil factory." Low water can also be good for the hook-and-line angler, for it makes the fish pack up tight in the available holes, from which a few big ones can usually be removed. I can't quite bring myself to accept these methods as sportsfishing, but nevertheless they are acceptable to some.

The sports-fish approaches to taking catfish include working with spinning rods, bait-casting rods and at times even fly rods. Fly rods are the least used for catfish, but plenty of sport can be had from 5-pounders on a stiff-action fly rod. Spinning has come into its own, and for 3- to 5-pounders very light rods are great fun. In fast water below dams where big channel catfish are likely to lurk, heavy-duty salt-water spinning rods with 45- to 50-pound test are needed to hold the big 20- to 50-pounders. This equipment can be strained to its utmost should a 25-pounder get a good run in fast water. Catfish love to ride a current and add their weight to the water pressure, so they can snap inferior equipment with reckless ease. Channel cats sit in the pools below dams and waterfalls and wait for stunned bait fish, who make an easy meal.

Glass bait-casting rods with stiff action, measuring 5 to 5½ feet in length, are fine weapons for catfish. They are excellent for working the banks of rivers or lakes. A reel capable of holding 300 feet plus of line is required. This is fine equipment when fishing from boats or from shore, for with a sturdy bait-casting rod the biggest cat can be struck and held. Another advantage is that long casts can be made away from the shore line, for catfish are shy; and many times an angler will unknowingly scare those close to where he is fishing.

Lines for fishing can be of 10- to 15-pound strength for usual catfish in quiet places, but strength must go up if the unusual is to be encountered. Hooks depend upon the size of the fish expected and the particular touch of the angler. Generally sizes vary from No. 4 to No. 1 for smaller fish and No. 1 to 4/0 for the larger ones.

Sinkers are important, for many times catfish strike lightly; and if the fish should feel a heavy sinker holding the bait, that will be the last seen of him for the day. For the line that flows freely, fishfinder rigs or sinkers with holes through the middle are used. Sinkers up to 2 ounces in weight are generally all that is required, because if more weight is needed, the current is too fast for good catfishing. Look in slow water for catfish. Even channel catfish below dams are for the most part in the quiet pools where the water moves much slower than in the center stream.

Another method used for taking catfish is float fishing, which resembles jug fishing in certain respects, except that rods and lines are used. Generally two lines are floated in a river. Fishing is just above the bottom, and depths are set by using floats, which indicate strikes. This method is less irritating than drift fishing, where baits are kept bouncing along the bottom. The use of floats helps, because the number of snags is far less. Float fishing can also be done while walking along the shore, while wading along a river or creek, or while on a boat.

Some important things to keep in mind are that catfish are shy and are spooked easily. They take baits lightly and can go up to 100-pound terrors. The fish like slow-moving water and avoid swift, roaring currents; daylight finds them deep and hiding, while nighttime brings them scurrying about for food. Also, when you're fishing, vary your baits. Chicken entrails are popular with the channel catfish, while natural baits take the biggest blue and flathead catfish. If a state allows it, a little chumming never hurts catfishing, for it may just put them on the feed the angler has planned for them; if not, slow-melting baits have the same effect. Then, too, remember to be reasonably quiet, for a clobberfoot marching on a bank can spook the shore line, and someone who wades through the water like the circus fatlady in a bathtub can spook hundreds of fish for hours. They are sensitive.

How are they for eating? Delicious, sir. They have a flaky, white meat that is a table delight. The mere mention of hush puppies and catfish will bring any Cracker running with a knife and fork.

Gar

The gar family of fish belongs in prehistoric times and would be right at home with trilobites, brachiopods, dinosaurs and prehistoric sharks. However, to put this fish in modern time settings with jet planes, sports cars and spinning tackle is like putting Whistler's mother in a Miss America Contest—it just doesn't belong.

Still, this prehistoric fish has survived the ages and may well survive the dynasty of man. Gar have protective equipment that has preserved them and that enables them to live in oxygenless or polluted water after every other kind of fish has died off. Equipped with a swim bladder that is connected with the pharynx and used as a lung, gar surface for air. Many times anglers are startled when they see one continually rising to the top as though taking flies. What he is doing is changing the air in the swim bladder.

They are extremely tough-skinned—so tough, in fact, that virtually no fish can harm a good-sized gar. They are covered with diamond-shaped scales that have a finish any paint company would be proud to duplicate. Some cheap jewelry is made from these tough scales, which, hinged together, serve the gar as an armored plate. Thus gar can never only be scaled but have to be completely skinned if the angler wants the meat.

Only young gar fall prey to predatory fish, while adult gar are active predators. They are useful in keeping trash fish in check, for they can gobble up astronomical amounts of fish in a day. In many Louisiana and Mississippi lakes, gar are the chief weapon for keeping down carp, pumpkinseed and other small species.

The longnose gar (Lepisosteus osseus) is the most widely distributed of the gar. This fish prefers the cleaner waters of the southern and middlewestern streams and rivers, and fish up to 5 feet long sun themselves in the rivers of Arkansas or Georgia. This gar is abundant in the southeastern states where schools of fish are common. The world record longnose is 50 pounds 5 ounces and came from the Trinity River in Texas. This fish measured 6 feet. The longnose gar is unusual looking, for its snout is approximately 20 times the length of its head.

The shortnose gar (Lepisosteus platostomus) has a beak only 5½ times the width of its head. It has a preference for dirty and muddy waters and is found throughout the Mississippi valley, mostly in the South.

The spotted gar (Lepisosteus productus) is found in the glacial lakes of the Midwest. It can be identified by the round spots on its head and body. It sometimes attains a length of 3½ feet.

The Florida spotted gar (Lepisosteus platyrhinchus), found in Georgia and Florida, has a spotted body but a clear head. This fish will attain a size of 3 feet.

The alligator gar (Lepisosteus spatula) is the big boy of the gar family. A world record alligator gar of 279 pounds, measuring 7 feet 9 inches, came from the Rio Grande River in Texas.

These fish are prevalent in all the rivers that empty into the Gulf of Mexico and 100-pounders never raise an eyebrow anywhere. Recently an oxbow lake of the Mississippi was drained, and much to everyone's astonishment half a dozen gar weighing over 150 pounds turned up. The fish are also found in brackish water and many times in bays; in Lake Pontchartrain or Mobile Bay they are often seen sunning themselves.

In spite of the awesome size the fish grow to and their fierce appearance, many people claim they are better fighters out of water than in it. They have the power of a dozen oxen, but they seldom use it. Gar have seldom impressed me with their fighting ability. They are just too slow and sluggish to be wild, active fighters. To rouse them to some action, we used to hit them over the head with an oar when they got near the boat.

Once while crabbing in some brackish water in Mississippi, I pulled in my crabline, which had fish pieces tied on by a wire. The line came in heavy-feeling, as if it were hooked onto the bottom and pulling in an ocean of seaweed. When I had it in a huge head popped out of the water; it belonged to a 100-pound 6-foot alligator gar which was holding on to my bait. The fish finally saw what was going on, and he casually let go of the line to sink back into the water like a water-logged log.

On another occasion, I had been salt-water fishing but came back into a bayou, even though the equipment I had with me was pretty heavy. I spotted a monstrous old alligator gar sunning himself as lazily as could be, and I flipped a big chunk of fish out to him. He took the bait, and I reared back, determined to set the hook deeply in his armor-plated mouth. He just spit it out, so I threw it to him again and again, with the same results. This little game continued with monotonous regularity: cast—nibble—strike—spit—curse.

The fish seemed to be enjoying it thoroughly, but on about the sixth cast something unexpected happened. There was an explosion at my bait. A good-sized bass had been watching our game from underneath. He decided that here was a meal for him, and belted the line. I hooked him all right, and we had ourselves a grandaddy of a battle; but when I pulled him in he weighed about 7 pounds. I think the gar out there weighed more than 20 times that much, but I'm sure the bass gave me triple the excitement and fight that the bigger fish would have. That, incidentally, was the most fun I ever had with gar.

Gar will take any kind of bait fish, and it can be served up to them dead or alive—it doesn't matter one bit. The bait can be floated along the surface or fished deep, for the fish will take it anywhere. When a fish takes the bait, hit the line with all your might; you'll find it's like trying to stick a hook in a wall of leather.

Hooks for gar vary from 2/0 to 10/0, depending on the kind of gar one is going for. Smaller gar are taken on hooks up to 4/0, shortnose gar on hooks up to 6/0, and alligator gar on hooks measuring up to 10/0. A good hook to use is an Eagle Claw No. 84. Steel leaders are recommended for the fish, while tackle, of course, depends on the particular gar to be fished. The 200-pounders take medium salt-water tackle with stiff action, while 20-pounders can be taken on most light fresh-water tackle.

Throughout most states gar are unprotected by game laws, so many ways have been devised to take them. One method is the snare, in which a minnow or a chunk of fish is put on a small hook that is part of a fiddle-string snare. When a gar comes lumbering up to the bait, the noose is tied, and the angler has a fish with a noose around his neck. Bow-and-arrow gar hunting has become popular. Here the quarry is searched out by moving a quiet boat about the water until a gar is seen. Then the job is to get close enough to hit the quarry. This can be done from shore or sometimes by wading, but the hunter should remember that when he hits a big one, he is in for a ride.

Gar will take plugs that are worked slowly in front of them. The closer to the snoot the plug is worked, the better the chance that the fish will hit it. Gar are also taken on bucktail flies, and many a snook fisherman has weighted his fly so as not to be annoyed by them.

The meat of gar is edible—flaky and white and said to be good-tasting. Not many people eat gar, and I must admit I, too, pass it up. The roe of gar is poisonous to both man and animal, so it should be discarded.

This old fish roamed the waters of the earth during the Triassic Age but now is found only in North America, Central America and the West Indies. It is the fiercest-looking beast of any in the water, but it is not intelligent enough to put up a wild fight. One thing I will say about the gar is that it can be dangerous. It has reptile teeth and breathes air, so it remains active out of water a long time. One fishing trip I had one in my boat an hour. I put my leg too close to it, and he decided to take a chomp. I heard the sickening click of his teeth and took a look down at my leg, half expecting to mimic Pegleg Pete the rest of my days. Luckily he just missed and only tore my pants. Watch out! Gar can be dangerous and should not be handled carelessly.

American Grayling

The American angler has few chances to fish for grayling because the species is currently found only in the mountain streams and lakes of Montana and very limited sections of Wyoming, Utah and Idaho. The Upper Peninsula and upper section of the Lower Peninsula of Michigan once had these delicate fish; but civilization encroached, and they quickly disappeared. Glacier National Park, Montana, and Yellowstone Park, Wyoming, are two areas where the fish are still available.

The grayling has one real stronghold left. That is in Alaska, where it can be taken from the coast all the way north to the Brooks Range Mountains. There is good grayling fishing in Mount McKinley National Park, the Chitina Lakes area and the Copper River area.

The American grayling (Thymallus signifer), sometimes called Arctic grayling, is a western North American species of fish that needs cold, clear water to survive. This is a beautiful fish, a relative of the trout, grayish silver in color, with a purplish iridescence on his sides and dorsal fin. The most distinctive feature of the fish is its extremely large, flowing dorsal fin, which is almost as wide as its body.

The fish spawn in the late springtime when the waters become ice-free. Females stir up the sandy bottoms of lakes or streams and deposit their sticky gelatin-like eggs there. The males fertilize the eggs but then abandon them. Eggs hatch in 2 to 3 weeks' time. Huge females are capable of depositing over 10,000 eggs in a year, while young spawners give only one-fifth this amount.

The world-record grayling, a 4-pounder that measured 19 inches in length, was taken at Clearwater River, Saskatchewan. Average catches in the Montana area are 10 to 12 inches long and weigh a pound or two, while Alaskan catches often approach the record fish. Grayling are not big, so standard light tackle of the spinning rod or fly-rod variety used for eastern brook trout is ideal. Fly rods weighing 2½ to 4 ounces measuring 7 to 8 feet in length are good. This outfit together with light line and 8 feet of leader tapered to 2x or 3x will provide barrels of fun for the fisherman.

The fish, which are primarily insect feeders, are taken on flies. Some recommended patterns would be Coachmen, Dark Cahill or Mosquitoes sizes 10 to 14. Actually grayling strike almost any fly that is worked in front of them. Sometimes they hit a floating fly gently and are hard to get on the hook, while other times they engage in acrobatics to strike at it. One rule is that they must be struck gently because of their soft mouths.

When the fish are not rising, flies should be fished wet, and the best procedure for lakes is to let a fly sink naturally. In a moving stream this is sometimes impossible, and pieces of shot have to be added. A fly should be moved very slowly and tightened gently on a hit. If missed, give the fly a rest before continuing to retrieve. Second hits are often the case. In lakes the fish tend to travel in schools, so the second hit on a fly might well be another fish in that school. It always pays to rest the fly.

Nymphs rolled along the bottom of a stream will bring hits. The fish feed both on top and bottom, and among their regular dinners are May flies, damsel flies, water fleas and mosquitoes. They also take some lures. A ⅛ ounce Flasher Spoon or a Wob-l-Rite, ⅟₁₀-ounce will do the trick.

Fishing for grayling can be done wading in streams or from shore. Lake fishing for them is good from shore or a boat, and in Alaska some superior catches have been made by boys fishing right off the pontoons of an airplane.

I have always found their white, flaky meat a real treat for eating, and fishing for them an exciting experience. They are truly exotic sports fish.

Muskellunge

The muskellunge (Esox masquinongy) is a true fresh-water prize—a rare fish, a tough fighter and a big fish, weighing up to possible 100 pounds. He is hard to locate, hard to entice on a lure, hard to fight and even harder to boat when fought out.

Fishermen who live right in the heart of muskie country will sometimes go a lifetime without ever catching one of these prize fish. I've known anglers who were virtually experts on pike, bass and trout, but somehow muskie always eluded them.

Many fishermen like myself enjoy striking out and fishing on their own; but with muskie fishing in strange waters, a guide is necessary if the chance for success is to be reasonable. The fish have to be located and have to be coaxed onto a hook once found. A local guide will know their haunts and what the best lure for a strike may be. He can see what equipment a visiting fisherman will have, and he will plan the fishing accordingly. If the angler is a fly-rod enthusiast, the guide could have the man troll a spinner-bucktail combination some 20 to 30 yards behind a slow-moving boat. Or he may permit the angler to work the fly into the weed beds, where a prize could be lurking.

Often a guide will recommend a special manufactured lure, or he may recommend a homemade one. Sometimes private lures can be purchased, while at other times they are only borrowed for the day. At any rate the angler can feel confident that whatever is recommended has been tested locally and works.

One word of caution about hiring a guide for muskie fishing: guides are not synonymous with a trip to a taxidermist. A guide will greatly increase one's chances for getting one of these rare prizes, but they certainly are no guarantee of success with the mighty muskellunge.

This big North American fish is present only in the cold rivers and big lakes of our northern states and Canada. He is found in no other waters of the world, and even here he is never over-plentiful. Generally in the United States the muskie states are Minnesota, Wisconsin, Michigan, West Virginia and New York. A few neighboring states have occasional catches, but mostly the ones listed are the best producers.

The world-record muskellunge, a 69-pound 15-ounce monster 64¼ inches in length, came from the St. Lawrence River in 1957. This beat out the previous record fish of 69 pounds 11 ounces, 63½ inches long, caught in Chippewa Lake, Wisconsin. A fish of 102 pounds was once taken in Wisconsin, but this was not a record, because he wasn't captured by sports-fishing methods. Compare these fish to the biggest pike caught, and the muskie is 33 per cent heavier and over a foot longer. No wonder we rank muskie so highly and go to such great extremes to preserve and propagate the species. Another species of muskellunge (Esox masquinongy ohiensis) is found in western New York, Pennsylvania and Ohio, and a 51-pound 3-ounce fish came from Chautauqua Lake in 1955.

Legend has it that muskellunge live 40 to 50 years, but this is not true—their life span is only 10 to 12 years. From birth they eat prodigously and grow rapidly. It takes a muskie about 5 years to reach one yard in length, and during the remainder of his life he may almost double this length. Older muskie, the real giants, are for the most part bottom fish, as it is an effort for them to move their big bodies around and the bottom provides them with ample food that is easy to obtain. Many of the big ones are blind or near blind, and their lives center around the immediate area about them.

Why the thousands of lakes that seem well suited for muskie will not support them is a mystery. Even in lakes in which they are present they are never in great number. A look at the female muskie, who can produce a quarter of a million eggs in a year's time, certainly would indicate they should be more abundant.

This species neither cares for the eggs nor its young; but neither do pickerel and pike, yet they are more abundant. One theory is that muskellunge destroy too many fish; consequently a lake can hold only so many muskie. Another theory is that the fish is too cannibalistic and finds his own young too good a meal to let the species thrive. This still doesn't explain why so often in plantings the fish will not take at all.

Much has recently been learned by the conservation departments of Wisconsin, Michigan and Minnesota about raising the fish, and now they are stocked. For anyone who has a lake he feels is sufficiently cold and large to hold muskie, he can buy the species commercially from Ken Fish Hatchery, Land O'Lakes, Wisconsin.

It is characteristic of the muskie to destroy other fish, which would immediately lead one to believe that they could be taken in any manner and at any time on almost any plug made. The sad fact is that they do not hit as readily as pike or pickerel. Many times they leave an angler exasperated when they trail a plug only to turn from it the last second, to drift back off into the deep like a sunken log. Unlike a pike, muskellunge will not trail a plug and hit it the last minute. Muskie only hit a plug as it goes by. When muskie are not hitting they are miserable fish and can lead one to one of the most disheartening afternoons imaginable. Sometimes, though, a succulent serving of live bait in front of one of these sleeping monsters will stir him into action—it's always worth a try.

A few years ago one lake had a 50-inch plus muskie that came to sleep under a big boat dock every afternoon. Fishermen soon heard of this, and they tried everything imaginable to get the big guy. All summer long he never looked at or touched anything. He was smart and stayed too far under the dock for snagging, and if something came too close he would move a few inches. No one ever caught him either, and finally he just disappeared, letting the local fishermen return to normal life.

For the fisherman the problem is how to catch this tiger-striped, olive-colored sports fish. One of the best ways is by live-bait fishing. Big, fat minnows, chubs, bullhead and dogfish are all prime muskie baits. Bullhead and dogfish should be about 12 inches in length, while minnows or chubs can be half that size. The baits are fished in water from 5 to 20 feet in depth, preferably where the fisherman has had some previous experience and knows where muskie are likely to be lurking. If he has no guide and no knowledge of the lake, then he might try near some weed beds, at sudden drop-offs, by rocky ledges, near sunken logs or anywhere else he feels a muskie is likely to be waiting to pounce on prey. In streams or rivers, he can try near fast water or in dips and curves.

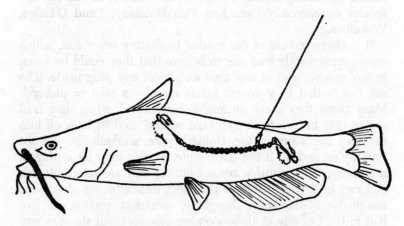

Hooking a bullhead for muskellunge. Two treble hooks are inserted into the fish's skin as shown. The hooks are connected by a chain or wire and tied to a swivel and to the leader.

The big super-sized muskellunge are old, big, slow bottom feeders, so live bait floated directly in front of them has the best chance of stirring some awesome activity. Cast the bait to the area and then let it swim freely about, advertising itself. A loose bait fish will lose no time swimming to the bottom to hide, so occasionally the rod tip can be raised to lift the fish up so others on the bottom are attracted. When a muskie strikes, don't strike

THE FRESH-WATER FISH OF AMERICA   239

back immediately, but give him time to swallow the bait. Like other members of the pike family, he sometimes only mouths bait before swallowing.

Rigging and live-bait fishing are important. A bullhead or dogfish should be rigged with two sets of 4/0 to 8/0 treble hooks. The hooks are placed into the fish's back—one set ahead of the dorsal fin and one behind it.

Smaller baits can be rigged up with only one set of treble hooks anchored into the back of the fish behind the dorsal fin. Many times smaller baits are fished with a float, but then it is important to set the depth of the bait correctly. Try to keep it within a few feet of the bottom.

Plug casters and spoon men should remember that big muskie tend to stay low and move slowly. For fishermen this means a deep, slow-moving lure has a better chance of taking a big one than does fast-moving top stuff. Some of the lures that can be worked successfully are painted spoons—the Daredevil of course, Johnson's Sprite, and such underwater plugs as the Creek Chub Pikie Minnow and the Creek Chub Jointed Pikie Minnow. Among top-water plugs that take them are the Creek Chub Top 'N' Pop or Fred Arbogast's Hula Popper or Jitterbug. When fishing plugs and spoons, remember that muskie are big fish and tend to go for big lures, some of which can be as big as the Giant Pikie, which is 14 inches long and weighs 4 ounces. Another successful lure for muskie is a spinner-and-bucktail fly combination. A Pflueger Fluted Spoon, which is red and nickle-spoon with a feathered treble hook, works. All these can be trolled successfully or worked casting. The fly spoon or fly-spinner combinations can be fished both with fly rods and spinning rods.

Equipment for muskie, of course, varies with the kind of fishing one plans to do for them. If big, heavy plugs are to be cast, a rod that can handle most of the requirements is necessary. Spinning rods call for at least a medium rod, and in many instances salt-water spinning equipment is fine. Lighter rods can be used if the lures are spinning lures or small spoons. Fly rods are successful of course. They should be 8 to 10 feet in length with a stiff action for striking a fish with light tackle. Precautions must always be taken to work a fish away from any weed bed. Line should be 15-pound test and a minimum of 200 feet long. Wire leader is essential for these big fish.

Muskie are edible, but for the most part they are primarily trophy fish, for there are many better-tasting fish in the lakes. The young, smaller muskie under a yard long are the best eating.

Muskellunge are big, fighting fish, so spirited they can take an unknowing angler completely by surprise. In Ontario, Canada, a Lake of the Woods guide once told me about a little Londoner who decided to do some fishing his first week over here. A muskie smashed into his plug, and a rousing battle was on. The little guy got so excited he waded in up to his chest to continue the fight, and after half an hour he finally had his fish close enough to see it. The sight of the muskellunge, almost two yards long with mouth open, flashing thousands of deadly white teeth, caused the little guy to drop his rod and hightail it out of the water.

His friend screamed, "What did you do that for?"

The little guy replied, "I expected to catch fish, not monsters. I want no part of anything like that."

If you desire some hard-fighting monsters, then I'd say you are a top candidate to be a muskie fisherman.

White Perch

Up New England way when you see a crowd of people fishing from a bridge, dock or shore, it's even money they will be pursuing white perch (Morone americana).

This little gamester goes up to 5 pounds, with the present record being 4 pounds 12 ounces and coming from Messalonskee Lake, one of the Belgrade Lakes, in Maine. The day-to-day fishermen will find fish weighing 2 pounds are good-sized catches. The white perch range almost the entire length of the Atlantic Coast, living in salt or fresh water; and they are also in many of the lakes of the eastern seaboard.

Fishermen going for white perch are apt to use every kind of equipment made. Handlines will be seen dangling from bridges

just as will cane poles, salt-water tackle, fresh-water spinning
rods, bait-casting rods, or fly rods. The fish are no particular
problem to take, and line for equipment can be 4- to 6-pound
test. Hooks vary from No. 8 to No. 3, with No. 6 being about
the most popular size.

White perch live in fresh as well as salt water and keep the
same habits in both. Once they were considered fine fish for
planting in lakes because they took so easily, but opinion has
changed, because in too many lakes and ponds they have over-
produced themselves and consequently have become stunted.
They make excellent forage for predatory bass, pickerel, or pike;
but if these fish are not about in ample number, the perch soon
begin crowding the water. Conservation departments beg fisherman to keep all perch caught, no matter what size, because this
practice can help keep them in check.

They are primarily school fish and the schools will travel
around a lake, bay or river searching for food. Sometimes dozens
of them can be seen passing an angler's bait without any of them
ever touching it. This is not a sign to change baits frantically
because 5 minutes later they may be attacking the line so rapidly
the angler can't bait up fast enough. When a school is about, the
action gets very fast and exciting, for the fish strike savagely
and fight hard. Still, at other times they will take nothing offered.
This characteristic comes from the fact that the fish are not perch
at all, but are actually members of the salt-water bass family,
which includes striped bass.

A springtime bait that is especially productive is the spinner-
garden worm combination. During the spring the fish are busily
feeding on worms and when one floats by with an attractive
spinner in front to show it off, it is just too much for one of the
hungry perch to pass up. Later on in the season, a spinner-
streamer-fly combination will take fish. White perch generally
hook themselves when a lure or bait is trolled or worked, so all
the angler must do is keep the line taut. A line that is struck
hard only takes the offering away from the fish. He will not hit
again if frightened, but, of course, others in the school might hit
the missed lure.

Chumming and fishing with grass shrimp in coastal waters will take lots of perch. Chumming attracts the fish, and the shrimp on a hook that is floated out into the chum line soon get smashed. Other baits can be small eels, crawfish or many of the spinning lures. If schools are about, an angler using this method should have no difficulty in taking all the fish he wants.

Sometimes perch can be seen breaking water, and then bass bugs are called into action. Throw the bug out into their midst and a perch will come and hit it. If he is missed, he might push the bug a few inches, and almost instantly another perch will splash up. Fish will hit the line continually, and some days they will chew up a bug in a few hours.

White perch are quite a treat in a pot, and on light tackle they are active and exciting fish. It's no wonder old New Englanders refer to the white perch as the prince of pan fish.

Yellow Perch

Every yellow perch (Perca flavescens) caught should be kept. This is true no matter where the fish is caught, no matter when it is caught and no matter what its size. If the fish is big, eat it, for it is a fine food fish; if it is small, feed it to the cat or use it as fertilizer. But don't throw it back!

Yellow perch are one of the chief culprits in overpopulating lakes. Some conservationists feel that perch are public enemy No. 1 in this respect. A friend of mine, a conservation officer, uses hard language when talking about yellow perch, because he spends much of his time straining lakes to get rid of them.

During a single season a family of perch can raise 40,000 fry. The fish do not protect the eggs or the young, but they have an uncanny habit of depositing eggs in protected places. The eggs are of a jelly-like substance that sticks to weeds or underbrush in coves, where the eggs lay protected for the 3 weeks it takes for hatching.

Perch grow rather slowly, taking 4 to 5 years to reach a size of 7 or 8 inches. A 1-pound perch will be 7 or 8 years old. The fish may reach an age of 10 years and could grow to 5 pounds—

the record being 4 lbs. 3 ounces, in Bordentown, New Jersey. In ponds or lakes where the fish are stunted, it may be hard to catch a single perch over 5 inches in length in a whole season of fishing.

This is a widely distributed fish, common in all the states and in Europe. The feeling among conservationists is that two perch in a pond are all that is needed to start an avalanche.

In states like Michigan, perch fishing is enjoyed by thousands, and the Michigan Department of Conservation states that in sheer number caught the perch ranks as the No. 1 game fish. A visit to Lake Michigan or Lake St. Clair quickly verifies this. These tremendous bodies of water can support perch, and predatory fish keep them in balance, so that here they are a welcome addition to the sports fish. Throughout the Great Lakes, perch are caught commercially and are sold in the Midwest markets.

Perch fishing takes no particular skill. During the springtime when the fish are close to shore, they are excellent fish to begin a child's fishing career, because the action is generally fast, and the fishing is not complicated.

Perch fishing requires no expensive tackle. Ultralight tackle of spin-, bait- or fly-fishing variety is fine for the sophisticated fisherman. Test line need only be 2- to 6-pound test, and hooks can measure from No. 8 to No. 4. The actual size of a hook, of course, depends on the size of fish expected and the fisherman's own touch; but No. 6 is generally conceded to be the most popular. A light clamp sinker or a piece of shot will take the package down into pay-dirt.

Baits for perch are headed by minnows, with the small ones being preferred. Shiners, grass shrimp or worms are other natural baits the perch takes readily. Natural baits can be fished dead or alive, for he is not fussy as to how he takes bait. When he is taking the bait, allow him all the time he wants to play with it because when he is ready to take it, he will hook himself. Perch seem to have an acute sense of smell, and natural baits are always best. Because of this sense, it pays the fisherman not to handle a bait too much before using it.

Streamer or bucktail flies that resemble minnows are fine for taking the perch. These flies should be worked close to the bottom in a slow, jerky manner so that they act like a minnow. The motion of the fly should be so enticing that the fish strike out at it without stopping to investigate it. All fish have a tendency to strike out at things swimming away from them, for fear they might be missing a meal, and this tendency is what makes them strike flies hard and fast.

Perch are, for the most part, bottom fish, and fishing should be done low. This is true whether one is fishing from shore or in a boat, for the hooks within 1 foot of the bottom will be the most productive. Multiple-hook fishing is a common practice, and some lines use as many as 6. Floats are used for multiple-hook fishing, while for single- and double-hook fishing the line is usually dropped to the bottom, and the angler feels the bites.

When perch are not easily located, troll a spinner-worm or a spinner-minnow combination around a lake until a strike or two is felt. Once strikes are felt, that area should be fished, for a school is lurking nearby. Give the fish plenty of time to hook himself, because he may strike very lightly often before being hooked. Sometimes a minnow worked through a weed bed or trolled over some submerged weeds will coax the fish into action. Floats can be used when trolling over submerged weeds, because with them the depth of the line can be properly set to avoid irritating weed tangles.

When trying to locate perch, fish the quiet side of a lake first. Quiet coves not getting hit by wind are where the perch will be active; then, as with so many other fresh-water fish, early-morning and late-evening fishing are more productive than noontime angling. Still this shouldn't keep the midday angler home, for perch can generally be coaxed onto a hook at any hour.

To the ice fisherman the yellow perch is a darling. No matter how thick the ice or how cold the weather, perch can always be counted on to be scurrying around for food. To catch them, cut holes in the ice, bait up with live minnows and then wait until the tip-up shows a fish on the line. Six tip-ups with 6 hooks on each line should be an active sportsman's limit.

An angler who catches yellow perch and cuts them up for frying is sometimes repelled because the fish are so wormy. These fish parasites are quite harmless to humans. Cooking destroys the parasites, and the meat is good to eat.

For the angler who wants fast action and big catches, the yellow perch easily fills the bill. Anglers and conservationists will thank the fisherman for every one he takes home, so here is an opportunity to take some really big catches and make everyone happy.

Pickerel

A pickerel is the smallest member of the pike family, but on light tackle he puts up a gallant scrap. Pickerel average only 1 or 2 pounds and 18 to 20 inches in length, yet their fight is worthy of the best, for they battle hook and line right to the end.

I have hooked pickerel all over the East and have never been disappointed with the little scrappers. Get them close to a boat which they know is danger and watch the high jinks; they will jump, flip, dive and even bulldog the line.

A pickerel fight begins when the fish hits a plug, for he smashes it, giving it a good, solid whack. From there it's usually a quick race to the weed beds, for he, like so many other fish, gets the feeling of security from weeds. This scrapper knows weeds give him a chance to foul up an angler's line, and a weed-tangled line is a ticket to freedom.

Most pickerel taken on plugs are caught while an angler is bass fishing. At times they take a plug as readily as bass, and I've seen some small pickerel with the audacity to hit plugs almost as big as themselves. Mostly, though, the larger members of the species will hit a plug, and when hooked they fight the hook, plug and line. Take a look at a wooden plug after a 15-minute battle with a 4-pound pickerel, and I guarantee the plug will look like it has been through a meat grinder. I've had plugs come back to me with dents and teeth marks on them, and with paint and wood torn right off them.

Pickerel are predators. They live by killing other fish for food, and their rows upon rows of sharp teeth have made their job of killing easy. When hooked, they use these teeth to try to bite and cut the alien object, and in this way they can chew a plug to pieces.

Some plugs that work well for pickerel are Creek Chubs or Flatfish; in fact, any standard bass plug will take them. Once while I was fishing Sebago Lake, Maine, I was using a deep-running plug trying for some smallmouth which weren't being particularly co-operative. Suddenly I had a whack on my line, and action started. It was a strange action. I knew it wasn't a bass, for it was too jerky. When I finally got the fish in, I discovered that I had hooked a pickerel outside of his mouth, way back on his head behind the eyes. The crazy flat-tire feeling during the fight was due to the fact that every time I exerted pressure I pulled the fish broadside. Hooking pickerel outside of their mouths isn't unusual, and can happen with plugs, spoons and bait. These fish love to grab at prey and then run with it, and it is in this grab-and-run act that they get hooked outside of the mouth.

Excellent lures for pickerel include Daredevil spoons—red-and-white ones, which are my favorite lures. Also effective are the Johnson Silver Minnow and many others. When pickerel are in a hitting mood, they will hit any lure and smack it regularly and hard. Other times they have to be coaxed, and the fundamentals one has to remember are to work the weed beds, in grasses, near logs and by sudden drop-offs. Seasons count too, for spring fishing is good near shore, while hot, summer-weather fishing has to be done deep. Early-morning hot-spots for them are the shallow weeds near shore.

Pickerel fishing is best with live baits. Minnows trolled into hot-spots or still-fished in a pickerel haunt will bring hits. It is important to remember when fishing with live bait to allow a pickerel plenty of time to take the bait. Very often he will grab it gingerly, tuck it in the front of his mouth, and begin to run with it, never really taking it. He will stop momentarily and let go of the crippled fish and then hit into it head on and devour it. If the angler makes the mistake of striking the line on the first run, he only succeeds in pulling the bait from the fish. It's that second run when the fish can be struck, for now he means business and is ready for capture. Since pickerel have soft mouths, horsing the fish after hooking it may mean ripping the hook from his mouth.

Pork rinds are the original pickerel lures of the country, and they are just as good producers today as they ever were. Cast or troll one through a lily pad, and be ready for action. Other producers are spinner-minnow, spinner-worm or spinner-fly combinations which are effective trolled. Frogs, crawfish, worms, strip-cut fish and small snakes will also take pickerel. Almost any artificial lure from plugs to spoons can take them; but remember to use bright-colored lures on dull days and darker-colored lures on bright days.

Trolled bucktails are fine producers and seem to be especially effective in Maine waters. Pickerel in streams will take both wet and dry flies, so any angler can readily see it is not so much the bait one uses as how well and at what time the bait is used.

Pickerel are year-round fish—they do not hibernate the way bass do—and consequently during winter months they become a fisherman's favorite. They take bait during the coldest months and are regularly fished through the ice. Lines are dropped through 12- to 18-inch holes in the ice and are lowered anywhere from 2 to 20 feet to where the fish are. Jigging for them through the ice is popular. Some states allow pickerel to be speared, but most fishermen frown on this as a method of taking sports fish.

Spring is breeding time for chain pickerel, and spawning takes place in the coves over soft bottoms. Two fish pair off and swim side by side, with the female dropping eggs while the male fertilizes them. This is the end of the parental responsibility, for the pickerel eggs are left to nature. If the eggs are not devoured by predators, they hatch in 1 or 2 weeks; and immediately the young fish dart off into the weeds and begin a lifelong search for food.

There are several species of pickerel. Chain pickerel (Esox niger) is the biggest and most important. This species will go to 10 pounds (the record is 9 pounds 3 ounces) but the average is 1 to 2 pounds, and 5-pounders are big.

Other species include grass pickerel (Esox vermiculatus), which is found in the Ohio River basin, and the redfin pickerel (Esox americanus), found in the Susquehanna and Delaware river basins of Pennsylvania. Both are pan fish, seldom going over 12 inches in length.

The chain pickerel has distributed itself throughout the eastern states from Florida north to Maine, west to Wisconsin and all the way south to Texas. The northeastern United States is the best place to fish them, for in the southern reaches they are scarce and are usually small. Hot-spots are all of New England, New York, New Jersey and Pennsylvania. My favorite places include the Delaware and Susquehanna rivers in Pennsylvania and the lakes of southern Maine.

Some anglers do not like to go pickerel fishing because they complain pickerel are not good eating. Actually they are good-tasting fish, but they are bony; and with the head and tail taking up more than one-third of the fish, there really isn't much meat left on a 1- or 2-pounder. I have a rule that whatever fish I keep get eaten (rough fish excluded), so in this way I aid conservation and also get to enjoy my catches. One thing to remember is that the pickerel is a soft-fleshed fish; and if he is headed for the pot, the sooner after catching he is cleaned, the better will be the flavor of the meat.

Tackle requirements for pickerel are strictly personal, but the lighter the tackle the better. An angler can use a bait-casting rod, a fly rod or a spinning rod for them, depending on his preference. The most important point is to keep the tackle light. Ultralight tackle seems tailor-made for pickerel fishing. Line can be as light as 2- to 4-pound test, but 5- or 8-pound test can also be used by the angler with less confidence in his fishing ability, or by one who may expect to hit something much bigger. Small pieces of wire leader with swivels attached for quick changes of lures are useful. Gut leader can also be used. Hooks can be 1/0 to 3/0, and hook size or test of line may depend upon what other fish could be hit in a particular lake, stream or pond. Many pickerel are taken in weed beds by the old cane pole method. This, too, can be fun and productive.

Opinions are varied as to the pickerel's place in the hierarchy of sports fish. The fish run all the way from trophy prizes right down to the level of pan fish or rough fish. Generally near big eastern cities pickerel are highly regarded as sports fish, and I even know of one angler who mounted one. Out in rougher country pickerel are quickly downgraded because of their small size, for anglers out in the woods are after bigger game, and pickerel only get in the way. But any angler who accepts these smallest members of the pike family for what they are—good, hard-fighting, light-weight scrappers—will find the fishing enjoyable and the catches good.

Pike

When a pike strikes a plug, his white teeth flash, and he hits in a short, hard smash. From there he dives for the bottom, where he can fight the battle on his own terms. If there are rocks around he will head for them, or he will try to twist around a stump or log. He may also make a headlong rush into weeds, where the line will become so fouled up the fish has to be cut. The northern pike is a fish with muscles, and he uses them. In dives or in hard, sideway runs paralleling the boat, and sometimes just to show his strength, he will thrust his head out of water and shake it furiously.

All of a pike's fight is strong, and an angler must be on the alert constantly for some new attack that could let the fish break away. But the biggest chance for losing the fish is through carelessness and horsing. Sometimes in a battle with a big one the tension is terrific, and the angler may find himself pulling his fish too hard and thus losing a prize. In spite of the pike's size and toughness it has a fragile mouth. Rod tips and star drags should be used to curb hard runs, because horsing only results in hooks being ripped from a fish.

The most dangerous time in fighting a pike is when he gets close to a boat, for the boat represents sure death, and the fish knows it. In close, he will take sudden dives, and many an angler has had his line parted that way. He may jump bulldog or charge right under the boat, for he wants no part of what is in store for him. An angler should refrain from forcing the fish's head out of water, for this can spur him into mad antics that spell trouble.

A big landing net or a gaff slipped under the gill is needed to bring a big one in. Some anglers use a 22-caliber bullet to quiet a monster, but a good stout club and a few detectivelike slugs on the head work wonders. When the fish is picked up, apply pressure over his eyes with a thumb and forefinger. This will paralyze him while he is being held. An attempt to remove the hook from a boated monster barehanded can end a fine day's fishing. Any northern pike can easily rip the skin of any hand brought within its reach, for his mouth is nothing but a mass of inverted needlelike teeth, and he would like nothing better than to use them on his mortal enemy—the fisherman. Pliers or, better yet, wire cutters are the best instruments to use to safely remove a hook from a fish.

Pike grow big—they are reported to go to 100 pounds—but the world-record catch is 46 pounds 2 ounces, taken in New York state. Thirty-pounders are taken yearly and 10-pounders, which are wonderful fighters, are never news. Strangely, the biggest specimens of northern pike are all females, for the ladies of the northern pike family grow to sizes 4 and 5 times bigger than their male counterparts. A catch of a 12-pound male northern pike would be close to a world record, if records were kept that way.

The pike is found in North America, Europe and Asia. Old European tales telling of 1,000-pound monsters have come down to us, but these are, of course, exaggerated.

When I was in the army of occupation in Germany right after World War II, I had lots of opportunity to fish for pike. We had a spot below a dam that was not too many miles from Heidelberg. The lake above the dam was fished, too, but there were too many torpedo nets strung out, which made fishing difficult. Furthermore, below the dam we could fish from shore effectively.

Our outfit had a topkick who had been raised as an ocean fisherman, and he scoffed at fresh-water sport—I love ocean fishing too, but I'll take my sport as it comes—so we could never get him to go with us. "Sardines," was his reply. One morning he wasn't doing anything, so just for laughs he accompanied us down the long steps to our hot-spot. He wouldn't even take a rod with him.

The morning mist still hung over the water, and we could see only a few feet in front of us. I tied an old silver spoon on my line and handed the rod to the sergeant. He shrugged his shoulders and cast. His lure hit. He let it settle and took two turns on the reel in retrieve when suddenly his rod doubled over, and he yelled, "*I got one!*" Instantly there was a complete transformation in him. Here was a man who had seen it all during the war, and now his pulse was up around 200 as he fought this fish. And what a scrap it was, for the two of them battled for what seemed like half an hour before he landed a 15-pounder. After that we didn't hear too much about "sardines;" in fact we had ourselves another fishing buddy.

North America has northern pike from Alaska through Canada and into the northern United States. There are good catches in Alaska, Minnesota, Wisconsin, Michigan, Pennsylvania, New York and Vermont, and marginal fishing is found in a few other neighboring states. Pike can be taken the year round, and ice fishing is popular in many states.

Spring is the best season for pike fishing, for pike are close to the shore during this period. While they are breeding they do not take food, but immediately afterward they are ravenous and will strike at anything. At this time they can be picked up easily by the angler who the works the weed beds with spoons, plugs or live baits. A big, fat night crawler on a 4/0 hook with a spinner in front is a good bet in the rivers during the spring.

Springtime, when the fish spawn, a big female will swim off with her pigmylike mate to the soft, grassy or muddy shallows. She will drop eggs here while the male fertilizes them. The female can lay over 100,000 eggs in one year. These fish neither care for the eggs nor the fry, so many are lost, but if 5 fish reach the age of 3 years—when they begin spawning—it is a successful hatch.

In the first year of life the young pike grow to 8 inches in size, and they will add another 8 inches of growth the second year. By the end of the third year a female could be 25 inches long, but after that growth is slower. Ten-year-old pike may be over 40 inches in length, and a fish may live to the age of 20.

As spring turns into summer pike begin retreating from the shore line to deeper water. In rivers they move out into channels, and in lakes they move offshore, and fishing has to be done deeper.

An angler must locate pike and get his offerings close to them if he wants results. A good rule-of-thumb guide to finding where they may be lurking is based on the following water-temperature scales:

Water Temperature	Depth Where Fish Are Located
40°–50°	Surface to 5 feet down
50°–60°	5 to 10 feet down
over 60°	10 feet down to the bottom

August is the worst month for pike fishing for several reasons. First, in August pike get sore mouths, or their teeth loosen and they get swollen gums. This puts them off feed for several weeks. Second, the fish are in deep water, and most fishermen don't get their lines down to them. Pike will not make a long run after a bait or plug, and seldom go after anything more than 10 feet from them. The closer a lure gets to the fish, the better the chances the fish will strike it.

Pikes are not fast swimmers as fish go, being able to swim about 20 miles per hour; but this is fast enough to enable them to hold their own, and almost twice as fast as a bass swims. The physical characteristics of a pike's long, cylindrical body make it difficult for him to twist around in the water, so that he goes straight for a prey and likes to take another fish on a broadside. He may follow a bait slowly, trailing it and then at the last minute strike out at it. Fishermen sometimes get the shock of their lives as a monster suddenly strikes up at a lure they were just about to lift out of the water. Other times pike lie in ambush and spring at an object, tigerlike.

One incident that clearly shows the viciousness of their hit occurred several years ago when one of them attacked an unfortunate swimmer in upstate New York. The man was wearing a medallion around his neck, and when a lurking pike saw the medal he charged into it; the result was a mangled chest and 32 stitches. Northern pike do not attack people, but they do hit flashy metal objects, and it's foolish to go swimming in any water while wearing such objects. This is especially true in tropical waters, where barracuda (the pike's salt-water relative) and sharks may be about.

The first cold weather in September finds the pike coming toward shore and getting active again. They are mean and hungry, and they take in prodigious amounts of food. Some estimate that at certain times of the year a pike will eat one-fifth his weight daily. That would be equivalent to my putting away a steak of almost 40 pounds in one day.

When the cold weather closes in and the leaves start falling, pike will be all over the shore line in pursuit of prey. They may be seen running minnows to shore, trapping them and gobbling them up in carefree abandon, or they will go after and gobble up a frog who's preparing to bed down in the mud for the winter. They will even attack rodents or smash up through the water at waterfowl. Generally any lure worked in front of them will draw a strike at this time; and for the angler who likes to fish with a fly rod, this is an excellent chance to work the shore line.

Equipment used to take pike can be a spinning rod, bait-casting rod or a fly rod. The choice is strictly personal; however, I do suggest using rods of at least medium stiffness, which help in setting the hook. Either a stiff rod or a medium rod is all right to work with. Line should be about 15-pound test for the average fisherman, while possibly as low as 8-pound test would be ample for an expert. A short piece of wire leader is a necessary protection against the fish's sharp teeth.

The choice of lures is a wide one, for pike fall prey to all kinds. They will hit big, wobbling spoons that may resemble a minnow to them; they take a jig, a spinner-worm or spinner-fly combination, feather-covered treble hooks, a bucktail fly and a large assortment of plugs. Generally speaking, underwater lures and plugs bring the best results, for pike are reluctant to come to the surface. A Flatfish, plug or a Creek Chub Pikie-Minnow are good producers. A big red-and-white Daredevil spoon is a good producer, and streamer flies work fine for river pike.

Among the natural baits for pike are whole minnows, suckers, and chubs, while strip-cut perch bellies take them too. Worms, frogs and mice bring hits. With natural baits an angler should give the fish time to really take the offering, for many times they only mouth it before swallowing.

Pike are a prolific fish. They are actually increasing in number in spite of the fishing pressure against them. They fight well, are edible and come to trophy size—in short, they are a good sports fish. Anyone who wants a memorable pike-fishing experience should take a float trip on the Menominee River that divides Michigan and Wisconsin, or the Kawishiwi River of Minnesota, and a few rodbenders here or elsewhere will soon add another member to the rapidly growing pike fan club.

Walleye Pike

The biggest walleye I ever caught I took trolling a spinner-minnow combination right on the bottom. I remember this incident, because I watched my rod bend over very slowly, and I thought I'd snagged the bottom again. Annoyed, I yanked my rod to try to rip the hook from the bottom and began reeling up. Nothing happened until the fish that was following me realized what was going on and burst into a fight.

The walleye dove, pulled at the line and tried to get his body into a run for the bottom. I gave him line, breaking it with my thumb, and I fought him all the way. Gradually I led him toward the boat again, and slowly his fight grew less and less strenuous. Still I remained alert for his sudden dives. When I had him, I boated a 15½-pound prize.

All anglers who fish for walleye (Stizostedion vitreum) probably have similar stories of snags and aggravations, but the biggest walleye are bottom fish and have to be taken among these annoyances.

In spite of my strange action in hooking this walleye, it really wasn't too far from proper procedure to take him. First, my having snagged bottom several times proved I was way down deep in walleye water, where the fish were likely to be. Second, walleye should be struck firmly—and believe me, no one has ever struck a fish harder. I still wonder why I didn't extract at least ten of his teeth on that yank. Hooks must be firmly imbedded in the walleye's tough cartilage mouth to hold.

Daytime walleye fishing should always be done on or near the bottom of any lake or river. Near-shore top fishing has good results only in spring and fall. Summer nights and very early mornings will find the fish near shore and topside, but for consistency of catches—go deep, young man; go deep.

Few people ever see a walleye in the water. They are extremely wary fish, and in the daytime they stay deep. The fish can be down as far as 60 feet, or they can be only 10 feet down. Generally they are in water 20 feet deep or more, somewhere close to the bottom. Their habit of daytime shyness is said to save millions of them yearly, for fishermen often get discouraged if they see no signs of fish, and others continually fish way over the heads of the walleye.

Walleye eat prodigious amounts of bait fish, especially gizzard, shad, carp and minnows. They are never able to resist a bait fish that swims close by. They also have a taste for worms, mice, frogs, tadpoles and young lamprey eels. Any of these delicacies make excellent bait for this fish, as do the all-American standbys—the pork rind and the perch belly.

Some very interesting walleye fishing can be done in rivers with the many small rubber lures that resemble tadpoles. During spring spawning, these lures bring phenomenal results if they are worked into holes. The lures are excellent to work rivers with. A fly rod and a 5-pound walleye on a 4-ounce rod can create quite a fuss.

The small rubber lures take fish in lakes, too, because rubber worms are so realistic they are capable of taking fish anywhere. I have had fish take these worms, miss them, and come back a second time. Work with rubber frogs along the shore lines, especially in the fall, or weigh them down and drag them through holes. If there are fish about, they will attack the bait. A rubber eel resembling a lamprey works, too.

The fish's protruding lower jaw gives him a pikelike appearance and a look of being all business. They are solidly constructed, and when they whack a line, there is a good fight ahead. They use their husky shoulders and strong body advantageously in order to get strength in their runs. The best fighters are the females, who grow bigger and faster than the males.

The fish's large, milky-white, bulging pearl eyes are the characteristic for which the walleye is named. These strange-looking eyes are functional, too, for they enable him to see at night and give him that excellent vision necessary for seeing in the deeper parts of the lake. Walleye are good swimmers, clocking in at a top speed of a little over 10 miles per hour; and they swim far and wide. Tagging experiments have proven walleye travel 300 to 400 miles up and down rivers, and experts agree that the fish is one of the wanderers of the fresh-water species.

The walleye is a table delight besides being a fine sports fish. It's hard to beat the white, flaky meat of a walleye fillet. Although walleye are sportsmen's favorites, there is always apprehension when stocking them into a new lake, for very often they will take it over. They reproduce rapidly and tend to be lake cleaners, for they are famous destroyers of other fish. Their appetite is insatiable, so they are excellent fish to have about to keep carp and pan fish in check. They are not recommended for stocking into a pure trout lake.

The walleye pike is a member of the perch family, and his Latin name (Stizostedion vitreum) verifies this. The word "pike" in his name is a misnomer, for closely related to the walleye pike are the yellow perch and black bass. Walleye are found only in North America, whereas their relative the yellow perch is also a native of Europe. If the Europeans wanted to introduce walleye to their waters, planting should be relatively easy. On many occasions only a few fish dropped into water produces remarkable results.

These fish are found east of the Rockies to New England and from Hudson Bay south to the Gulf states. Lakes in Minnesota at the headwaters of the Mississippi River have all the requirements for the fish—clean water and clean, sandy bottoms—and consequently they rank as the walleye center of the country. The upper Mississippi River is a hot-spot for them, as are its tributaries. Another important walleye center is the TVA lakes.

Walleye are spread over a wide area and have acquired countless local names. In Pennsylvania they are known as Susquehanna salmon, in Missouri jack salmon or jack, while in other places they may be known as white salmon, grass pike, blue pickerel, hornfish and a host of other names.

No matter where the fish are, the same general principles are used in taking them. A lake should be worked in its deep pools, over rocky ledges and over sandy bottoms; dirty, muddy places should be avoided.

They are active night feeders, and in the still of night an angler can often hear them splashing around, chasing bait fish. At night they can be taken with many noisy top bass lures.

Lures that take this fish are weighted spinner-minnow combinations, which are trolled slowly 125 to 175 feet behind a boat. These or spinner-night crawler combinations are then worked into the holes. Spoons or deep-running plugs are good, as is the popular June Bug spinner. The important thing is to get down to where they are without spooking them. If a strike comes, keep working that depth and area. They are school fish, and chances for a second, third and fourth strike are very good.

Tackle, of course, depends upon the methods of angling. A casting rod is most commonly used when trolling, but sometimes fly rods are used. Rods should be of medium size and firmness. Spinning tackle is best used with the rubber lures and small spinning lures up to ½ ounce. Line from 6- to 12-pound test is sufficient except when fishing in weeds or places where snags are inevitable; then a higher test is recommended. The sinker need only be the clamp type, and heavy enough to take the line down into pay-water. A small piece of wire leader, and hooks varying in size from No. 1 to 4/0, make up the complete outfit.

Walleye pike are good eating, good fighting; and I agree with the anglers who say that from lake to line to pot, walleye are all sports fish.

Atlantic Salmon

Atlantic salmon (Salmo salar) were once thick in the rivers of the Northeast. They thrived in rivers from the Delaware north including the Passaic, Hudson, Connecticut and Charles, all of which were salmon streams in the eighteenth century. Then progress and industrialization came, and with it the pollution which killed off the salmon in river after river. By the end of the nineteenth century no major river had salmon. The twentieth century completed the eviction, for salmon were chased from minor streams until today they are present in only 7 rivers in the United States. These rivers are all in Maine, but even there fishing is spotty. The serious salmon angler should go to the northeastern Canadian provinces.

The Atlantic salmon cannot live in even minutely polluted water, and raw sewage and industrial waste have proven too much for him in our country. Add to that the new dams that cut him from his spawning water, and it is not hard to understand the loss of one of our finest sports fish. The state of Maine is now desperately trying to save and propagate the species.

Atlantic salmon are really tremendous fish, going to a record of 79 pounds 2 ounces. Forty-pounders are not uncommon in good salmon waters, and it doesn't take much to imagine how a 40-pound hellion that can jump up and over 10-foot waterfalls will act on a 4-ounce fly rod. Battles with the fish regularly last 3 hours, for it is never caught, but beaten. A salmon is through fighting only after he is half dead and is lying on his side too exhausted to move.

Atlantic salmon go to fresh water to spawn. The young fish migrate to sea when they are 4 to 8 inches in length. There they feed heavily and grow quickly. The next year the fish could weigh 2 to 5 pounds and be ready to join a spawning run up-river. Spawning runs into fresh water start as soon as the ice is out, and some fish come in. These will stay in the bays, rivers and brackish water for a time, but by the middle of June they will have made their way to the salmon holes in fresh water. Other fish come out of the sea and join them from time to time, and runs generally follow high water. The fish actually spawn in the fall, and the early fall run is usually a good one.

When the fish are in fresh water they are taken only by work-ing salmon flies over their heads. This is a rule of nature and law, for actually the fish are not feeding here, so the fly must annoy them into striking. Sometimes 50 to 100 to 1,000 casts are made over a pool without a strike. Other times a fly is re-peatedly floated over a fish, only to have him slowly move away. When a salmon comes up at a fly, hit slowly and easily, give him plenty of time to take the fly before setting the hook. When he is on, get ready for action!

Sometimes fights cover half a mile of stream, because anglers often walk a fish to slow the runs. The fish has to be guided away from any obstructions or rapids, where he can get leverage and tear the hook from his soft mouth. With this fish it's no simple job to change his direction, because he is as stubborn as he is strong. When the fish is beaten he is landed in a huge net, large enough to hold top-size salmon.

Equipment usually consists of hollow glass fly rods 8 to 9 feet in length weighing 4 to 5 ounces and using floating tapered line. Bright-colored flies are tied on No. 4 to No. 6 hooks. Some popu-lar fly patterns include the Parmacheene, Golden Witch, Super-visor or the Gray Ghost. Patterns number in the hundreds, and any good down-East tackle shop will have all the specials.

The beautiful Atlantic salmon is recognized as a prize wherever he runs, from Scandinavia, where fishermen pay high premiums for the privilege of leasing salmon holes to northeastern North America, where he is considered the top sports fish.

King Salmon

The Chinook (Oncorhynchus tschawytscha) is the king of the western salmon, sometimes growing bigger than the legendary 100 pounds. This is a fish with the power to ascend rapids few other fish could survive descending; a fish that can hurl his 50 pounds plus through the air to jump over 7-foot waterfalls; a fish that can cut up schools of bait fish like a canning operation. This is the sports fish that is called the terror of the Pacific Coast.

The Chinook or king salmon is a native of the Pacific. It is found from Monterey, California, north all along the coasts of California, Oregon, Washington, British Columbia and Alaska. He is also eagerly sought in the streams of Siberia and northern Japan during spawning runs.

The salmon has its complete cycle of life very definitely plotted out for it by nature. Life starts early in spring with the hatching of eggs that have been lying alone on the stream bottoms for 2 to 4 months. The parents of the fish have long since died, but nature aids the young fish to remain in the comparative safety of the nests for another month. During this time they live off the pink-colored yolk sac that is attached to their stomach. After the yolk is absorbed, the fish rise and start feeding on the plankton in the water.

Most fish start the trek toward salt water within a few months after hatching, but others stay in fresh water for a year. This first year is most precarious for the young Chinooks, because they are gobbled up by birds and fish whenever they cannot move fast enough to get away. Many die on the run to the sea, for they can be seriously injured in falls over dam spillways, or cut up going through the giant electric turbines. One recently completed study showed a 30 per cent fatality rate for all young fish running through a turbine. Many others die of pollution, since raw human waste and industrial waste are deadly to the fish. Others will die when they run up irrigation ditches that have no escape. Those yearling fish will often be taken by trout anglers, for the salmon will be 7 to 8 inches long and will appear very similar to trout.

The remaining fish work their way down to the base of fresh water, where they pause. At first they take only short cruises into the salt water, until their bodies become accustomed to it, but finally they head out into the ocean, wandering along the coast. At first they use their speed to avoid being eaten, but as they get bigger, they use it more and more for hunting out and killing other fish. The salmon will remain at sea the rest of his life, coming inshore only in quest of bait fish. Sometimes he will even follow schools of herring into fresh water.

Some king salmon reach maturity in only 3 years, but most take 4, and a few take as many as 6 years. When it reaches maturity, this anadromous fish will prepare itself for its last and final run into fresh water for spawning.

A month or two before starting upstream the mature salmon gather at the mouths of the rivers and in the bays. Here they eat fiercely, fattening up and gathering strength for the strenuous run upriver to the spawning grounds. Some mature males will weigh as little as 3 pounds; these are referred to as jack salmon. The average fish will weigh 15 to 25 pounds, but some affectionately referred to as sockdolagers weigh over 50 pounds. One netted at Petersburg, Alaska, weighed 126 pounds, and a 92-pounder was taken by a sports fisherman in the Skeena River in British Columbia.

The color of the fish begins to change, and he turns a dark red that on some fish appears muddy or even black. His jaws show signs of becoming distorted, and begin to curve, and his teeth grow bigger.

A fascinating homing instinct exists in salmon, who return to spawning the stream where they were born. Tests have proven that some fish enter wrong tributaries to spawn, but few fish are known to run up wrong rivers. When artificial propagation of salmon first started, there was some concern about where the fish would go on their spawning runs, but it was soon found that they returned to the water where they were planted. How the fish do this, no one knows.

There are two upstream runs of salmon, one in spring and one in fall. The spring run will go to the spawning waters and remain there through the summer before spawning in the fall, while the late run spawns on arrival.

When the kings move upstream they slip past commercial nets, past an assortment of hooks and lures, past rapids and up the fish ladders around the new dams that have been built. This is an exhausting trip run against some of the stiffest currents in the world, but at last they arrive at the breeding rivers, which could be as much as 1,000 miles from the sea. The good summer fishing is done hundreds of miles from salt water in the Snake and Salmon rivers of Idaho.

Once spawning begins, females rest their bodies on the gravel beds of the streams and by wriggling and moving furiously they dig a craterlike nest. The eggs are laid, and a nearby male will fertilize them. Then they are carefully covered with gravel by the female. A Chinook will lay from 3,000 to 12,000 eggs a year during the time of spawning. Each batch of eggs is carefully covered, because some trout are in these waters and they are always ready to feast on salmon eggs. When all the eggs are laid the fish will still stand guard over her cache for a week or two, but the salmon's strength is gone, and gradually the current drifts the fish downstream where it dies. The carcass of the salmon does not float, for it remains free of gases. Still the meat of the fish is not wasted in the wilds, for fish and the birds will eat it, and animals are always ready to make a meal of it. And so goes the cycle of a king salmon's life.

Salmon fishing starts in the oceans, where trolling of whole herrings or flashing spoons will bring hits. At river mouths and in bays a great deal of fishing takes place. Here a favorite method is mooching, which is done from a small boat that can be anchored at a river outlet or kept moving. A plug-cut herring, with the head cut off at an angle and with 2 hooks inserted in its body, is used as bait. The herring is let out by the angler and is then alternately moved up from the bottom and sunk to the bottom again in imitation of an injured fish. Some fishermen let it drift freely in the current and tides, which gives it a life-like motion. Still other fishermen troll. Here, stopping and start-ing the boat or changing speed will cause the bait to rise and fall as would an injured herring.

Spin fishing is often done from a small boat that is anchored or drifting. The bait (herring or anchovy) is left to drift away from the boat, and the fisherman relaxes until a hit tells him there is work to be done.

All along the shores of the bays and rivers, jetty men, surf men and river-bank fishermen have a good go at the fish when they are about. Catches are good, and it is no easy job for an angler to land a 25-pound wriggling package of muscle while he is standing at a 50-degree list on slippery, jagged rock. Gaffs or monstrous nets are necessary to land a king salmon. Some men used to put a bullet or two into the head of a big one to make landing easier.

In the rivers the fish are the targets for thousand of anglers. Small skiffs are available everywhere, and boats can often be seen anchored side by side strung out across a whole river. Tackle varies because of the different natural state of the rivers. On rivers like the Willamette where currents are extremely fast, sinkers weighing a pound or more are required, and tackle has to be scaled accordingly. King-salmon fishing is generally done with tackle capable of handling a minimum of 200 yards of 15-pound test line. This has to be scaled rapidly upward if:

1. The angler is new at the sport
2. The current is very swift
3. The fishing is in extremely crowded water.

The third point is important, for in some places the fishing is done with boats practically one atop the other; and a 35-pound salmon bullying an 8-pound test line will elicit no friendly comments from the natives.

The spring run of salmon is most important for the inshore fishermen, for the fish are on their way to spawning waters and will stay there all summer. These fish will take salmon eggs which are dropped into the deep holes the fish lie in. They can also be taken on spinners and spoons like a big Daredevil, or a Super-Duper or a Spinner with a big red feather covering a treble hook. Unfortunately Chinook do not hit a fly. They would be ideal fish to take this way.

Salmon running upstream to spawn do not feed. Luckily the fish can still be taken on hook and line, and even the fall run, which is physically ready for spawning, will strike. These fish retain their carnivorous nature; they have lived all their lives by killing, and the urge does not leave them even when they won't eat what they kill. Thus spoons and other flashing hardware will annoy the fish into striking.

The most unspoiled salmon fishing can be done in Alaska, where fishing on the Alaskan Peninsula is phenomenal. Other equally good places are on the Kenai Peninsula and in the straits and rivers of southeastern Alaska. Coos Bay, British Columbia, is famous for them, and in the continental United States the state of Washington has Chinook in Puget Sound, the Skagit River and, of course, the great Columbia, where they run up for hundreds of miles. They also travel up the Snake River, a tributary of the Columbia, and into the Salmon River in Idaho. Oregon hot-spots include the Willamette River and the world-famous Rogue River. California has a good run of fish, too. They enter the Klamath, Eel and Sacramento rivers.

They say a man never forgets the first king salmon he takes. I know I will never forget mine. He was a 29-pound beauty taken in Winchester Bay, Oregon. He hit my line lightly, but before I had him boated he fought me arm-weary. I'm proud of this king just as every angler is who takes one, for the king salmon are sports fish, every pound of them.

Kokanee Salmon

The Kokanee (Oncorhynchus nerka kennerlyi) is the smallest salmon of the Pacific Coast, growing to a maximum weight of 3 or 4 pounds while measuring up to 20 inches in length. The average fish weighs only 1 pound and will be approximately 12 inches in length.

Kokanee are landlocked sockeye salmon, and live in the western lakes. These fish hold to the same basic life pattern as other western salmon. A Kokanee will be born in a stream adjoining a cold, clear lake, and will descend into the lake almost immediately after birth. For four years the lake will be the fish's home, and it will feed there on plankton. This little red salmon serves an important function in the life of these lakes, providing excellent forage for big Mackinaw and kamloops trout. Fishermen find the Kokanee small, but even those who classify him as a pan fish agree that he has a pedigree.

One look at the dark color of the inside of the fish's mouth shows him to be a true salmon. He is silver-colored for three and a half years; then during the summer of his fourth year, he changes to a muddy red or bright reddish-green color. This change is accompanied by increased aggressiveness, as the fish is readying itself for its spawning run. When fall arrives the fish begin to congregate along the shores of lakes and at stream mouths, in preparation for their one and only spawning run, at the end of which they die. A large spawn will be 3,000 to 4,000 eggs.

Fishermen get their best chance for Kokanee during the early fall, when the fish are near shore. These salmon will strike virtually any fly made at this time, and it is never hard to bring home the limit of fish if the schools are milling about. If a lake does not have a suitable stream to run up for spawning, the fish will spawn right in the lake. One such spot is Flathead Lake, Montana, where fish come to the shallow, gravel-bottomed shores for spawning. Fishermen can have a fall heyday here.

Other times of the year the little red salmon are a problem to fishermen, for the fish are neither in shallow water nor in deep water. They prefer the open water of the lakes, staying in a medium depth of 10 to 50 feet. The shore fishermen are fishing too shallow, and the lake-trout fishermen are too deep for them. The fish has one natural protection: if there is a chance to hit a 30-pound kamloops by bottom trolling, who will bother trolling for a 1-pound salmon? Nevertheless, when a salmon school is located, the fish readily hit hooks baited with worms and maggots or even hooks just covered with some red twine— and catching 20 to 30 fish is no problem.

Most salmon are hooked in their final year of life. They are aggressive then and will go after small bait fish, so the fisherman can use a variety of small plugs and spoons to bring hits. Small pieces of bait or bait fish can also be used. Equipment must be very light, for the fish are small. Hooks will be No. 10 to No. 6. Some angling is done by snagging the fish while the Kokanee schools are near shore.

The Kokanee is native to the lakes of British Columbia, Idaho, Oregon and Washington. It has been planted in other areas and is now found in many western states. Some waters with Kokanee include the impoundments of the upper Missouri River in Montana, Lake Pend Oreille, Priest Lake and Island Park Reservoir of Idaho. Wallowa, Davis and Odell lakes of Oregon and Freemont Lake, Baysen Reservior and Crystal Reservoir of Wyoming have the fish, as well as Donner Lake, California, and Lake Tahoe of California and Nevada.

True sockeye salmon are ocean-going fish, and their cycle of life has them spawning in streams with lakes at the headwaters. The young fish spend one year in fresh water before they descend to the ocean, where they live until full maturity. During their fourth year they trek back to the spawning grounds and complete their cycle. The sockeye are not important as a sports fish, for they are seldom caught by anglers, but are a relatively important commercial salmon.

The small Kokanee or the ocean-going sockeye is universally accepted as an excellent eating fish, and many people claim it is the best tasting of all salmon.

Landlocked Salmon (Eastern)

Thirty thousand years ago Atlantic salmon roamed the cold waters of the North Atlantic and came inshore to breed. The area was much colder then, for that was the age of the last great glaciers, and ice extended south beyond New York. The salmon spawned in the streams and lakes at the foot of the glaciers until one time the melting glacier left morain debris at its base, which cut the inshore fish off from the sea.

Many of the trapped young fish lived and died without reproducing, but some did reproduce, and thus began the strain of Atlantic salmon which was to become the modern landlocked salmon (Salmo salar sebago). Another species of landlocked Atlantic salmon also survived, the ouananiche (Salmo salar ouananiche), but these are small and are found only in Canada.

The landlocked fish kept the strong bodies and all the wild, free spirit of the ocean salmon. The only change was that they got stunted because of the adjustment to their new environment's food supply. The biggest landlock ever taken by fishing weighed 22 pounds 8 ounces, and a 35-pounder was taken in a net. The average fish weighs under 5 pounds. Originally the landlocked salmon was found in only a few Maine lakes, including Lake Sebago and Grand Lake, but they are such highly-thought-of sports fish that they have been transplanted to many new areas. Maine has over 80 lakes and rivers with landlock, including the Fish River chain of lakes, Moosehead Lake, Chesuncook Lake and Rangely Lake. Vermont has them in Lake Memphremagog, New Hampshire in the Connecticut Lakes and Lake Winnepesaukee, and New York has some in Schroon Lake and Lake George.

Not all salmon transplantings were successful; in fact, many were not. One famous failure was that at Crystal Lake, Michigan, where smelt were planted as salmon fodder. The salmon failed, and the smelt thrived. Smelt were in turn planted in the Great Lakes, where they are popular little sports fish, while salmon plantings in the Great Lakes also failed. The basic requirement for a successful plant is cold, clear water with a high oxygen content, but even under such conditions there is no guarantee of success.

The fish are pursued all season long by northeastern anglers, who fish them with fly rods in the spring and fall and troll for them in the summer. Each way can be productive if done correctly.

Landlocked-salmon fishing begins as soon as word comes that the ice is out. The fish are on top then, and are in perfect position for the fly-rod enthusiasts. To get one the angler has to realize that these fish are wary, and the fisherman working the bank should be conservative in his motion, always trying for long casts so that he doesn't have to go too close to the fish. They are shy and scare very easily.

This fishing calls for hollow glass rods 8 to 9 feet in length and about 4 ounces in weight. Torpedo line and fine leader with a minimum length of 10 feet are necessary. Generally salmon flies are used. These could include the streamers, Gray Ghost, Green Ghost, Gray Smelt, Warden's Worry or Supervisor. Bucktails such as the Mickey Finn and the red-and-white bucktail are fine producers. Small flies of standard wet and dry patterns also take the fish in clear water, as will spoons ⅛ to ¼ ounce that imitate bait fish.

Spinning is another popular fishing method during spring and fall. The long casts and the low-visibility line are perfect for the fishing required. Lures are generally those that imitate smelt or other bait fish, or spinner-fly combinations will bring hits.

When warm weather begins the fish slip back into the lakes and retreat into the depths, because they like water about 50°. During the summer, fishing methods change completely, and the only way to take the fish is to troll in deep water. Deep trolling lines with heavy sinkers or monel wire are necessary to get down to the fish. A series of deep-trolling, flashing spinners followed by a small one and a bait fish is the standard rig. Bait fish are regularly a smelt or a big minnow, while other times the spinner-streamer fly is trolled. This deep fishing takes much of the fight out of the fish, but it's the only way to take them in the summer, so it is extensively used.

The cold nights of early fall bring a sigh of relief from light-tackle anglers, for they know the landlocked will again be available in shallow waters. The fish are spawning then, and in some areas conservation laws protect them at this time.

Salmon are slow-growing fish, and it takes them 4 to 5 years to reach sexual maturity. They are rare fish found only in the Northeast but fine ones that are avidly pursued by anglers. Any angler who hooks and holds on to a landlocked that is doing 7-foot leaps through the ozone and hard runs over 100 yards in length will know what a sports fish this is.

Silver Salmon

The silver salmon (Oncorhynchus kisutch) is a beautiful sports fish that will bolt at a fly trolled in a bay and will put up a real display of fireworks that can leave an angler breathless. Ten- to 15-pound fish will give any light-tackle man a frantic 15 to 30 minutes' display of speed, runs, leaps and dives that will be hard to contain.

When the fish enter fresh water they do not readily take a fly, but some anglers insist on taking them only with streamer flies. The best fishing is with spoons and spinners. Good takers in the hardware department are silver and brass spoons. Anglers will paint one side of a silver spoon red or use a Daredevil spoon. A good-sized glob of salmon eggs dropped to the bottom of a river is a steady taker. Fish are actually not eating at this time, although they strike gobs of salmon eggs; fish experts say that they are not eating but are actually fighting the bait. In brackish water and in bays, mooching or baiting with a herring or anchovy gets fish.

The silver salmon do not make the thousand-mile trek into fresh water that the king salmon make. They prefer to spawn further downstream in medium-sized streams near the mouths of the main river. Also silvers do not have a spring run of fish that will be available for fishing fun all summer. The silver-salmon runs start in September and continue on through to December in some areas. There is good fishing during the runs, but since the silvers do not go as far upstream and are available for a shorter period of time, fresh-water fishing for them is more limited.

The silver salmon, as his name implies, is a silvery, bluish-colored fish that may have an almost metallic hue on its back. During spawning the fish's appearance change, and they turn a dark reddish color. The jaws of the males are harshly curved, and in some areas the fish are referred to as hookbills.

Most silver salmon live 3 years but a few may go to 5 years. Some males live only 2 years. Young cohoe remain in fresh water a year before they go to sea, and on entering salt water they will be 5 or 6 inches long. The salmon grow gradually at sea until the summer before their sexual maturity, at which time they may well double their weight. It is in the late summer and early fall that fishing gets hectic in the bays and river mouths, for the fish are attacking fiercely. An average spawning fish will weigh 8 pounds, with many being 15 pounds. A few young males weigh only 2 pounds, while the record fish was a 31-pounder from Cowichan Bay, British Columbia.

The best silver-salmon fishing takes place during September in bays such as Coos Bay or Puget Sound. At these times the fish are at the river mouths and can be taken near shore. In some areas the fish have to wait for high water because sandbars block the upstream migrations. This is especially true of some of California's smaller streams such as the Del Norte or the Humboldt.

Most used for silver-salmon fishing are fly rods measuring 8 or 9 feet and weighing 4 to 6 ounces. Spinning rods 8 feet in length holding 6- to 10-pound test line are just as popular. Heavier equipment is needed if there is a good chance of hitting a big Chinook, for it will be twice as big as the average silver.

During river migrations silvers are fished the same way as Chinooks. They are sought by anglers in skiffs, by anglers from the banks and by anglers who stand shoulder to shoulder on the bridges. This is an acrobatic fighter, a high-spirited fish always ready to attack a bait fish—it's a sports fish all the way.

Sauger

The sauger (Stizostedion canadense) has the misfortune to be a smaller relative of the walleye. The sauger also frequents the same water, has the same fighting and eating qualities as the larger fish and is therefore unjustly overlooked in the sports-fishing picture.

The record sauger was a whopping 8-pound 3-ounce fish taken from gigantic Garrison Reservoir in North Dakota. This huge body of fine, cold water allows the fish to grow to a good size. Sauger are found in the waters of Minnesota, Wisconsin and down the valleys of the Mississippi and Ohio rivers. They also live in the Tennessee River and throughout the TVA lakes. They are taken all the way from the Canadian border to the Gulf states, including Florida, Alabama and Texas.

The best time to fish sauger is spring, when they are busy on spawning runs up rivers and creeks and can also be found in the shallows of lakes. They are all over the shore line, and many times an angler will have no trouble taking 50 to 100 fish in a day. After spawning and during other times of the year they make themselves relatively scarce by spreading out and swimming into deeper sections of the lakes. Most of the time they can be found in water 20 feet deep or more.

An average sauger caught is from 12 to 15 inches in length and weighs about a pound. Some sauger are taken weighing several pounds, but many more weigh under a pound. It is the great number of small ones about that arouse the chief complaint against the fish. Sauger have a tendency to overpopulate a lake and cause fish in it to become stunted. This is always a danger in small, enclosed lakes.

Breeding takes place where the female lays her eggs over the shallows of a lake. The males closely behind will fertilize the eggs and then leave them. They will hatch in approximately 2 weeks' time.

The fish that survive will reach a length of 3 to 5 inches in 1 year and reach maturity in 4 years. At maturity they weigh only 1 pound, unless of course, they become stunted, in which case they could be half that weight.

Sauger live on crawfish, larvae, crustaceans, insects and smaller fish. They take live bait, spinner-minnow combinations, an assortment of spinning lures, spinner-fly combinations and small bass plugs. Like the walleye, they will often tear into rubber lures of frogs, worms, tadpoles and other aquatic delicacies.

Equipment calls for light tackle, with monofilament for leader and hook sizes from sizes No. 1 to 3/0.

These small fish make fine food and are scrappy fellows.

Shad

Shad are anadromous, spending their lives in salt water and coming into fresh water only for spawning purposes. They are important sports fish on both coasts, and come into major rivers from Maine to Florida in the East and from Washington to California on the West Coast.

Shad, like so many other fish, are off feed when they come in on spawning runs, so that they have to be cajoled and teased into taking baits and lures. Small red flies with tinsel or red beads are favorite shad lures, and small, fast-moving spoons have proved effective. The West Coast shad regularly take sea worms.

The Connecticut River shad are famous sport in that state. Anglers line up in the springtime to throw out their lures to the fish. The flies are allowed a long float, and many hits are just at the end. Then the hooked shad runs downstream and rips line from the fisherman's reel, putting the unwary angler in trouble. A hot-spot is just below the Enfield Dam.

It is often said that the shad of the Hudson and Delaware rivers are unco-operative and can only be taken in nets. I decided to disprove this, and I set about to write an article telling how to catch Hudson River shad on a hook. I spent 3 whole days on the Croton River, a feeder to the Hudson, fishing in holes crawling with shad. I used every method and tried every lure imaginable. I used all prescribed methods from fishing just below the surface to fishing the bottom. I threw spoons, spinners, dry flies, wet flies, nymphs, beaded flies, streamers, bucktails, wobblers, spinner-fly and spinner-worm combinations, tinseled hooks, hellgrammites and even pieces of liver at them. After the third day I just threw my tackle box, after becoming thoroughly convinced that Hudson River shad do not take a hook.

Other areas have shad that are catchable and give fine sport. Some of the good fishing places include the Susquehanna, Potomac, Chickohoming, James and St. John's rivers. In the more southern areas the shad run in late winter, while in northern areas shad run in the spring.

The shad of the West Coast were introduced in 1871, when they were planted in the Columbia and Sacramento rivers. They took very well there, and are prime forage for big salmon as well as being sports fish in their own right. They are taken in most of the rivers from Monterey Bay north to the sounds of Washington.

There are two kinds of shad, the hickory shad (pomolobus mediocris) and the larger white shad (alosa sapidissima). Males of the species will come into fresh water first, and then will head up to the spawning grounds and await the bigger, ripe females. A female of the white or American shad has weighed up to 20 pounds, but generally an 8-pound fish is large, with most weighing under 5 pounds.

They seem to be an indestructible fish, for neither pollution nor excess fishing has ever slowed up the hordes of fish that come in every year. A single female can deposit up to 150,000 eggs a year and can make 6 or 7 spawning trips in a lifetime. Under perfect conditions this could amount to 1 million offspring from a single female—no wonder the fish are increasing.

Shad are delicious food fish, heavy with rich, white meat, but it is suggested that, because they are bony, they be cut into fillets. Shad roe is, of course, a well-known delicacy that ranks close behind caviar in the epicurean department. Then too, these shad, which are members of the herring family, have the same wild spirit on a hook as do their close relatives, the tarpon and bonefish.

Smelt

Smelt (Osmerus mordax) came to the Great Lakes area as an experiment and were first introduced to Crystal Lake, Michigan, in 1912. They were originally supposed to be forage for some landlocked salmon stocked there. With new fish plantings, success is sensational or failure is complete. The results of the smelt stockings were that the smelt thrived, and the salmon disappeared. Smelt were then put into Lake Michigan, where they did just as well.

Smelt were originally an Atlantic seaboard fish living in both the salt- and the cold fresh-water lakes along the coast. They are now in the Great Lakes and many adjoining lakes of the area. Occasionally smelt population will drop radically in the interior lakes, but to date the little sportster has always proven himself capable of making a strong comeback.

In the springtime anglers get out in the water for the fish and use dip nets to catch them on their spawning run. The fish come into the shallows or run up streams and rivers to their spawning grounds. Anglers wade out and net the 6- to 8-inch fish while they are in the shallows. Night is the best time for dipping. In Chicago the little fish create quite a stir when they are about. Fishermen stand elbow to elbow on the breakwaters along the lake, dropping dip nets or using special nets on trolleylike devices to catch them.

The smelt will grow to a maximum size of approximately 12 inches, and 8 or 10 of them will make an excellent meal for any fish lover.

Sturgeon

During the eighteenth and nineteenth centuries the waters of the West crawled with sturgeon. Indians used them for food and leather, while the white man abused the fish, catching it, milking the roe and then throwing the carcass away. The slaughter was on a level closely akin to the buffalo slaughters. Then, as with all abused natural resources, the sturgeon began to decline, at first slowly, then at a highly accelerated rate until finally they were on the brink of extinction.

About the turn of this century conservation departments started putting the fish under strict protection to save the species. Sturgeon have made somewhat of a comeback, and today there is sports fishing and even some commercial fishing for them. There is no denying the restoration has helped, but the sturgeon is still my No. 1 candidate for eventual extinction. None of the six species of sturgeon found in our country is so plentiful that the ugly head of extinction is far away.

Sturgeon appear to be prehistoric beasts, with snouts for faces and suckerlike mouths with barbels hanging down from them. The really strange thing about sturgeon is the heavy bony plates that give the fish an armor-covered body. This hard body helps protect sturgeon from other fish, but it doesn't protect the fish from his worst enemy—Man.

The Atlantic sturgeon (Acipenser oxrhynchus) comes into the rivers from the Atlantic Ocean or the Gulf of Mexico to breed in the low inland waters. This fish occasionally grows to awesome sizes, with some scaling over 800 pounds. Every once in a great while a river fisherman on the Hudson or Delaware will get a real monster in his shad net. The fish will rip the net to pieces, but if he is taken it is a worthwhile catch, for sturgeon meat draws fancy prices.

Another eastern seaboard sturgeon is the shortnose sturgeon (Acipenser brevirostris). This fish will attain a maximum size of 3 feet and possibly weigh 50 pounds. Pollution has been the prime enemy of these fish, for our country's population is crowded along the East Coast. The rivers here have become too filthy to support the fish, and today eastern seaboard sturgeon are rare.

The shovelnose sturgeon (Scaphirhynchus platorhynchus) is taken in the rivers emptying into the Gulf of Mexico. This fish is in the Mississippi, Brazos, Rio Grande and the other Gulf rivers. The shovelnose feeds on crustaceans. He will take worms and is often taken by catfish fishermen while trotlining. This is one of the smaller species of sturgeon, going only to 8 pounds, with common catches weighing 1 or 2 pounds. Other names for the fish are switchtail, hackleback, flathead sturgeon or sand sturgeon, and in a local area they may be known only by one of these names.

Another Midwestern sturgeon, the pallid sturgeon, (Scaphirhynchus album) is found in the Missouri and Mississippi rivers. This fish may attain a weight of 40 pounds, and is a rare species.

The lake sturgeon (Acipenser fulvescens) was once the most common of Midwestern sturgeon. This fish used to be taken weighing up to 300 pounds and measuring 7 feet in length. The ancient fish lives in the rivers and lakes of the area, for it prefers shallow water where it can grub around the bottom for food. Huge specimens of this species are rare and the fish is fast disappearing. There are several items stacked against the lake sturgeon and each of them contributes to its decline.

This fish, like other sturgeon, is prehistoric, stupid and sluggish. It cannot adapt itself to a changing environment, nor has it even learned that a hook is a danger. The fish is a slow grower, which means that reproduction is slow, because it takes a fish from 15 to 25 years before it reaches maturity and begins reproducing. In this time the fish may weigh 8 pounds and be up to 3 feet long. A 100-pound lake sturgeon would be 50 years old and could live another 50 years if left alone. Nevertheless, slow-growing fish are penalized, for only a minute percentage reach maturity. Another big contribution to the decline of lake sturgeon is the pollution of so much of the water that once supported the fish.

The lake sturgeon, which in some areas is known as rock sturgeon, will spawn in the springtime. They put on quite a show in spawning, for they rile around in shallow water like a tag team of wrestlers. Females let their caviar sink to the bottom, and the males fertilize it.

The fact that the fish are easy to get on a hook hasn't enhanced their hopes for the future. A hook covered with a worm dropped in front of a groping sturgeon invariably brings a hit, and more often than not a landed fish. They are not spectacular fighters; in fact, they often seem to lack any spark for a fight. It seems to me that when on a hook the fish are completely unaware that there is danger involved, for they often follow the line, sheeplike. Spring is the best time to fish for them in the Mississippi and Missouri valleys.

The prize American sturgeon is the white sturgeon (Acipenser transmotanus) of the West Coast. One monster weighed 360 pounds, and it was the biggest fish ever taken in fresh water on sports tackle. This sturgeon was caught in the Snake River, Idaho. In 1959 a fish weighing 320 pounds and 9 feet 7 inches long came out of the Snake River below Swan Falls. Deep-sea angling techniques and deep-sea tackle are needed to boat these monsters. When a fish is hooked, the angler must follow the run of the fish with the boat, so the strain is taken from the tackle.

The area of the Snake River above Lewiston regularly yields sturgeon 6 to 7 feet in length. Fish under 4 feet in length are released by sportsmen here.

This sturgeon is on the decline, too, for the great dams of the Pacific Coast have cut off the fish from his spawning grounds, and industrial pollution has chased it from other rivers. The state of Washington is making a gallant effort to stock the fish in the Columbia and Snake rivers with hopes of propagating the species.

Because fishing for sturgeon varies from 300-pound white sturgeon down to 2-pound shovelnose sturgeon, equipment must be scaled to the expected catch. Out west the need is for heavy-duty, salt-water tackle with 50-pound or better test line, steel leaders and hooks size 10/0. Reels should hold a minimum of 200 yards of line. Midwestern sturgeon can be fished with standard fresh-water rods with medium to stiff action. Line up to 15-pound test is ample, and hooks varying from No. 2 to 4/0 can be used. Actually there is very little sportsfishing for sturgeon, for most of the catches come in commercial fishermen's nets.

It is a shame that this excellent eating fish and source of caviar is disappearing from our country. At least we are not alone, for Russia, the home of caviar, is experiencing the same misfortune. Russia once had sturgeon weighing up to 3,000 pounds, but now fewer and fewer of the big fish are found— the reasons, hydroelectric dams and industrial pollution. Possibly in another 50 years the sturgeon will be a fish of the past for both countries. Let's hope not.

Bluegill

One spring morning I watched a dude take a brand new salt-water rod from the trunk of his mile-long car. He put on a pair of waders (why, I'll never know) and got into a boat. Curiosity made me watch him to see what was next. He tied on a plug that seemed big enough to take whales in the Arctic. He cast away. About the third cast I saw his face grimace, and I could have fallen off the dock, for he brought up a bluegill battling the block-and-foil tackle every inch of the way.

This incident and some others make me feel that bluegill in springtime are just about one of the easiest fish possible to get on a hook. They will jump out of the water for cigarettes, especially filter tips, pieces of wood, or even paper.

Bluegill (Lepomis macrochirus) are all over the shore line during breeding time, which is May and June. Males, identified by their handsome bright orange or yellow chests, are really busy then making nests on the bottom and cleaning the area over gravel. They push the silt and dirt around until a clean crater-type hole is constructed for the nest.

The male is the maker and guardian of the nest, and he coaxes a female into his nest to deposit her eggs. After that the female may swim over to another nest, depositing more eggs for another male. Any male will welcome any ripe female to the nest, and Sigmund Freud might classify these fish as totally happy fish, for they practice free love.

After the female has left a nest the males stand guard over the eggs and later the fry. Any fish coming near the nest to sample some sunfish caviar is soundly attacked by the parent-to-be. The larger predatory fish often take advantage of nesting bluegill and come into the shallows for fine sunfish dinners. Fishermen also make use of spawning time, and fish along the shore lines among the nests. The best and largest catches of sunfish are taken in the springtime.

Water 2 inches to 1 foot deep is all that is required for the nests of the small bluegill and pumpkinseed sunfish. Here nest after nest can be seen in a small area. The bigger bluegill, ½ pound to 2 pounds, make their nest in water from 2 to 4 feet in depth, and an angler searching bluegill will generally find them a short way from shore. Some nests are in marshes or near weed beds, but one thing is sure—if an angler comes upon one nest he should fish that area extensively, because there will be many other nests about. Sometimes there are as many as 75 nests in a radius of no more than 50 feet.

These are prolific fish, with an average female giving 20,000 eggs in a year, and big ones almost doubling that figure. The fact that the fish take care of the eggs and spawn allows a high percentage of fish to survive, and as many as 20,000 fry may come from a single nest. Once bluegill get started in a lake or pond, it isn't long before they are everywhere. An angler should never have the slightest pang about taking them from a spawning nest, for no amount of hook-and-line fishing could ever eliminate bluegill from any lake. They simply reproduce too rapidly.

Fly fishing is productive and fun. One method of fishing is with cheap flies that have plenty of hackle on them, because the fish ruin a good fly quickly. A bass bug, which is a fly tied on a hook with a piece of cork on it, is a producer. This bug is worked just like a regular dry fly, and it is retrieved while in the water. After a cast the bug is permitted to rest, and then a lifting of the rod tip, jerks the bug a few inches and allows it to make ripples on the lake. The bluegill will be watching from below and it will not be long before one will come bursting up out of the water at the bug or fly. The angler never knows what fish will hit a bug next, for a big old bass could come lumbering up at the bug.

The stocking of bluegill and bass together in a lake or pond is known as the Alabama method, for this fine combination was started there. The theory behind this is that young bluegill feed on vegetation and algae, and big bass feed on young bluegill— a perfect combination.

One man tried this perfect combination in his private farm pond but he made one mistake: there was already a supply of mature bass in the lake. Consequently every time he stocked bluegill the bass thought it was feeding time. They simply did not understand the rules of stocking. Small bluegill make fine bass takers, but an angler should study his state's laws *very* carefully to make sure bluegill are not classified as sports fish and are not taboo as bait.

During hot summer months bluegill retreat to water up to 25 feet deep, but they never go into extremely deep water. In the evenings and mornings they can always be taken inshore, and during fall they are in close again until the freeze-up.

Down south where there are no ice problems the bluegill fatten themselves up all year. They are known south of the Mason-Dixon line as bream (pronounced brim), and they are highly thought of as sports fish and edible delights. The record bream came from Ketona Lake, Alabama, and weighed 4 pounds 12 ounces.

Cane-pole fishing is still popular, and small pieces of shrimp, garden worms or crawfish or grasshoppers are productive baits. Lines are thrown out and tip-up floats let the angler know where there is activity at the hook. Hooks should be set so they are riding just off the bottom. When a big bream takes the bait, he will not only pull the tip up, but he will yank it down under the water. These little scrappers average about ½ a pound each, but they will put up such a big fuss that anglers will honestly swear they weigh well over a pound each.

These are really welcome fish to have about, for what angler hasn't said during the hot days of August, "Ah well, let's get some bluegill; at least there we will get action." During this dog weather, fish around weeds, sunken logs and generally in water up to 15 feet deep until you find some; trolling often locates hot-spots.

My favorite piece of equipment for bluegill is the fly rod. A light rod with soft action is fine for bug fishing and fly fishing. As already said, the fish will take flies of almost any pattern, but flies with plenty of hackle will produce best. Streamer flies rarely take fish, for in many instances they represent minnows bigger than the fish generally go after. Flies can be tied on No. 6 to No. 12 hooks or even on smaller ones.

Spinning equipment of the ultralight variety is excellent for bluegill fishing. Ultralight rods weighing only 1 or 2 ounces are perfect for these fish. These can be used with small spinning lures, popper plugs or spinner-worm or spinner-fly combinations. Line for the fish is 2- to 4-pound test unless other game fish are about. Then heavier test line is necessary. Bait-casting rods can be used to advantage too.

A small spinner-worm combination is deadly when worked into bluegill waters. The fish will go after it every time. A worm need not be large; in fact, smaller ones are more productive, for the fish have small mouths and cannot get at a snake-sized worm. This type of lure may be cast and retrieved, or it may be trolled, as is often done in summers. Jigging up and down in bluegill waters with spinner-worms brings in many fish.

Hooks generally used are long shank hooks No. 6 to No. 2 in size. Sinker is generally only a piece of shot or a small clamp sinker. The weight of a small spinner is ample to get the bait down, and in most instances this is the only sinker necessary.

Bluegill (or bream, if you prefer) are pugnacious and battle a line all the way. They are plentiful, never hard to catch and make excellent eating. The next time you come home and tell everyone you took some 2-pound bluegills, you'd better weigh them first. Chances are the fish will weigh under a pound, although they probably will have fought like 5-pounders.

Crappie

If there is an angler who never caught a crappie, I would say he just isn't a fisherman. These plentiful scrappers are found in all the 48 continental states, and millions of American fishermen get their piscatorial delights from them yearly.

There are two kinds of crappie: black crappie (Pomoxis nigromaculatus) and white crappie (Pomoxis annularis). Both are members of the sunfish family. They have spread into all states, since they spawn heavily and are easy to stock. The black crappie females weighing only from 1 to 1½ pounds lay 20,000 to 60,000 eggs a year, while some very big species will give up

160,000 eggs in one springtime. Black crappie average twice as many eggs as white crappie. The male crappie fertilize the eggs in the family nest, which is found along the shore lines. Their habit is to spawn by new weed beds or by rock ledges, with the nests of many families close together in typical sunfish style. The male is keeper of the nest, and many times he has the eggs of several females there. Young fish are cared for by the male parent, and this gives a high percentage of them a chance to get a start in life.

Fishermen find spring spawning of crappie important because the spring season is the easiest time to take the fish. They are easy to find then because they are seldom in water more than 15 feet deep and are often in only 5 feet of water. They are close to shore, and the angler who drops a minnow down into a brood will find that the fish tear into it. Secondly, it is at this time of year the fish are best eating, for their flesh is firm and hard after a winter in cold water.

After the spawning season schools of crappie continue to travel together around lakes and rivers searching for food. Lakes such as Kentucky Lake sometimes have unbelievable numbers of schools swimming about. The schools do not break up until the hot summer sets in, and then they retreat with other fish into deep water. Summertime fishing should be done in water 15 to 25 feet in depth. Fall again finds crappie congregating and actively swarming the shore lines. This keeps up until the winter gets very cold; however, in the South crappie are taken along the shore line all winter.

Crappie are carnivorous, feeding on fish, insects and crustaceans. They have an insatiable appetite and are always ready to grab at a bait that is conveniently close to them. Hot-spots to work a bait for crappie are near sunken brush, logs, fallen trees or sudden drop-offs. Minnows on a hook dunked at the end of a cane pole are a sure-fire, standard method of taking crappie.

Using artificials brings crappie fishing to a fine sportsfishing level. One way to fish is with bucktails that resemble minnows. A gray or white bucktail fly on a No. 4 to No. 6 hook is placed behind a very small spinner. The fly is cast and allowed to sink to the bottom. When it is on the bottom it is pulled in, in a jerky fashion, making it act like a scared minnow in a crappie trap.

A small, narrow strip of pork rind attached to a hook and trailed behind a spinner will take fish. A worm behind a spinner and No. 2 to 2/0 hook is also attractive.

Spinning equipment of the ultralight or light variety is fine for this type of fishing. Daredevil spoons, small Johnson's Silver minnows or other minnow imitators are cast away from a drifting boat. This is continued until a strike is felt which would indicate a school of fish is about. The angler then fishes this place until there are no more strikes, for then he knows the school of fish has moved off. Retrieves of casts should show the fish plenty of action or flutter, for the live-wire crappie are attracted by flash.

Nighttime finds the fish close to shore, sometimes in only a few inches of water. This is the time a dry fly or a bass bug worked along the shore line brings hit after hit. The fisherman often cannot see his fly being hit, but he should have no trouble feeling it; and fish are struck on noise and touch instead of visual contact. Any experienced wet-fly or nymph fisherman will have no trouble at night. Give crappie plenty of time with a fly, for they seldom recognize it is artificial and dangerous. If they want it, they take it.

Topside bass plugs such as Pflueger Baby Scoop can be worked with a spinning rod and bring good action. It is best to stick with smaller plugs for crappie.

Some states have stopped their hatcheries from raising crappie. They have stopped stocking the fish in an attempt to control them, not because they do not want the species in their waters. Crappie are such prolific breeders that many times in captive areas they will take over the lake through their amazing reproductive capacities. This of course, leads to stunting and on several occasions has forced conservation departments to get rid of them so that other fish in the lake could grow to decent size. Once the crappie was found only as far west as Lake Erie, but stocking has been so successful that they are everywhere now.

The record goggle-eye (popular name for white crappie in

the South) weighed 5 pounds 3 ounces and came from Mississippi. A black crappie or calico bass weighing an even 5 pounds came from Santee-Cooper Lake, South Carolina. Three-pound fish are good catches for the average fisherman, and they make a wonderful meal when brought home and put in the frying pan.

This is a good, active fish with plenty of spunk and fight and is a fine sports fish.

Rock Bass

The rock bass (Ambloplites rupestris) has a large mouth, a red eye, a mottled color and is a member of the sunfish family. He is sometimes known by the popular name of northern rock bass, or by goggle-eye, after his red eye.

The fish is primarily a nighttime feeder, staying in water 20 to 40 feet deep during daylight hours. He is a school fish, and hitting one indicates that more are about. He is often found in smallmouth-bass streams and can be taken by the angler in quest of smallmouth.

Rock bass will take small minnows, other bait fish, worms, spinner-minnow or worm combinations. Daytime fishing in lakes calls for trolling baits in fairly deep water, under overhanging banks or near underwater obstructions. Known hot-spots should be still-fished because the fish often stay in their favorite haunts; other times trolling will find migrating schools.

Nighttime fishing, near shoreline, can be done with natural baits including grasshoppers or other bugs. Artificial bass bugs or flies take fish near shore after dark, as will small bass plugs.

Equipment can be standard light tackle, and hooks are generally No. 4 to 2/0.

The rock bass spawns in typical sunfish fashion, except that his nests are widely separated and poorly constructed. He is a small fish, going only to 10 to 12 inches and weighing about 1 pound at maturity. It ranges throughout the Midwest from Canada to the Gulf and provides good sport on light tackle for anglers of this area.

Warmouth Bass

The warmouth bass (Chaenobryttus coronarius) is a popular southern favorite that ranks right up there with crappie and bluegill. Throughout Alabama, Georgia and Florida this big member of the sunfish family is considered a prize catch. The fish is easily recognized by his large mouth and red eye and is another fish often called red-eye or goggle-eye. His color is green, and he has reddish bars and other colors on his sides. His belly is yellowish.

The warmouth bass, or warmouth perch as he is sometimes called, frequents warm, muddy, slow-moving water. A good place to look for him would be around cypress trees and in heavily vegetated water, because he spends much of his time in weeds.

The fish is carnivorous and is even a more vicious battler than the bluegill. Many anglers consider his fight to be even harder than that of a bass of equal size. He hits live baits such as minnows and worms, and puts up a gallant scrap on light tackle. Flies or bass bugs floated above him can also be used to get him on a hook.

Light tackle of your favorite type and hooks No. 2 to 2/0 are fine for warmouth. It grows to a size of about 10 inches and adults weigh about a pound. The fish is found from New Jersey south, throughout the southern portion of the Midwest, and has been successfully introduced on the Pacific Coast. His flesh is edible, but the most outstanding thing about the warmouth is his scrap, and that is what we sportsmen are looking for.

Brook Trout

The story of stream fishing in America is the story of brook trout (Salvelinus fontinalis). These fine sports fish are found in cold-water streams throughout the country. They are native to the East Coast from Maine to Georgia and were found as far west as the Midwest. Anglers here loved them, and they lost no time in transporting the fish to other areas. By the beginning of the twentieth century they were firmly established through-out the Rocky Mountains. The squaretails took to these cold, clear mountain streams as though they were havens created especially for them. They thrived to such a degree that in some areas within a few years the problem of overpopulation and stunting became acute.

During this same period many places in the Northeast had a different experience with brook trout, for the fish was destroyed and depleted near cities. Today fishing near Boston, New York, Buffalo, Baltimore and Washington is done only for bathtub fish. These are brook trout that have been reared to maturity in a hatchery and then are dumped into streams near cities so local anglers can pull them out. These fish are dumped in waters that have long since been unable to support native fish, for they have been ruined by pollution and increased water temperatures that resulted when native timber was cut down for factories and houses. Brookies cannot survive in water that goes over 65° for any period of time. Therefore they die in city streams, which heat up like Turkish baths in the summers.

One could almost look at any map and with only a few facts should have no trouble pointing out good spots for brook-trout fishing. The angler should note the warm states and densely populated areas as places to avoid. Then if he can find mountain streams on the map, he should have good brookie waters. Generally brook trout and people do not get along well, so the more sparsely the area is populated, the better the fishing will be.

Mr. Squaretail is not a sophisticated fish like the brown trout, and he never inspects a fly with microscopic precision before striking. If he is in a mood to hit, he will smash it with carefree abandon. Out west where it's considered proper to fish 2 or 3 flies on a rig, doubles and triples are not at all uncommon.

It has been proved that brook trout as well as other fish can see colors—especially bright colors like red and yellow—and brightly colored flies are a brookie's undoing. He goes for patterns such as the Royal Coachman, Parmechene Belle, Montreal Grizzly King and other bright flies. These can be size No. 6 to No. 8 and in very clear water hook sizes go down to a No. 12.

Seldom are the No. 18 to No. 20 microscopic size flies necessary.

Fly fishing for brook trout is about as fine a sport as there is. The methods of fly fishing vary greatly according to terrain. On a very small stream the fly fisherman may have great difficulty trying to cast, because on many occasions back casts are impossible. On small streams fly fishing is not eliminated, because there are fish still sitting under the underbrush ready to pounce on any fly that floats by. Sometimes there may be room for a bow cast. Then the angler merely bends the rod like a bow and lets the fly shoot out under the underbrush to a particular strip of water. Many times even this luxury is forbidden.

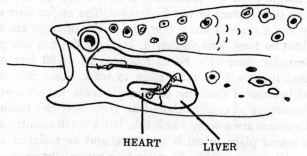

HEART   LIVER

Dangers of live-bait fishing for trout. Note that the deeply swallowed hook is lodged in the trout's vital organs. This leads to certain death even if the fish is released.

Most fishermen would pass up a spot too heavily vegetated and head for a stretch of open water; but it is an isolated place like this that affords the best fishing. This is especially true on streams closest to population centers, because here the densely thicketed wooded section of streams gives the best chance for trout. This is because these sections get surprisingly little fishing pressure. Take any 10 anglers working a stream, and 9 will move from one easily accessible hole to another, hardly ever pausing at rough places. The tenth angler will stop at outlandish spots, and he will be the best fish-catcher of that group. Fish know top cover gives them safety, and they go there to be protected or to stay cool.

Heavily thicketed streams are easiest to fish downstream, because without casting room it is virtually impossible to cast a fly upstream. Still it pays to try to work just upstream, for the fish face upstream and by coming in behind them the angler is not likely to spook them. One way to work upstream is by leap-frogging from one spot to another and actually leaving the stream when moving to the next location. The angler can steal quietly and slowly to the stream's edge. He should try to remain hidden, for many times he can take fish right at his feet if he is still enough. After the immediate area is fished he may let his fly work downstream in wet-fly fashion. The angler now moves his fly like a nervous water bug, and if the brookies are taking they lose no time pouncing on it. Hooking the fish can pose a problem, for there may be as much as 20 or 30 feet of line out, and there will be little room to work. Some fish will be missed because of slack line or entanglements, but with practice the percentage of catches should be good. Brookies taken from small streams are usually small fish, but a small country stream is the surest place to catch the limit, and an unfished section of a small stream within 50 miles of a major city provides the only opportunity to take a native in these areas.

Larger streams with open casting room make fishing more comfortable. Here the fisherman's immediate job is to locate the fish. Brook trout, contrary to popular belief, do not stay in the middle of a current ready to pounce on food. It would be impossible for a fish to buck the main current for any length of time, for the energy needed to swim against this water power is beyond the strength of any fish. The fish lie behind boulders or rocks, or on the bottom in the quiet water that may be in the vacuum behind a submerged rock. A hot-spot in a stream will be wherever the current slows up, and this could be at the base of a waterfall or at a sharp bend in the stream. The fish will stay under a bank or behind some obstruction that slows the water up. Man-made dams, beaver dams and natural pools make good brook-trout hot-spots, and the best fact of all is that there are more fish where the first one came from, because these fish tend to school loosely.

An angler picks up trout by working a fly to the waiting fish. The best way to work dry flies is to cast upstream and then allow the fly to float back to the fish. It is important to keep slack out of the line, for slack gives the fish a chance to spit out the hook. When a fish takes a fly he holds it loosely in his mouth, and the instant he knows it is not real he spits to get rid of it. That instant while the fly is in the fish's mouth, you need only move the fly a fraction of an inch to imbed it in the brookie's paper-soft mouth. The slightest twitch of the rod tip will do. A correctly hooked trout will have the fly imbedded in the corner of his mouth. Sometimes while brookies are hitting aggressively, hooking is no problem, for they hook themselves.

Many times the squaretails will be fly-feeding but will not be making even a hint of a ripple. At these times they are underneath, taking the drowned flies and aquatic insects carried in by the water. Wet-fly fishing using the same bright fly patterns is worth a try on every brookie trip. Wet-fly fishing is best done across and downstream. As the fly floats through the water, twitch it by moving the rod tip. A piece of shot added 6 to 12 inches in front of the fly is sometimes necessary to get the bug deep enough in the water.

If the fish are sulking, the angler might well try nymphs. This procedure is like moving the mountain to Mohammed, for sulking fish are usually on the bottom and have to be fished there. Fishing a drab nymph is not as exciting as watching a fish take off through the air after a fly, but nevertheless it is productive. Before starting, it may be wise for an angler to turn over a few rocks to see the size and shape of the nymphs present, and then try to match these from his fly box. An autopsy of a caught trout, of course, quickly reveals the day's meal and an angler should learn to recognize the nymphs of caddis flies, May flies and two-winged flies.

Proper procedure is to fish upstream about a quarter-turn and let the nymph float down, not bothering it as it bounces past you. When it gets past, start twitching it in wet-fly style, giving it added life. Nymphs will have to be fished right at the bottom; therefore, a piece of shot is necessary for weight except in the laziest streams. It is hard to recognize a hit; therefore, I suggest that the rod tip be raised gently on every suspicion. Many times a sinker bouncing off a rock will feel like a hit, but the angler will also bring in his share of fish that have been hooked right at the edge of the upper lip.

Sometimes brookies will seem to want no fly at all, but before giving up the angler might try a small black gnat. A small spiker on an 18 to 20 hook may help on other occasions.

When brook trout reach 12 to 15 inches in size, they begin to change their basic diet from aquatic insects to small fish. These big fish-feeding trout can be taken with streamer flies that are worked into the big holes. Streamers are fished to imitate a minnow. They should be moved in short jerks, like a minnow nervously changing positions. Streamers can also be trolled through lakes, and the big-lake residents of the brook-trout species may boil into one.

Brookies will take bait fish eagerly, and a small spinner in front of a minnow that is floated in front of a brookie will bring a fast hit. Rigged bait fish can be fished dead or alive, but the angler using dead ones should try to give them lifelike motion to attract the fish. A spoon which looks like some kind of bait fish flashing through the water is a good attraction for the brookie.

Other natural baits for brookies include hellgrammites, grasshoppers, live nymphs, crickets, salmon eggs and small frogs. All of these are generally floated down and permitted to swirl into the holes. The fisherman shouldn't give the fish too much chance to play with the soft baits, for trout can be good bait thieves. A quick movement of the rod tip at the feel of a strike is the surest way to hook them.

The worm is the one bait that comes before all others in taking brookies. Trout will strike any time of year when a worm is floated in front of them. The best worms are those with plenty of wiggle. They should be hooked loosely and be allowed to float down to the trout. The fish will hit them in a matter of seconds, and they will continue to hit as long as they are not spooked. The only problem with worm fishing is that small fish will many times get to the worm first. The best way to avoid this is to get down into the deep holes directly to the big fish, thus bypassing the small ones. Worms should be fished on No. 6 hooks, which are small enough to hook a fish and still are plenty large enough to hold a worm. Worms can be fished with fly rods or spinning equipment, but the most important thing is to keep the rods light. Worm fishing is not highly thought of by fly purists; still, none deny it is productive.

Sometimes an angler may be fishing, and suddenly the water will get cloudy. This cloudiness could be caused by a local storm or some man-made disturbance upstream, but nonetheless it is a signal to switch to some highly visible lures. This has happened to me several times, and in each instance I took fish with spinners and streamers. Once it happened during a heat spell in August, and I was still able to take 4 fast brookies.

Brook trout are easily planted, and they generally take well if the water is cold enough. But although it is easy to get brook-trout waters going, it is just as easy to ruin them, too. I knew of a small but wonderful brook-trout lake tucked away from the beaten trail in the Adirondack Mountains. It was over a mile walk from the nearest road, so not too many people knew about it. Every time we went there we could count on getting our limit of fish.

One summer we came, and to our surprise we caught nothing. At first this was hard to believe, but on a return trip my friend took two pickerel, and it all became clear to us. Someone had indiscriminantly fished the lake with young fish so he could hook into the trout. He wasn't careful in his selection of minnows and must have thrown the unused ones into the lake—thus a lake that only a short time before had contained only trout soon had pickerel and carp. This angler, whoever he was, committed an unpardonable crime—he ruined a trout lake by simple care-lessness. Thousands of trout lakes have been ruined by such carelessness, and jail sentences would be too lenient for the culprits. Never release fish of unknown origin in any lake, especially a trout lake, because such lakes are hard to come by and easy to ruin. This lake did keep some of its brookies, but it was never the same Shangri-La again.

The brook trout is an all-year fish. He is generally the first fish to surface feed actively in spring, and he will continue feeding all season. During summers he still feeds, but he looks for cool places such as spring outlets in lakes and headwaters of streams. He remains active through breeding time in the fall and only slows up in the ice cold of winter.

The fish spawn in regular trout fashion by building nests in the gravel. The male then turns a dramatic crimson. A female will deposit between 500 to 2,500 eggs a year which will hatch in about 2 months.

Some brook trout of the Northeast run into the ocean for part of the year and then return, bigger and fatter. All of them have strong migratory habits. They will go up- or down-stream depending on their desires. The average trout will weigh up to 3 pounds, with a big one being a 5-pounder. The biggest ever taken was a 14-pound 8-ounce fish from the Nipigon River, Ontario—a record that is now almost 50 years old. Even though fish that approach this record size are seldom caught, they all are good scrappy sports fish. Even the small 10-inchers are scrappy, and in a frying pan these cold-water fish have no peers. They are all-around fine fish. Best of all, they can be taken in almost any cold-water stream in the country.

Brown Trout

The brown trout (Salmo trutta) is as wary a fish as swims in any water. It has thrived for centuries in the streams of Central Europe, where it has learned to be suspicious of anything that comes near it.

The brown trout, who were introduced to the United States near the end of the nineteenth century, like all immigrants, were not acceptable in polite circles at first. In fact they were blamed for the disappearance of brook trout in the East. Although it was the increase in cities and population, and industrialization and pollution, that were responsible, because brown trout were new and were known to have cannibalistic habits, they were blamed. The brown trout, with a history of survival in civilization, took to warmer water much better, and thrived as the brook trout faded. Fishermen didn't like the browns for several other reasons. They were harder to catch, and they fought less spectacularly under the surface. They were looked upon the way Dolly Varden still are in some areas.

The German brown trout was the first to be introduced here, and later the Loch Leven trout of Scotland was added to American waters. These fish were almost identical and soon crossed into the modern brown trout. Gradually they were upgraded, for Scot anglers taught us how to catch them, and they soon gained a following.

During my tour of duty with the army of occupation in Germany, I constantly fished the streams not many kilometers from Heidelberg. Here I had 1 solid year of fishing for brown trout, and in that time learned their habits intimately.

These streams of Germany were unbelievably filled with fish, for there had been no fishing at all during the war years. The fish were here, but we had no equipment, and this infuriated us. Finally a friend and I managed to appropriate two bamboo fly rods and some line. Leader was impossible to get, but we discovered that violin strings were made of gut and we dissected one. This was tied together into some of the finest ¾-pound test leader ever used.

Flies were not only scarce—they were impossible to get. The only ones available were the few sent us from the States. None of us had landing nets, either; therefore, we learned to pick the fish up out of the water with our bare hands. This meant many lost fish until our skill increased, and virtually all fish were landed safely. We landed them by putting our hand over the trout's back and into his gill and slipping one finger over his mouth to tighten the hold. This way he was lifted up without further fuss. The fish was handled gently but firmly, and I'm sure those we released were handled far less than many which are netted and mauled.

What I remember most clearly is that we fished without waders. Instead we donned sneakers. When we waded into the cold water we took a deep breath, stepped, and waited for a kind of numbness to take over; after that it wasn't too bad. Many years later I was caught on a Montana stream without waders, and I tried that stunt again; but within a minute I almost froze to death and hotfooted it out of that water. It was harsh, but it proved to me that Montana trout live in much colder water than Central European brown trout.

I fished 4 or 5 times a week, and I really came to know the browns. After a while I could gauge by a few looks at the stream just how well we would do on a particular day. It was simple, because we just looked at some of the big pools, and if the fish were rising or if the big ones were making some big lazy ripples on the surface, then all the fish were feeding. I found the fish of the States have the same characteristics.

At first brown trout frustrated me, too. I was fishing in water that had them up to a yard long, but for a long time I could never get the big ones. Little ones were easy to catch, for it simply meant dropping a fly into a ripple and whacko—there would be a short, fast strike and a 6- to 8-inch brownie would be battling the line. These small fish were never fussy about what fly patterns they hit, for we caught them on Light or Dark Cahills, Coachmen, Dark and Light Hendricksons, Black Gnats and some other unidentified local patterns I wasn't familiar with. I even took a few small ones on flies I tied myself, and the fact that fish hit those early flies I made would certainly indicate their willingness to hit anything that vaguely resembles a fly.

Those big lunkers measuring 20 to 30 inches in length would stay in the deep pools, and we could sometimes see them feeding on top. Brown trout over 15 inches in length generally become minnow feeders and cannibals, but they never really lose their appetite for bugs and aquatic insects; therefore, they can always be taken on a properly presented fly.

The lunkers would leave wide-rolling ripples whenever they lazily broke the surface for a fly. We fished them by wading into the water about waist high to chest high; then we would start working a fly over an area in front of us. We would work upstream, across stream and finally downstream. Our selection of flies depended upon whether the fish were near the top or were feeding under the fine surface. If they were on top we dry-fly fished, and we kept the fly on top or just an inch or two below the surface. For wet-fly fishing the fly was brought down very deep, and many times we attached a piece of shot in front of the fly to insure a deep sweep for the fish.

We never fished with nymphs over there but we fished our wet flies in a nymph-like manner quite often. The results were the same—those tiny hits that were virtually impossible to be sure of. This was trying fishing, and it wasn't too successful until we learned to tighten up line on any slight touch. Later I fished nymphs in the same manner and found them good brown-trout takers for the alert fisherman. Some patterns that will take brown trout include Stone Fly Nymph, Green Drake, Dark Hendrickson and Gray Fox.

These brown trout were as wary as a minnow in a bass nest. It always seemed we could cast almost to where the big fish were feeding and needed just one more step to reach them. I soon learned that if I took that additional step it was no trout, for they would instantly stop feeding. This meant that I had to get more practice fly fishing to enable me to squeeze that necessary 1 or 2 more yards out of the fly. This wasn't as easy as it sounds, because we were using that miserable low-test (¾-pound) violin-string leader. Dozens of times when I tried for that little extra distance I'd hear a snap on my back cast, and I knew immediately that another fly had snapped off the line. Gradually I became very skilled on the fore cast and back cast. As I think back I realize this was the best training in fly fishing I could ever have received, for I learned to float a fly anywhere with the softness of the evening breeze.

When I mastered fly fishing to a degree I never dreamed possible, I began to get strikes from some of these lunkers. Then the leader presented another problem, for holding onto a 5-pound brown trout that can exert at least 25 pounds of pressure against the line that tested out less than a pound, tests an angler to his limit. Each run of the fish had to be braked apologetically, allowing him to bully the line. Then, if he pulled into fast water, we scampered along with him, trying to lead him in gradually but surely, never giving 1 ounce of slack, for with such low-test equipment slack was fatal. We learned to hold the fish too, and by the time we did manage to obtain some store-bought leader, we were sorry to see the homemade equipment go.

Under no circumstances should an angler think big brown trout are restricted exclusively to the deep lazy pools and never enter fast water. True, they are not in fast water 98 per cent of the time, but when they do come into rapids, they can give an angler some of the best fishing he will ever have.

I recall one day my friend and I fished with only mediocre success, and a lightning storm closed in on us. We packed up to go home, and while backtracking on the stream we passed the fastest section of water. Our eyes almost popped out of our heads when we saw several big brownies leaping out of the water like salmon on a spawning run. Lightning or no lightning, we assembled our rods in record time, and on my first cast my rod almost jumped out of my hand as the fish hit my fly. I fought in a 25-inch brownie, added a 23-inch fish and finally finished the hat trick with a 26½-inch fish—then it was over. My friend had done just as well, too. These fish had come into the fast water for the swarms of flies that had been pushed there by the rain, and they were feeding like gluttons. This doesn't happen often, but the mere fact that it does happen makes it worthwhile to be on the alert, because when it happens to an angler he will never forget it.

The brown can also be taken on small spoons. We found those about 1 to 1½ inches in length were fine. My favorite was a small red-and-white peppermint-striped spoon, while my fishing buddy swore by a slight silver-and-gold-plated one. These could be worked through the ripples and fast water for fish of average size, or they could be worked laboriously in the deep pools in an effort to entice some big fish to take them. My luck with spoons has always been good, and both here and in Germany I've never failed to take my share of brown trout with them. The fish attack one of these spoons as they attack a minnow—they hit with a crisp, sharp smash, ready to swallow the meal.

Our duties for Uncle Sam took up many of our days, and we couldn't get out to the stream until dusk. This was some of the best fishing I had, for I would go to one of the bigger, better holes and station myself there. I would maneuver myself into the exact position so that I could easily reach the spot where the big ones were. Sometimes I'd put a small piece of tape on my line at the exact point where I would reach the fish. On occasion I had as many as 3 small bits of tape on the line, each one measuring the distance from where I was standing to a particularly good spot.

I found it wasn't worthwhile to move around a lot on a stream in the evenings, for I stumbled about too much. I didn't care for moving about even with a flashlight, and jacking fish wasn't my sport. Also, wading a stream actively at night isn't fun, and I don't recommend it.

Brown trout are basically night feeders, and I could hear them smacking up out of the water. When they fell back in, they sounded like a brick wall collapsing. Sometimes they would jump to within a few feet of me, for they seem to throw caution to the winds at night, probably thinking the cover of darkness their safety. It is never an easy job to hook a striking fish at night, for the strikes cannot be seen. Two things aid an angler: (1) sounds carry very well, and many times the sound of a breaking fish is enough to tell the angler to strike the line; and (2) the fish hit much harder at night, and they hook themselves easier. Holding the hooked fish is another problem, for after dark the fish can see, while the fisherman stumbles blindly. With this advantage the brown trout gives an angler an awfully rough time. Sometimes though, when the moon is full on a warm summer night and the fish hit, it's sport hard to match anywhere. At night, use flies with plenty of tackle and feathers, for they are easier for the fish to see.

I very seldom fish for brown trout with live baits, for I enjoy the challenge of trying for them with flies or spinners. However, I see nothing wrong with them, and some of my fishing buddies have had remarkable results with worms. They use either big night crawlers or the small, active wiggle worms. These are fished downstream and permitted to work into the holes and along cuts in banks. They are often fished with a shot added so the package will take down deep to where the fish are sitting. Other natural baits used include salmon eggs, hellgrammites, June-bug grub and a host of insect baits. Rubber artificials of these baits will take fish as readily as the real baits.

Live minnows trolled through lakes with the big brownies are fine fish takers. It is wise to use rather large minnows, for big browns like big baits and are known to swallow fish as big as a yearling trout. Chubs up to seven inches in length are fine meals for big ones. Spinners in front of the baitfish are sometimes added as an extra attraction. Live or artificial frogs will get browns to a hook in a hurry.

Brown-trout fishing, like most fishing, is best in the spring and fall. During springtime when the big hatches of insects start coming out, browns may get very active for a few weeks, but as warmer weather approaches they slow up. During the heat of July and August, early mornings, evenings and nights may be the only time to fish, for during the day the browns are virtually asleep and nothing interests them. In the fall they construct saucer-shaped beds to breed in. One female lays between 200 to 6,000 eggs, depending upon her size. Eggs will hatch in 2 to 3 weeks, varying with water temperatures. The fish are active feeders during breeding time and can be taken where the law permits.

Some tackle recommendations for brown trout: start with light fly rods 3¾ to 4¾ ounces that measure 8 to 9 feet in length. I like the long fly rods so that I can get the extra distance in working a fly. Torpedo lines and tapered leader up to 12 feet should be used in clear, low water. Hooks are No. 8 to No. 4, while fly sizes vary from No. 18 all the way down to No. 4. An average fly would be tied on a No. 8 hook. Light spinning rods also make good brown-trout rods if live bait or lures are used.

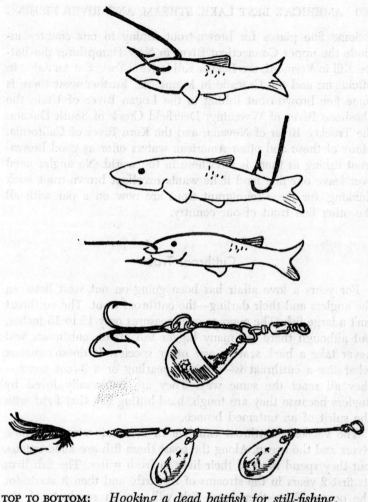

TOP TO BOTTOM: *Hooking a dead baitfish for still-fishing.*
Hooking a live baitfish for natural swimming.
Often used while still-fishing with live bait.
Hookup for trolling. Hook may also be inserted through lower lip first.
A Colorado spinner. Good for trout.
An Indiana spinner and fly. Good for trout, bass, walleye, perch, etc.

Some fine places for brown-trout fishing in our country include the upper Connecticut River in New Hampshire; the Batten Kill in Vermont; the Beaver Kill in New York; the Au Sable in Michigan; and the Cascade in Minnesota. Further west there is some fine brown-trout fishing in the Logan River of Utah; the Shoshone River of Wyoming; Deerfield Creek of South Dakota; the Truckee River of Nevada; and the Kern River of California. Many of these and other American waters offer as good brown-trout fishing as there is anywhere in the world. No angler need ever leave our fine land if he wants excellent brown-trout hook dunking, for these immigrant trout are now on a par with all the other fine trout of our country.

Cutthroat Trout

For years a love affair has been going on out west between the anglers and their darling—the cutthroat trout. The cutthroat isn't a large fish. The average one measures only 12 to 15 inches, but although there are many bigger fish about, cutthroats will never take a back seat to any other species. It doesn't matter what size a cutthroat is—a 6-inch yearling or a 3-foot terror—they all react the same way. They are universally loved by anglers because they are tough, hard-hitting fish that fight with the spirit of an untamed bronco.

The versatile cutthroat can live in mountain streams, lakes, rivers and the ocean. Along the coast these fish are anadromous, but they spend most of their lives in fresh water. The fish lives its first 2 years in the streams of its birth, and then it starts for the ocean. Even then some fish will remain residents of the streams all their lives. The majority of the fish that go into the ocean never seem to make up their minds to stay there, for they will be in and out of brackish water regularly. The cutthroat will leave the ocean within 1 year and come back to the streams to breed. The short stay in salt water is the apparent reason they weigh only 2 to 4 pounds at maturity, while steelhead weigh twice that much. If the fish had stayed longer in the ocean, where there is plenty of food, they would return as bigger fish.

The fish are considered spring breeders, but they may breed anywhere from December to March depending upon the fish and the area. Many of the fish returning from the ocean will breed only once, but others are known to have bred 3 or 4 times. There seems to be no general rule as to the times they breed except that the long, hard treks upstream exhaust the fish and consequently cause many fatalities. Inland fish live much the same lives as their sea-going counterparts; they leave the lakes and head into streams for breeding when the season is upon them.

Cutthroat are taken regularly in the ocean and bays and in brackish water. They come into the western bays after the salmon rush and they are available in Puget Sound after the spring salmon run and again after the fall run. Peak fishing in Oregon and Washington is in September and October. Fish are caught by trolling streamer-flies or small herring or silver spoons. It is not necessary to fish deep, for cutthroat cruise at shallow depths.

The fish continue to take the hook on their fresh-water migrations and anglers try them with flies, lures or baits. Cutthroat fishing methods are similar to steelhead. A favorite natural bait for these fish is the salmon egg, which is drifted down to the fish. A good time for them along the coast is in April and May, when the fish return to the sea after their spawn.

Resident fish and the mountain fish are taken by fly fishing in the streams. They readily take wet flies and patterns that imitate a May fly, caddis, stone fly or beetle.

There are many anglers who reverently remember old blackspot because he was the first trout they ever caught. There is reason for this, because cutthroat are less shy than other species of trout. When an angler approaches a hole of feeding trout he may spook them easily enough, but even then they swim away more in annoyance at being disturbed than in fear of the fisherman. This small extra margin is all a fledgling angler may need for his first prize. And what a prize is this fish that is named for the two red spots on his throat, for no matter if he fights it out topside or doggedly under water, he always lets an angler know that he has hooked a sports fish.

Pyramid Lake, Nevada, used to boast the biggest cutthroat trout in the world. Fish of 20 to 30 pounds were common, but gradually poor conservation and waste combined to make fish of this size virtually unknown. The world-record cutthroat trout came from Pyramid Lake—a monstrous 41-pounder that measured 1 yard and 3 inches and was caught in 1925. However, no one expects to see a fish of this size again.

The big fish in the lakes are best taken through deep-trolling methods. Anglers just troll a bait fish-and-spinner combination or a spoon until the rod bends in two. Then action starts.

The cutthroat trout is adaptable to many waters. It is sea-run and comes out of the Eel and Klamath rivers of California, the Umpqua and Rogue of Oregon, and the Columbia, Skykomish and Kalmama rivers of Washington. Alaska has them throughout its southern reaches. Some fine inland cutthroat fishing can be found in Priest Lake and the Salmon River of Idaho, in the North and South forks of the Flathead River and in Flathead Lake in Montana, or the Gros Ventre River and Jackson Lake of Wyoming. The fish also thrive in the eastern Wyoming prairie lakes, which are quite alkaline. The fact that the fish can live in the ocean, in vodka-clear streams or in alkaline lakes shows their versatility.

The cutthroat is as succulent a fish as ever hit the pan, and it is a beauty on a line. It is a fine trout.

Dolly Varden

The Dolly Varden (Salvelinus malma) is probably the most underrated sports fish of the country. This species of trout is a char closely related to brookies and Mackinaw. It has many of the same characteristics of the latter fish—brightly colored and big—yet by many anglers it is rated hardly more than a rough fish.

The fish started off fine. It was named Dolly Varden, after

the colorful women's hats of the last century. The fish has a
green back and a yellowish belly, but it undoubtedly was the
yellow and orange spots on its back and sides that led to its
inspiring name. From there on the Dolly went downhill, for in
many areas it was netted out of lakes and streams and destroyed,
being accused of destroying more acceptable species of game
fish.

The Dolly Varden is a western trout found along the coasts,
but it will also thrive inland. The fish is not exclusively a North
American species—it can be taken in Siberia or Northern Japan
in cold waters. In the northern reaches it is anadromous, going
to sea to live but returning to fresh-water streams to spawn.
Strangely, near the southern portion of its area the fish never
goes to sea but stays in the streams and lakes of its birth.

A 32-pound fish from Lake Pend Oreille, Idaho, holds the
world's record. They grow big, and 15- to 20-pounders are not
uncommon from the big, cold northwestern lakes. They are
found in Oregon, Washington, Idaho, Wyoming, Montana and
Alaska.

There are several reasons why fishermen are still prejudiced
against the Dolly. The chief reason is that he is primarily a
bottom fish. Because he is not a spectacular topside fighter, he
is overlooked in favor of the wilder rainbow and cutthroat trout
that inhabit these same waters. I have had some rough moments
with Dollies, and although their fight is subsurface, it is always
a determined struggle.

Small Dolly Varden running to possibly 7 pounds can be taken
in streams. These fish will be found in the deep pools of the
western or Alaskan rivers. They can be taken from these haunts
in several different ways. Wet flies are a fine attraction for them,
but the flies must be fished down deep. Some patterns that will
take them include Coachman, Cahill Fletcher and Professor.
Nymphs are good for getting Dollies on a hook, for they are
fished deep.

Another way to take the fish out of the pools is to use spinning equipment. Here the angler approaches a pool and casts
directly across toward the other bank. He allows sufficient Ken-

tucky windage so his retrieve will be directly through the spot
he wants to work. First the angler must allow the lure or spoon
time to sink to the bottom, and when it is worked back it should
constantly be kept bouncing off the bottom, for this is pay-dirt.
I have found the selection of lures is not nearly as important as
keeping the package down. I once had hits on 5 different lures
while a friend of mine had nothing; it wasn't because we used
different lures, but merely because I kept mine down and he
didn't.

Another way to catch Dollies is with salmon eggs. The fish
will take them whether there are salmon living in their waters
or not, for they have an insatiable appetite for fish eggs.

When they see attractive, round salmon eggs bouncing along
the bottom toward them, it is virtually impossible for Dollies
not to suck them in. Use light rods, monofilament line and
inverted-eye salmon egg hooks from No. 8 to No. 4. When sinkers are necessary, use them by starting with split shot, for it
is important to keep the egg bouncing along the bottom. Some
anglers will flip occasional loose eggs in the area being fished,
for this creates activity.

A point where a stream empties into a lake is a fine place to
set up shop if fishing with natural baits. Let a rigged bait fish
float from the mouth of the stream into the lake, permitting it
to swish in around sand bars or holes behind gravel beds, and
the size of the catches could be a pleasant surprise. Sometimes
20-pound-plus fish can be taken by just such a method.

The big Dollies are found on the bottom of the cold lakes of
the west, and they are taken by trolling along the lake bottoms.
Methods and equipment used are the same as for Mackinaw and
kamloops. When an angler has one on the line, he can never be
sure what fish it is until it finally breaks water, for all three of
these fish put up a similar determined underwater fight.

Why then are Dollies so downgraded? Anglers would do well
to remember it wasn't too many years ago that lake trout were
strained out of lakes with the excuse that they were a menace
to other sports fish. There was a time when brown trout were
downgraded to the level of pan fish. We have changed com-

pletely in our thinking about these fish—what state isn't proud of its man-sized Mackinaw or Loch Leven trout? Unfortunately we haven't come that far with the Dolly Varden trout. But I feel it won't be too much longer before anglers give this fish his due. Then suddenly everyone will discover Dollies, and the rush will be on. They meet every qualification of a fine sports fish—so why not treat them as such?

California Golden Trout

The California golden trout (Salmo aguabonita) is one of the most beautiful and most rare fish in the country. It was once found only along the South Fork of the Kern River in California. Anglers from other states besieged their conservation departments to get the species stocked elsewhere, and considerable planting has been done. The fish is still restricted to high mountain lakes, in streams over 9,000 feet in elevation, but it can now be taken in Oregon, Montana and Wyoming. California has them in many waters, including those in the Bear Creek, Fish Creek and Mono Creek.

The golden trout are brightly colored fish, rich in a deep golden tone that is further highlighted by the fish's bright red belly and the red band along their sides. They are close relatives of the rainbow and cutthroat trouts, but the golden's colors so far exceed those of any other trout that it makes other fish appear dull.

The goldens spawn in July, because at the elevation these fish live the water is too cold for the eggs during the rest of the year. Many of the lakes are so inaccessible that they can only be stocked by airplane. Trout have been stocked at altitudes lower than 9,000 feet, but their coloring dulled and they lost their identity. No one drives to a golden-trout lake. It takes a western pack train to ascend the rugged mountain to the lakes, which can be as high as 14,000 feet above sea level. These trains leave from places like Jackson Hole, Wyoming, Dillon, Montana, and many other western spots. Write the California Department of Fish and Game for their pamphlet *Golden Trout and Where to Get Them*—it lists over 40 California hot-spots.

Fishing the lakes or mountain streams for golden trout is done with regular fly tackle and small No. 8 to No. 12 flies. Patterns used include the Black Gnat, Red Ant, Mosquito and Royal Coachman. Anglers fish from shore, and flies are worked over an area. Tackle should always be of a type that is extremely easy to carry, for during the long climbs to the waters, tackle can get awfully burdensome.

Spinning tackle is popular for goldens. The long casts of which this type of rod is capable are helpful for reaching to the far corners of the lakes. Small silver spoons worked through the lakes with the aid of spinning equipment have proven to be good fish takers.

When a golden trout is caught, it should be cleaned immediately and wrapped up. Later when the fish is eaten it should be fried in a practically dry pan, for the fish is naturally greasy and provides most of its own oil in cooking.

California golden trout are not sensational scrappers. They are not exceptionally large fish—the biggest ever caught weighed only 11 pounds, and it came from Cook's Lake, Wyoming. Neither are they exceptionally good eating fish. They are a rare fish whose waters are extremely hard to get to. Why then are they so sought after? Any angler need only catch one and see it in all its brilliant color to know—for like some women, these trout are a prize because they are beautiful and hard to get.

Sunapee Golden Trout

Near the end of the nineteenth century it was discovered that Lake Sunapee in southern New Hampshire contained some exotic trout which were a beautiful golden color. This trout was quickly referred to as the golden trout and later identified as Sunapee Golden Trout (Salvelinus alpinus), to distinguish it from a different species of golden trout found in the mountain lakes of the high Sierras.

The golden trout is a relative of the Arctic char, and indications are that this fish is an ancestor of the char left in the lake by retreating glaciers. These landlocked fish survived, and in this one lake the fish gradually became a new species of trout— the golden trout.

For the most part of the year goldens stay in deep water. They come topside only for a week or so after the ice is out in early spring. After this they prefer the depths of this famous cold lake.

The fall season is spawning time for the fish, and they come into a section of the lake called Loon Island Reef. The New Hampshire Fish and Game Department sends some men to the lake annually to net the spawning fish. The roe is stripped from the females and is milted by stripping captured males. Those fish left in the lake will spawn naturally, but unfortunately many of them have crossed with lake trout, another ancestor of the char. There has been worry that the strain of golden would die out because of this crossing.

A female will lay about 2,000 eggs in a season, but unless these eggs are fertilized within a few minutes after leaving the fish they become sterile. Artificial spawning has raised the percentage of births from about 2 per cent to about 80 per cent.

The fertile eggs hatch in 2 to 4 months, and the fry come to life. The fish grow relatively slowly, because it takes 3 years for a fish to reach maturity. They can live up to 10 years of age, possibly reaching a maximum size of 15 pounds, with the record fish an 11-pound 8-ouncer.

An angler's best chance to take golden trout is in the spring when the fish are near the top. Fishing is done by trolling various spinners, metal spoons or spinner-fly combinations. A visit to Lake Sunapee and a quick talk with any tackle-shop proprietor will bring an angler a healthy list of the sure takers.

Another way of getting a golden is to use a smelt as bait. This can be still-fished by hooking it through the back and letting it sink into the deep spots of the lake. Other bait fish will take them too.

Sunapee golden trout have been stocked into Tewksbury Pond,

New Hampshire, and the Averill Lakes of Vermont. These exquisite fish are one of the rarest sports fish in America and a catch of even one is a lifetime trophy.

Lake Trout

The mighty lake trout (Salvelinus namaycush) is the biggest trout in our country. The record catch of 80 pounds 8 ounces came from Lake Athabaska in Saskatchewan but wasn't taken by sports-fishing methods. A 63-pounder was taken in Lake Superior on sports-fishing tackle, and it is a long-standing record.

The lake trout is available to light-tackle anglers only in the spring and fall while the water is cold. When there is even the slightest hint of warm weather, the fish dive down into the depths of the lakes. Lake trout cannot survive in water that is warmer than 65°; therefore, they are found only in our nation's large northern lakes.

New England refers to these native lakers as togue, and they're proud of some of the monsters that come out of lakes like Moosehead or Chamberlain in Maine; the Connecticut lakes and Lake Winnepesaukee, New Hampshire; or Lake Memphremagog, Vermont.

The laker was once the predominant fish of the Great Lakes. These spacious bodies of cold water were ideally suited for the fish, which is called gray trout by the populace of Michigan and Minnesota. Lakers thrived here, and tons of them were taken commercially for marketing; but then a few lamprey eels went through the Soo Canal at Sault Ste. Marie. These lampreys bred in the streams feeding the lakes, and soon they were attacking all the trout in the Great Lakes. They attach themselves to a mature fish, and with their vacuumlike mouth suck the blood from it. Strangely the attack never bothers a host fish, for he swims about with the lamprey without struggling. I've had lamprey attach himself to my legs momentarily, and he feels like a vacuum. The lamprey immediately lets go of any warm-blooded body, for he wants cold blood only.

The laker drained of its life's blood dies within a day or two after a lamprey attack. Trout were ideal prey for lamprey, for all trout have soft gills and the eel finds it easy to get the fish's blood. This scourge was so bad that the commercial catch of the whole Great Lakes fishing industry dropped to less than 5,000 pounds in one year. There is hope for the future, for a new chemical, Lampricide, should greatly aid in killing off lampreys; and with these parasites in check the laker population will increase again.

In other areas the fish have fared much better, and the big Mackinaws of the West are the pride and joy of many anglers. Once in my youth I was thoroughly confused by the word "Mackinaw," and it wasn't until I boated one from Jackson Lake that I recognized him as my old friend—the lake trout. The fish is easily identified by its grayish over-all color and white mottled spots. It can also be recognized by its oversize features, the eyes, mouth and head or its deeply-forked tail—all help spell out lake trout. Some well-known Mackinaw lakes include Jackson Lake and Fremont Lake in Wyoming, and Lake Tahoe in California and Nevada.

Whether found in the Northeast, the Great Lakes, the Northwest or Alaska, lake trout are always fall breeders. They have a regular ritual of breeding. Male trout come into the spawning grounds first and set up shop while waiting for the females. The male busies himself cleaning off rock ledges where the eggs will be deposited, and he impatiently scurries about the spawning grounds, which are usually at a depth of 25 to 75 feet. Finally the ripe females come in and begin depositing their eggs that could number up to 20,000 in one year. After the eggs are milted they are left unattended by the fish, and they will lie there from 2 to 4 months until they hatch. Many eggs drop into rock crevices where they are safe, but many others are lost when other fish make meals of the uncovered, unprotected eggs.

The most exciting time of the year for lake-trout fishing is in the spring, for then the fish are near the top. But even then they are seldom taken right on top for they just do not surface to feed. During the spring, lakers go cruising around in schools, and they swim about anywhere from 5 to 25 feet down. Fishing is best over rocky-bottomed shoals and near reefs. Wobbler spoons or deeper-running plugs can be worked either from shore or from a boat. Boat trolling is still most productive, and an angler will find that jerking his lure in almost a jigging fashion while trolling will increase hits, for it adds speed and change of pace to the trolled lure, and it attracts the fish.

During springtime fishing lakers will take any number of lures and baits. They can be taken on spinner-fly combinations, trolled streamer flies, bait fish, spinners or even big night crawlers.

As soon as the weather begins to warm up, the lakers dive into the subterranean, not to be seen again until fall. Now the only way to get them is by deep trolling. Two important points to remember about laker fishing:

1. The fish are near the bottom, generally over rocky bottoms, and

2. They are almost exclusively bait-fish eaters.

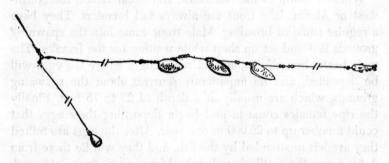

Rig for deep trolling with cowbell-type spinners. Line from rod goes to a three-way swivel. The bottom line leads to the sinker. It is relatively short and is usually a lower test strength than the baited line. Thus when the line snags the sinker section breaks while the remainder of the rig is saved. The top line has 5 to 10 feet of line from the swivel to the spinners. This is followed by the wire (sometimes nylon) leader, usually 1 to 5 feet in length. The bait is connected to the leader.

Mackinaws live on minnows, perch, bait fish, walleye, trout or any other fish they can capture. To the angler this means bait fish or imitations of them have to be used. A popular rig is a cowbell, which is a big row of Indiana-type spinners strung together with rows of red beads between the spinners. This gaudy piece of hardware is the advertisement for the bait fish that is trolled through the depths for the big ones. A few times bait fish are fished without spinners. A way to keep the package in pay-dirt is by hitching up a three-way swivel with the sinker on one line and the trailing hook on another. Big 50-50 spoons of bronze or silver are used regularly in trolling.

Keeping down in a lake for these fish can pose a problem, for in some places in Lake Superior it takes almost 10 pounds of sinker to get down to the required 100 to 200 feet. Because the lakers of the deep are often over rocks, snags are inevitable. If a lighter line is attached to the sinker it will break and save the rest of the rig. Some anglers use a break-away line so that a hooked fish will put up a better fight and not have to battle with several pounds of lead being dragged around.

I prefer monel wire to any other kind of line for deep fishing. Monel has the advantage of sinking down at a steeper angle, and it doesn't have the stretch or slack ordinary line can build up. Monel also gives the fisherman close contact with his fish, for it acts like a telegraph wire between fish and fisherman. Other lines used will be from 20- to 50-pound test, depending on the requirements. Rods for this kind of fishing call for medium salt-water boat rods, for they take the strain of deep trolling. Three to 5 feet of nylon usually connects the hook to the wire line. Hooks vary in size from No. 6 to No. 1 and should be extra-strong, short-shanked hooks.

Another method of taking lakers off the bottom is through drift fishing. Here live bait is lowered over the side, and the angler stays in his boat, drifting over the hot-spots. This usually requires less weight than trolling, so more fight comes from the hooked fish. The unfortunate thing about lake trout taken from deep water is that they have only a minimum amount of spirit. Small 3- to 5-pounders are often overwhelmed with the terminal tackle and hardly fight at all, but even large ones may appear lacking in spirit. This fish is affected by pressure changes, and a sudden reeling to the top injures him and saps his strength so that by the time he gets to the boat he may be half dead. In the fall the fish come in closer to shore again for breeding and feeding. They feed actively just before the actual breeding takes place, but once this gets under way fishing will slack off until it is over.

The thing to remember in lake-trout fishing is that the angler who stays near the bottom, whether fishing in the shallows in spring or fall or fishing the depths during the warm weather, is the angler who will bring home fish consistently. And the finest thing about taking home lakers is that one or two 20-pounders can really fill up a freezer with delicious trout meat for a year.

Rainbow Trout

The rainbow trout (Salmo gairdneri) are the most widespread and most versatile of all our trout. These fish can live in the cold streams of the Northwest and abound in Alaska, and they can also survive in water up to 75°. They live in the warm waters of Georgia, Arkansas, Tennessee and Oklahoma if the water is running swiftly and if there is sufficient aeration.

The rainbow trout is a native of our western states. It has been easy to raise in hatcheries and has been able to adapt itself to all sorts of environmental changes; consequently the fish is now found in all states except the extreme southern ones. Other countries have planted rainbows, too, and Argentina, Australia and New Zealand boast some fine catches. The legal minimum size in the mountains of New Zealand is 18 inches. Japan now exports frozen rainbow trout that are grown in their fish farms.

These trout are easy to identify, for a red stripe down the side of any trout readily spells rainbow. They have black-trout spots all over their bodies including their heads and caudal fins. They are generally greenish in color except when they come from alkaline waters or from deep lakes, when their color is almost silvery. Males of this species can be differentiated from females by the cartilagelike button on the lower jaw.

Unlike other trout, the rainbow are spring breeders. The big fish come out of the lakes or reservoirs (and ocean with steelhead) and head up to the spawning grounds, which are the small gravel-bottomed streams. Females lay from a few hundred up to several thousand eggs, depending upon the health and size of the fish. The big steelhead that come up from the sea may lay 10,000 eggs. They will hatch in 2 to 4 months, depending upon the water temperatures. The young begin life by feeding upon plankton, but gradually their diets change to larvae and insects and later to small fish.

This species of trout is relatively fast-growing, and will grow almost 10 inches in 2 years. A 3-year old fish will be a 15- to 17-inch beauty that anglers will love to hook into. Sea-going and lake rainbows grow even faster, for the waters these fish live in hold an abundance of food that nourishes them.

The rainbow trout's uninhibited acrobatics are very popular with anglers. Rainbows jump during practically every battle, and many a fight takes place exclusively on the surface. This fish puts up a strong fight, and in an open stream or lake his full strength is displayed, which often amazes even veteran anglers. If a fish is taken in very shallow water during a spawning run, it has to do its fighting from closed-in quarters, and much of the free swinging spirit of the fish is lost. They are best in open water.

One place a spring run of rainbows draws anglers in droves is Catherine Creek in Watkins Glen, New York, where there is an annual opening-day party for them. Fishermen line up shoulder to shoulder along the shore of this arm of Seneca Lake and throw out an assortment of flies, spinner-fly combinations, salmon eggs, bait fish or big night crawlers, hoping to hook one of the big beauties. I stood out there one opening day in over 8 inches of snow, and my reward was one of the reddest, coldest noses ever seen on any snowman. What brings anglers back year after year is the fact that just down the line someone will be seen taking a 15- or 20-pounder, and the mere sight of such a fish can make anyone forget cold feet and a frozen nose in a hurry.

Methods of catching rainbow trout run the whole gamut of fishing methods. Fly fishing is the No. 1 sportsman's way. Here, too, methods vary, for rainbows will strike dry, wet, and streamer flies as well as nymphs. My favorite way of fishing is with dry flies, but this wouldn't be the most productive method for most anglers, for the fish either have to be rising or coaxed into rising before any will be taken. Flies for taking the fish are a duller color than those used for other trout, and some like the Olive Quill, the Quill Gordon and the Adams are standards. A rule of thumb is to use smaller, dull-colored flies the higher one gets into mountain areas, for up here the water is clearer and insects fewer. When the fish are on top they are wary, so the successful fly angler moves deliberately and fishes upstream so as not to spook them. Casts generally have to be long, and leader should be fine.

Wet flies take many fish. These flies can, if desired, be fished downstream. In very clear water, nymphs are rainbow-killers. Nymphs have to be fished so that they roll along the bottom directly to the resting fish. The trout will only nudge the nymph, simply sifting it in the way a sucker might. They spit the package out immediately, and herein lies the sport, for the angler must tighten line on any hint of a fish. Many false strikes are made even by experts, but a taut line on a mere breath of a hit has already brought in some amazing fish.

Streamer flies worked downstream and in open water will act like minnows, and it's a hard task for any rainbow to pass up a minnow meal. This fly has to be made to dart around the water like a scared minnow.

Some of the hardest strikes at a line will be at natural bait. Big night crawlers or a glob of small, high-spirited worms on a hook will attract a rainbow from the far corners of a pool. Worms are best fished downstream, and the bait should be floated from ripples into big holes and back into fast water. Many times the fish will be sitting in white water, and they will smash at a bait or fly as it passes them. Worm fishing is most productive in the springtime during high water, for the fish see many worms in the water then.

A live minnow dropped among rainbows is always a taker of fish. Other natural baits that can be used include salmon eggs, grasshoppers, hellgrammites or grubs. One friend of mine does very well catching freshly stocked fish by using small pieces of liver as bait. He argues that the fish are used to this food, and liver stays on a hook better than other baits.

Spoons and plugs will take rainbows in the big rivers and in the lakes. A Daredevil or other red-and-white spoon will get the fish to hit. This lure can be worked through medium-fast water, or it can be worked in lakes or open sections of running water. I have caught some nice rainbow on flatfish that were worked slowly.

Steelhead

They say that when a Westerner is missing from home for a week or more, his wife shouldn't get too excited. If he is a fisherman it's even money that he just happened to stop at a stream for a little steelhead fishing, and he just had to get in that one more cast before starting home. No other fresh-water fish of the Pacific Coast draws fishermen the way this sea-going rainbow trout does.

These rainbow trout of the Pacific Coast are anadromous. They are born in fresh water, sometimes over a thousand miles from the sea, remaining there one or two years before coming downstream to the Pacific Ocean. Once in salt water the fish grow rapidly, and within one or two years they are mature, weighing 5 to 10 pounds. These mature fish will come back to small streams and spawn just like regular inland rainbow trout.

Many steelhead die on spawning runs, but unlike the salmon it is not the fish's nature to die then. Some fish will spawn as many as 4 times in a life span that could stretch to 7 years.

Steelhead enter the rivers of the coast almost any time during a year. Their spawning time is late winter or spring, but if they come upstream out of season they merely set up shop and start living in the stream. They are a different color when they return from the sea, for they look like a piece of well-tempered steel. Color and size are all that have changed in the fish, for they are rainbow trout, and luckily for anglers they still keep their feeding habits.

Fishing for steelhead was once done exclusively with salmon eggs as bait. These were weighted down and dropped into the water, and then the angler waited. Sometimes eggs were fished singly. Other times they were fished in a clump held together by cheesecloth or in a net. Steelhead were always on the lookout for this tasty morsel, so catches were productive. Later on, tackle became less cumbersome, and anglers experimented with new baits. It was found the fish would take fresh-water clams, worms, herrings, and cherry bobbers. But even today the old salmon egg is still the No. 1 taker of fish during the big winter runs.

Somewhere someone found that rainbows returning from the sea took flies, and then the sport became an art. A steelhead on a fly rod will quickly show an angler he is fighting one of the strongest, wiliest fish in fresh water. Flies for them include such favorites as the Royal Coachman, Mickey Finn and Green Drake. Small standard flies and big salmon flies take fish. Fly sizes vary from No. 4 down to No. 8, and a good general rule to follow is to use progressively smaller sizes as the water gets lower and clearer. The fish hit flies lightly, so strikes should be made on mere suspicion.

Good steelhead tackle must meet certain specifications. First, it must enable an angler to make long casts to reach the fish; and second, it must be sturdy enough to handle the fish's long hard runs. Fly rods are generally 9 to 10 feet in length and weigh about 6 to 9 ounces. Reels should be capable of holding 100 yards of line.

Drift fishing where the bait is sent downstream rolling along the bottom calls for long rods and monofilament line. Sometimes spinning outfits are used, and sometimes 9-foot casting rods are the equipment. Minimum line length for this fishing should be 150 yards, because the bait is often allowed to roll a long way. The important thing is to get the bait low enough to

the bottom so the fish see it there. When working a drift, the
hot-spots are the ripples at the base of rapids and those before
new rapids. Fish love to rest there on their way upstream, and
many times there may be a congregation of fish waiting there.

Steelhead will take spinners and spoons that are worked in
front of them. Sometimes chrome, chrome-brass or a red-and-
white spoon measuring up to 2 inches in length will work wonders. The lures should be put low in the water. They should be
given time to sink and, once near the bottom, worked constantly.
Raise and relax the rod tip so that the lure works in a jerky fashion. A moving spoon on or near the bottom will always pay
dividends.

The winter run of fish is the heaviest, and it is the time the
biggest fish come in from the ocean. The big females will be
heavy with roe, and the males will be active and mean. Fishing
at this time is more difficult because of adverse weather and high
water. Salmon eggs are the favorite winter bait, but fluorescent
flies have already proved themselves.

But no matter what the bait or what time of year the fish
is taken, a steelie is always quite a fish. Once hooked, he ex-
plodes like a bronco out of a gate, and he'll run and jump and
sometimes do 1½ gainers in the air. I've seen fishermen struggle
along the shore trying to follow a long run of a fish. A friend
of mine fell down in the icy water and got up scratched, bruised
and wet, but in the excitement of the battle he didn't notice his
own condition. His only thought was of the fish, and he battled
it without complaint for another 20 minutes before he landed a
15-pound beauty. It wasn't until after he had his fish that he
even realized he'd fallen.

Some nationally famous places for this popular fish includes
the Nushagak and the Kvichak rivers of Alaska, and the Skagit
River of Washington, and the Deschutes and Columbia rivers of
Washington and Oregon. Oregon is well known for its steel-
head runs in the Umpqua and Rogue rivers, while California's
Big Eel and Klamath River runs are a legend. The inland state
of Idaho is well known for its steelhead fishing in the Snake and
Salmon rivers.

The states around the Great Lakes have another form of steel-head trout, but these trout, instead of going to the ocean, spend a year or more in the Great Lakes. Michigan is especially well known for these rainbows that go into Lake Michigan to return twice the normal size. The lamprey eel has cut into this supply of fish, but trout should be on the increase, for the fight against the lamprey is really making headway.

Kamloops

The biggest of all rainbow trout live in the cold, clear lakes of the Columbia River basin. The world-record rainbow was a Kamloop that came from Lake Pend Oreille, Idaho, and weighed an even 37 pounds. Every year fish over 20 pounds come out of the cold, deep northwestern lakes of this area.

These fish are generally taken by deep-trolling methods similar to those used by lake-trout fishermen. Occasionally in springtime they can be taken trolling along the shore line, but during warmer weather deep trolling is the only method that can catch them. Equipment used: 100 to 200 yards of line of 20-pound test or better, hitched onto a sturdy rod.

The rainbow is the most versatile of American trout and is now spread over the greatest area of the world. He is a beautiful fish and a wonderful sportsfish, and because he can adapt himself to so many environmental changes he should be around to provide anglers with excellent sport for years to come.

Great Lakes Whitefish

The ciscoes of the Great Lakes is the names commonly applied to chubs and whitefish of the area. The biggest of these white-fish, the lake herring (Coregonus artedi), are found in the Great Lakes and many nearby lakes, and also many lakes of the upper Mississippi valley. They are also taken in the St. Lawrence River and throughout much of Canada.

Many of these herring are caught commercially in nets, but

the angler can also get them. One acceptable way is to troll a small minnow until hits are felt; then fishing should be active until the school moves off. These fish can on rare occasions attain a weight of 8 pounds, but the average fish will weigh only 1 to 2 pounds. The herring are usually taken in water over 20 feet deep and are sometimes over 150 feet down.

The round whitefish (Prosopium cylindraceum) is also common to the Great Lakes area. These fish range throughout North American cold water from Alaska to the northern United States. They are also present in Asia. The round whitefish can be distinguished from other whitefish in having a single flap (rather than two flaps) between its eyes. The best time to take these fish is during their fall spawning migrations, when they are in shallow water. They can be taken on a small minnow or a fly. The average fish weighs only 1 pound, while large ones may go to 4 pounds.

The whitefish (Coregonus clupeaformis) is a native of New England, the Great Lakes region and Canada. This is an important commercial fish that can also be taken by sports fishermen. Baits should be fished near the bottom. These fish are generally in water more than 20 feet deep, and this is the minimum depth for fishing them. The fish hit worms or very small pieces of cut fish on a hook. Baits and other lures take them if the angler gets down to them. Hooks for these and other whitefish have to be small because of the fish's soft and small mouth. Sizes No. 6 to No. 8 are standard. On some occasions the fish are on the surface, and then they may be taken with flies—generally size 10 to 12 flies are used, and many anglers like some red in the fly pattern they use. This whitefish is 2 to 4 pounds in weight but could go to 15 pounds.

Whitefish are closely related to trout, and they are fine eating fish. They may either be smoked or broiled.

Rocky Mountain Whitefish

Throughout much of Colorado, Utah, Idaho and Wyoming, Rocky Mountain Whitefish (Prosopium williamsoni) thrive in the streams and lakes. The fish average about 1 foot in length and weigh about 1 pound. The whitefish is an important fish of Jackson Lake, where it is forage for the big Mackinaw trout. Other hot-spots are the Snake River and its tributaries, and the Clark's Fork River.

The fish have the appearance of grayling and are many times confused with it. Whitefish can easily be distinguished, for they lack the long, flowing dorsal fin of the grayling. The fish is generally a grayish blue on the back and has silvery sides. Its lower jaw is shorter than its upper jaw, which gives it a sucker-like appearance.

Rocky Mountain whitefish can best be taken on extremely small size 16 to 18 flies. They rise to gray-colored flies, and the angler must strike his line very lightly. The fish must be struck gently, too, for hard strikes only rip the hooks from their paper-like mouths. Flies can be fished wet or dry, or nymphs can be used. They also take hellgrammites and small minnows.

The fish puts up a reputable tussle, and a good-sized 3-pounder will really scrap. The whitefish is related to trout and grayling and holds its own in the epicurean department with those more glamorous fish. He is a good scrapper, is plentiful in his area, is available all year and is a welcome member of western sports fish.

White Bass

Out on the Tennessee River or the Kentucky River, anywhere in Kentucky, Tennessee or Alabama, a springtime catch of over 100 white bass (Roccus chrysops) wouldn't surprise anyone. Other hot-spots for white bass are the upper Mississippi River, Lake of the Ozarks in Missouri, and Lake Erie. At Sandusky Bay in Ohio a recent survey showed 17½ per cent of all fish caught were white bass. The fish ranges from Canada to the Gulf states throughout the Midwest.

Springtime is the time to fish these white bass (or striped bass, another name for them), for at this time the fish school up in phenomenal numbers and swim upriver to their spawning grounds. In lakes without feeding rivers they come into shallow coves near stream inlets to deposit their eggs.

During the spawning season the fish can be taken on almost any lure in the angler's tackle box. They will strike hard and fast at top plugs or low-running ones. Two plugs I've found that bring strikes regularly are the Midge-Oreno and the Hawaiian Wiggler. There are many others, for in a big school they strike anything. White bass will take virtually any spinning lure made or will smash at streamer fly-spinner combinations.

When the white bass breed, females drop their eggs over rocky or gravel bottoms in rivers, and males cover them with milt. A full-grown female can deposit ½ million to 1 million eggs in one season. These eggs and the young are left unattended, for the big fish immediately head back into deep water.

Young bass are left to their own ingenuity to avoid starvation and disaster. They feed on insect larvae and insects, and those fish that survive grow rapidly and soon head downstream to deep water of the lakes, where they will spend their lives. The white bass will grow to 4 or 5 inches in 1 year and will be almost a foot long the second year. They live only 4 years, but they can attain a weight of 3 pounds in this short time. The average catch weighs 1 pound.

The adult fish are carnivorous. They feed primarily on small fish, including gizzard shad, perch, minnows and crawfish. These natural baits or spinner-fly combinations should be trolled at a 20- to 40-foot depth to take the fish during daytime, when the fish prefer open water. Evening brings schools of white bass out of the deep water, and they go on patrol along the shores of lakes in search of bait fish. A plug splashed over the head of a school in the shallows will bring a sure strike, as will a minnow, if it is thrown in front of a school.

Tackle can be any of the standard rods, with 8- to 9-foot medium light fly rods, bait-casting rods 5 to 5½ feet, or spinning rods measuring 6½ to 7 feet with medium-light action all being good. Line should be 4- to 6-pound test, and hooks can be No. 4 to 1/0. Those preferring maximum sport should use light and ultralight tackle. Sinkers should be just heavy enough to take the bait down to the desired depth. Two-ounce sinkers are often adequate in a lake, while shallow fishing calls only for a piece of shot.

White bass are not members of the fresh-water bass family but are relatives of the sea bass. They are poles apart from black bass, and their habits are totally different. The white bass is a fresh-water fish today because thousands of years ago some sea bass became landlocked and, instead of dying out, survived and reproduced their own kind in the fresh water. The white bass can be distinguished from other bass in several ways. First, white bass have two separate dorsal fins, while black bass dorsal fins are connected by membrane; and secondly, 4 or 5 longitudinal lines on the sides of the white bass's body clearly identify them for fishermen. They are a silvery-white fish with a yellowish underbody and are easy to recognize. Then, too, their spawning habits in no way resemble the nesting habits of black bass.

The white bass is a good eating fish, very plentiful, sporty on light tackle, a prolific breeder, a fast-growing fish, and all in all a fine light-tackle sports fish.

Yellow Bass

The yellow bass (Roccus mississippiensis) is found all along the Mississippi and Ohio rivers and their feeder streams. The fish are also in the lakes throughout this area, and lakes such as Clear Lake, Iowa, have large populations of the fish. Yellow bass are distinguished by their bright golden-yellow sides. They are olive-green on the back, white on the belly and have longitudinal lines on their sides.

Angling for yellow bass is generally productive all year long except during extremely hot weather, when the fishing falls off badly. Trolling in a lake or river to locate the whereabouts of a school is a logical way to begin fishing, and where a school is located a dozen or so fish may be picked up in short order by a skilled angler.

Baits often begin with naturals, and minnows are always a sure bet. Artificials can be used, and lures like a Red and White

Flasher or a Silver Minnow will bring in fish. Flies or bass bugs will take fish that are playing at the surface, while trolled spinner-worm or spinner-fly combinations are best used if the fish are not visible, and trolling is the order of attack. Many youngsters bring home big catches of yellow bass by still-fishing with worms or night crawlers.

Tackle should be kept light, for the fish caught generally do not exceed 1 pound. Hooks are No. 4 to 1/0.

The fish are good eating, plentiful and scrappy.

Basic and Advanced Fishing

Bait Casting

Practically every American angler lives within a short drive of
a river or lake, and therefore almost all anglers keep a bait-
casting rod handy. The bait-casting rod is ideally suited for
heavy-duty work and can cast an assortment of plugs and spoons
for bass, pike, muskie and sturgeon. It is an ideal weapon for
pulling monsters out of weed beds, for a sturdy rod will, if
necessary, haul both weeds and fish out together. Another job
for which the rod is ideally suited is a slugging match with a
stubborn overgrown carp, for a bait-casting rod can bring any
fish to bay.

Bait-casting rods can be of either solid or hollow glass construction. They vary from light- to heavy-duty, and their construction depends upon their ultimate use.

A light bait-casting rod is capable of casting ¼- to ½-ounce
lures. It is thin, measures from 5 to 6 feet in length, and feels
springy. It can handle test lines up to 10 pounds and can be used
to take pan fish or sports fish weighing up to 10 pounds. The rod
is used most frequently with light test lines to take fish of pan-
fish size. Lightweight reels are made to match the rod.

A medium bait-casting outfit is usually no more than 5½ feet
long, but it has a stiffer action than the lighter rod. It is sturdier
than the light rod, and it has a heavier, stronger base. The rod
should be capable of handling lures from ⅜ to ¾ ounces, and lines
for this outfit go to 12-pound test. The rod can comfortably
handle fish weighing up to 18 pounds. This rod will not give the
play of the light rod, but for anything bigger than pan fish its
added strength is a help.

Heavy-duty rods throw lures from ½ ounce to monstrous 1½
ouncers. These rods are short and stiff, usually measuring only
5 feet in length. They are ideal for taking big, balky muskie,

catfish and pike out of weeds or other obstructions. Lines for this outfit can be 15- to 25-pound test or more if necessary. With this rod the angler can handle any fish that swims in fresh water. Heavy-duty trolling is another specialty of this rod because it can stand the strain of a deep troll.

The bait- or plug-casting rod is the work horse of fishing tackle, and if I ever had a chance to break a world record, my choice of tackle would invariably be a bait-casting rod. This rod gives any angler the best chance for landing a fish no matter what problems may arise in the ensuing battle.

Some bait-casting rods of today are neither light-, medium- or heavy-duty, for they are made to do the work of several sticks. A relatively new concept is a rod with a solid, heavy base and middle, and a light, flexible tip. It has the sturdiness of a heavy-duty rod, while it gives some of the play of a light rod. Longer rods are now being made, and some light rods now measure 6½ feet in length. Some that can be used interchangeably as spinning rods are becoming quite popular.

When choosing a rod for a trip, it is best to take as light a rod as possible because the light, springy ones are easier to cast and are sportier. Heavy-duty rods are the order of the day when:

1. There will be deep, heavy-duty trolling;
2. The fishing will be done in weed forests; or
3. The fish will be of exceptional size.

The bait-casting rod is capable of throwing a lure up to 100 feet with accuracy. Anglers take great pride in their bait-casting ability, and they become proud of their accuracy, for casting is a skill that must be learned.

Many beginners do quite well casting if they keep their range within 75 feet. They tend to lose accuracy and develop painful backlashes when they try to cast beyond this point. Backlashes come when an angler doesn't thumb his reel and the rapidly unwinding reel travels faster than the line going out. Spinning tackle would never have had such a swift acceptance if it weren't for baitcasting's backlashes; actually, though, even a beginning bait caster should have only a minimum amount of trouble with backlashes if he stays within his range.

Proper thumbing of a reel is the best assurance of avoiding backlashes. The danger point in most casts is at the end of the cast, when the lure has reached its maximum height and speed and is coming into the downward arch. The lure will begin traveling at a slower speed, while the precision-made reel, which is unwinding, continues at the original fast speed. Gradual thumbing (by exerting pressure on the unwinding reel with the thumb) should begin before the lure reaches the point where it is traveling at a slower speed than when it left the rod. The thumbing is done exactly as a car is braked—easy pressure is applied at first, then stronger pressure as it slows to a stop. Many of today's reels have thumb brakes built into them, but most experts prefer to use their thumbs and consider the brakes as gadgets.

The most important point in choosing a reel is to get one that is fast-winding and has smooth motions. The reel is of the utmost importance because it is an integral part of the cast. It is just as important in fighting the fish, because the fish is fought directly from the reel. Heavy-duty reels should have star drags to help wear out big fish when they are hooked.

Line for this fishing can be of several different products—silk, dacron, braided nylon, or monofilament. Monofilament lines are fast becoming the favorites.

Bait casting is a fine sport, and every angler should have a bait-casting rod because it is a fine piece of equipment. It does many jobs well—and some better than any other piece of fishing equipment.

Understanding Lures

A typical tackle shop will have hundreds of lures to choose from, but to an angler who doesn't understand them, they can present a totally confusing picture. The only way to pick lures is to understand exactly what their job is and then to gauge their ability to do that job.

Each lure acts in a characteristic way which is supposed to

SOME BAIT-CASTING TACKLE RECOMMENDATIONS

LIGHT RODS

Manufacturer	Model Name	Model No.	Length	No. of Pieces	Remarks
Enterprise Mfg. Co.	Pflueger	R1260	6 ft.	2	A light tubular rod.
Garcia Corp.	Gold Bond	474 LCT	6 ft.	2	Handles line 4 to 10 lb. Also used as spinning rod.
True Temper Corp.	Flipline	4025	6 ft.	2	Light action. Also used as spinning rod.

LIGHT REELS

Manufacturer	Model Name	Model No.	Length	No. of Pieces	Remarks
Enterprise Mfg. Co.	Pflueger Trusty	1923			4 to 1 ratio. Holds 200 yds. 10-lb. test line.
Enterprise Mfg. Co.	Delux Nobby	1960			Weighs 5 oz. and holds 145 yds. nylon line.
Garcia Corp.	Garcia	ABU 2300			A fine reel for thin-line and light lures. Holds 140 yds. 11-lb. test.
True Temper Corp.	True Temper	1925			4 to 1 ratio lightweight reel.

MEDIUM RODS

Manufacturer	Model Name	Model No.	Length	No. of Pieces	Remarks
J. Heddon's Sons	Mark III	6255	5½ ft.	2	Made with fast-tip action.
Enterprise Mfg. Co.	Pflueger	R1450	5 ft.	2	Solid glass medium rod.
True Temper Corp.	True Temper	3144	5½ ft.	2	Hollow glass with fast tip.

MEDIUM REELS

Manufacturer	Model Name	Model No.	Length	No. of Pieces	Remarks
Enterprise Mfg. Co.	Pflueger Trump	1943			4 to 1 ratio. 175 yds. 15-lb. Mono.
Garcia Corp.	Garcia	ABU 2100			A beautiful, expensive reel. Capacity 110 yds. 12-lb. braided nylon.
True Temper Corp.	Ocean City	N1600			An aluminum-spool chrome-plated reel.

HEAVY DUTY RODS

Manufacturer	Model Name	Model No.	Length	No. of Pieces	Remarks
J. Heddon's Sons	Musky S. P.	6273	5 ft.	1	A sturdy muskie rod, as name implies.
Enterprise Mfg. Co.	Pflueger	R1556	5½ ft.	2	A solid glass rod capable of taking any fish.
True Temper Corp.	Montague	3860	4¼ ft.	1	For heavy-duty bait-casting and trolling.

HEAVY DUTY REELS

Manufacturer	Model Name	Model No.	Length	No. of Pieces	Remarks
Enterprise Mfg. Co.	Pflueger Bond	2000			Reel capacity 200 yds. 25-lb. test braided nylon or 300 yds. 15-lb. Mono.
True Temper Corp.	True Temper	1700			Has free spool and star drag. Holds 150 yds. 15-lb. Mono.

COMBINATION BAIT-CASTING-SPINNING RODS

Manufacturer	Model Name	Model No.	Length	No. of Pieces	Remarks
J. Heddon's Sons	Viscount	5000 to 5008	5½ ft.	1 or 2	Inexpensive, sturdy, solid glass rods.
Airex Corp.	Airex	171–174	6 to 6⅞ ft.	2	Tubular glass rods.

attract fish to it. It attracts a fish by being appealing as food, by momentarily confusing him, by annoying him, or by scaring him; or its job may merely be to bring attention to a trailing meal. Then each lure does its work either on the surface, near it or deep down.

The size of a lure is important in only one respect—it must be able to be worked comfortably with the equipment used. It was once thought that only large lures take big fish; but this theory has been exploded by the advent of spinning, for time and time again some real monsters have whacked the daylights out of ¼-ounce lures. And the opposite holds true too, for what angler hasn't taken a high-spirited sports fish on a lure that was as big as or bigger than the fish that attacked it?

For maximum efficiency the lure must be able to be worked easily by the rod used. With fly-fishing tackle, lures should not weigh more than ⅛ ounce. Various kinds of fresh-water spinning tackle take lures weighing from $1/16$ to 1¼ ounces; bigger salt-water-type spinning rods can take lures over 1 ounce.

Bait-casting weights for lures are about ⅝ ounce, but these rods can comfortably throw lures up to 1¼ ounces. Twenty-pound test line is of course required for the big lures like the Giant Pikie. Lures down to ⅜ ounce can be used with 8- to 10-pound test line when fished on bait-casting rods.

Metal lures fall into 2 categories—spoons and spinner. Most spinners are advertisers of baits that follow, for they are seldom fished alone. They are successful in getting more fish to come in close for a look at the worm, minnow or bucktail fly that might be attached behind it.

Spinners are made so that a silver or gold blade spins around a shaft, causing a bright flash in the water. The Indiana-type spinner is most common. Here the blade is fastened by a collar and turns around the shaft. The hook is attached in the rear, where it carries its own bait or lure. The popular June Bug spinner works on the same principle. A variation of this lure is one with blades set at fixed angles, so maximum rotation is effected. These types of lures are used to attract fish ranging from pan fish to bass to lake trout. The big, deep-trolling spinners used for the lakers are a large version of this type spinner.

A Colorado-type spinner is often used as a complete lure for trout fishing. Here the blade is attached to a ring, and it rotates and gyrates around in the water. The ring which has the blade attached is only one of several rings, and a hook is attached to the last one of this chain. This spinner is fished behind a swivel. There are many sizes of Colorado spinner. Blades vary from a fraction of an inch to almost two inches; hook sizes vary accordingly.

Another type of spinner extensively used is the propeller. It is generally used in conjunction with another lure and is built into many plugs. It attracts fish by its rotating blade.

Spoons are self-contained lures that attract fish by their metallic shine and their strange spinning, wobbling motion. The spoon was invented when Julio T. Buel dropped a silver spoon in the water and watched fish dart out and hit at it while it sank to the bottom. It wasn't long before spoon-shaped pieces of metal were thrown in the water, but these were on a line and had hooks attached. They proved amazingly successful, and today the variety of spoons numbers in the thousands.

A basic spoon is Johnson's Silver Minnow. As the name implies, this lure simulates a minnow in the water; and with its wobbling motion, it appears that the small fish is injured. The attack from the game fish comes because the lure looks like an opportunity for a good, easy meal. This lure can be bought with feathers attached, or a strip of pork rind can be added, trailing the hook; but neither are necessary.

Spoons of the Daredevil design are also popular fish takers. These spoons also wobble and roll in the water, and fish are attracted by their motion. Daredevils are generally enamel-painted on one side and have a shiny, metallic surface on the other, and in fast-running streams they create quite a fuss. There are many colors and designs, but the red-and-whited striped one is the popular favorite. Trout regularly go for the small ⅛ ounce ones, while lake and river fish take the bigger ones. Other spoons which very closely resemble Daredevils are Sprites and the

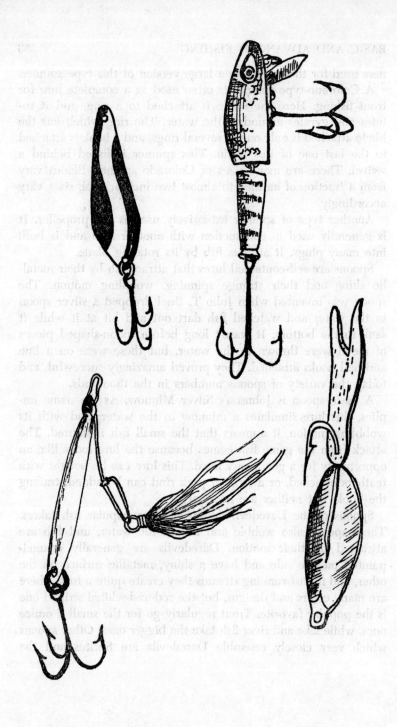

Flasher series. These can be bought in sizes of ⅛ ounce to a big ¾ ounce. Another spoon that works on the same principle —except that the body is shaped like a fish—is Wright-McGill's Right-Fish. A good tip for spooning: work them slowly, and let them hit bottom once or twice in a retrieve.

Plugs are lures with bodies shaped and painted to attract fish. Hooks are added to hold the fish. Plugs were invented by James Heddon, who added a bottle cap and a hook to a whittled piece of wood and surprised everyone by taking fish with it.

In the old days plugs were made exclusively of wood—hence the name plug. Today the plug is made of wood or plastic and can be in a million and one shapes. It can have all kinds of feathers, rubber, beads or pieces of metal sticking from it; but it still has the same purpose as Heddon's first crude lure—to fool and catch fish.

Three basic kinds of plugs are on the market today: surface, subsurface and deep-running.

Surface plugs, or top plugs as they are often called, are made to float on the surface and by their allure have fish come up to take them. The Injured Minnow is a well-known surface plug that attracts fish because it leans on its side like a hurt bait fish. Another type of surface lure attracts fish because it makes a commotion on the top. The Jitterbug falls into this category as do the popper plugs. A Plunker or a Hula Popper have stirred many a bass to their last breath. These plugs are good for fishing at night and in murky water wherever commotion is attractive. They are best for near-shore and shallow-water fishing.

The smoother riding plugs like the Injured Minnow and other torpedo-shaped plugs bring better results in clear water with

UPPER LEFT:	A *red-and-white spoon of the Daredevil type.*
UPPER RIGHT:	A *Miracle Minnow.* A deep running plug.
LOWER LEFT:	A *Silver Minnow and Fly.* Excellent for pickerel or pike.
LOWER RIGHT:	A *silver spoon with a piece of pork rind attached.* Pork rind adds to the attraction of the lure.

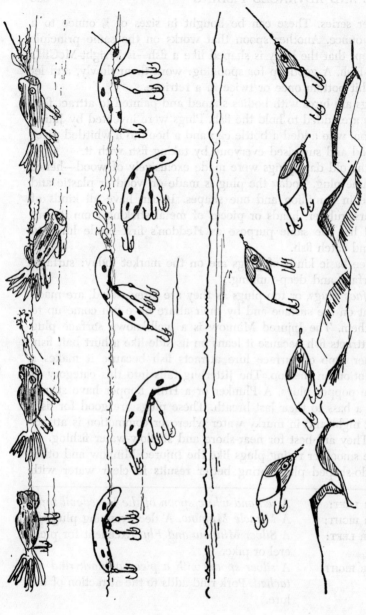

TOP: A top-popping plug such as this Hula Popper is worked in short jerky motions so that it pops and creates a disturbance which soon attracts the fish. MIDDLE: This Flatfish plug dives, dips and wiggles through the water and attracts fish by its peculiar action. It may be worked slowly with pauses for it to come to the surface or it may be worked in a steady retrieve. BOTTOM: A bottom plug generally works best when the retrieve is fast and the plug is kept bouncing off the bottom. An angler must be sure to give the plug time to sink to the bottom before beginning retrieve.

high visibility. Rod tip action like a jerk, a jerk and another jerk while reeling helps with these plugs.

Subsurface plugs are basically floating lures that dip and dive under the water when they are retrieved. Some of the most famous lures made fall into this category, including both the Bass-Oreno and the Flatfish. The Flatfish's shape makes it dive and wiggle like a belly dancer in an Arab tent, while the Bass-Oreno's shape makes it move erratically, like an injured fish. Other subsurface lures are constructed with metal-shaped fronts which make them dive even harder. Some of these lures are made in several sections, like the Jointed Pike Minnow; and this adds to its realistic appearance as an injured fish.

With subsurface lures the faster the angler retrieves, the deeper the dive of the plug. Anglers must vary the speed of their retrieves constantly to get these lures to maximum efficiency.

Deep-running plugs or bottom plugs are designed, as the name implies, to sink and run deep in the water. They are the best for taking fish like walleye, sauger, catfish and summer bass. Some of these types look much like subsurface and surface plugs except they are constructed of plastic and are heavier than the specific gravity of water, and therefore sink. Plugs like the Miracle Minnow attract fish by acting like an injured fish looking for a hiding place in deep water. Some deep plugs have propellers, whose job is to disturb the serenity of a deep hole and get the fish to hit the agitator.

Jigs can be classified as deep-running plugs or they can, because of their special features, be put into their own category. The jig has a small body and long trailing feathers. It has to be made to jump off the bottom by an up-and-down motion of the rod and rod tip. Successful jigging depends upon the motion of the jig in the water; and when an angler gets tired of jigging, which can be work, he had better switch lures, because without work they are not producers. With work they bring some excellent catches.

Plastic lures are rushing into prominence. They duplicate live baits in appearance as closely as possible, and in some instances they even feel like live bait. The plastic lure is better than live bait in some respects, for it will not fall off a hook.

Plastic lures are made to resemble worms, eels, frogs, tadpoles, lizard, bait fish, hellgrammites, etc. They should be fished the same way as live bait. Frogs can be made to jump from the shore into the water, and eels can be made to crawl along the bottom. Worms can be floated down a river or stream as though just washed off a bank. Fish hit them the way they do live bait; and many times when they are just mouthing a lure they will come back to it two or three times, for they can't seem to tell the difference between it and the real thing.

All lures are only as good as the water being fished. If there are no fish, there can be no catches, no matter what lure or bait is used. Very often it's not the lure being used but the spot being fished that is wrong, for if fish are on the bottom the angler doesn't have much chance using a top lure. In the wrong place even a drag net would come in empty. The first rule is to find the fish and then experiment with different types of lures until one is found that will take them. When the strike comes, it's all fun, because you will feel as though this fish has really been outwitted.

Fly Fishing

What greater thrill is there than to stand on a stream with a rod, line and a few feathers tied on a hook and with this be able to catch fish?

Fly fishing is an art; it is the kind of fishing a new angler will be least successful with; and it is the kind of fishing that takes the most time and practice to master. But once skill is acquired, it is hard for a fly fisherman to use any other piece of tackle. However, even a beginner could, with a little instruction, be able to take some fish even though it will be years before he really masters the rod.

Tackle for fly fishing begins with the hollow glass rod. When the glass rod first appeared in the stores I objected to them very much, because I felt that the bamboo had a much finer action. I have since changed my mind, for the glass rods of today are far superior in every way to those first ones on the market. The well-made rod today has all the fine, subtle motion of a bamboo, while being many times stronger and sturdier, and with minimum care can be kept for years.

The ultimate in fishing is dry-fly fishing, for here the angler tempts a fish by floating a fly over the water. The angler must induce the fish to come to the top to take this tiny morsel, and this can only be done by perfect presentations. Rods for this kind of fishing generally are from 7½ to 8½ feet in length, are of light action and weigh under 4 ounces. Dry-fly fishing generally takes smaller trout; therefore, the equipment should be kept as light as possible, so sport can be felt from the hooked fish. The rods generally are not extra long, for 95 per cent of all dry-fly fishing will be done in a 40-foot radius of where the angler stands.

Reels for this fishing can be either automatic or single-action, hand-operated reels. I don't care for the automatic reels, for I think the reel is the least important piece of equipment on a fly-fishing outfit. Reels do not control casts as they do bait casting, for fly-rod casts are made by using the weight of the line and the momentum of the moving rod to get the fly out. Line is hand stripped from the reel, and many fishermen will not use the reel even when playing a hooked fish, for they prefer to pull the line in with the left hand. The line is left loose at the reel until after the fish is netted. Therefore, the reel is merely an auxiliary piece of equipment, acting as nothing more than a convenient tool to store line until it is needed. Buy the cheapest, and it will be sufficient.

Tapered floating line is generally used for fly fishing. It is thinner and more nearly invisible as it approaches the point where it meets the leader. The leader should be a minimum of 6 feet with as much as 12 feet being used in low clear water. This leader should be tapered, with the stronger tests being near the line and working down to almost invisible leader at the fly. For beginners I suggest that leader of no less than 4-pound test strength be used. Some finesse will be lost with this heavier

Fly casting.

(1) Start by positioning rod 20 degrees forward and strip line from reel.

(2) Move the rod back over the head in a steady motion to a minus-20-degree position. Then snap rod forward back to number (1) position in a false cast. Allow slack line stripped off the reel to work into motion. Return rod to number (2) position while stripping more line from the reel.

(3) Snap rod forward in the cast and allow slack line to run through guides.

(4) Point rod at target and prepare to retrieve fly or strike the fish. Accurate casts of 40 feet and more should come with practice.

leader, but this is more than compensated for by the number of flies that can be saved. When the fly is stuck in a tree or a bush a few pounds extra strength will be a big help to retrieve it. Also, flies will not snap off on the back casts.

Nymph fishing in small streams uses this very same equipment, with the substitution of nonfloating line for floating, because nymphs have to be fished deep.

Wet-fly fishing includes the use of standard wet flies, streamers, bucktails or small spinner-fly combinations. It takes sturdier equipment than dry-fly fishing, for where dry-fly fishing calls for finesse in taking fish, wet-fly fishing may call for brawn to take a record-breaker out of the water.

Rods for wet-fly fishing can be 8 to 9½ feet in length and may weigh anywhere from 4 to 8 ounces. The longer, heavier rods are favored by anglers in the West where chances for a 20-pound fish are great. Reels for this fishing should have a capacity of 100 yards so the line can be floated way downstream into the holes. Reels are important here, for the big fish are fought directly from the reel. It pays to get a good piece of equipment.

Line may be either level or torpedo, with the level line favored when a great deal of line is used, and the torpedo line when under 100 feet is used.

The art of fly fishing depends generally upon the ability of the fisherman to cast. A beginner should get on a stream where there is plenty of elbow room for forward and back casting. The casting of a fly by the standard overhand cast takes almost as much room behind the angler as it does in front of him.

The overhand cast must be the first one mastered, for this cast is essential to all kinds of fly fishing. After this becomes second nature, the angler should begin working on other casts to bring more versatility to his fishing. Another important cast is the roll cast. It is necessary near heavily vegetated streams where there isn't room for back casting. In the roll cast the rod is tilted back to minus-22 degrees and then snapped sharply forward to plus-22 degrees, and the line is permitted to shoot out. This is repeated, and each time more line rolls out, taking the fly further into the stream.

STANDARDIZED FLY LINE WEIGHTS

Line Number	Weights in Grains
1	60
2	80
3	100
4	120
5	140
6	160
7	185
8	210
9	240
10	280
11	330
12	380

Types of Lines:

DT	Double taper
L	Level
WF	Weight forward
ST	Short single taper
F	Floating
S	Sinking

(Lines used to be measured in diameter, with the C-line measuring .05 inch. Then .005 inch was added or subtracted for each size larger or smaller than C. This became confusing with the new materials, and inaccuracies developed between brands, so lines are now differentiated by weight.

The tolerance allowed manufacturers in weights of lines is not shown.)

Sometimes in very badly covered streams a bow cast is necessary. Here the rod is bent in bow-and-arrow fashion, and the angler holds the line and the rod tip in his left hand. The rod

SOME FLY FISHING TACKLE RECOMMENDATIONS

DRY FLY RODS

Manufacturer	Model Name	Model No.	Length	No. of Pieces	Remarks
Airex Corp.	Airex	191	7⅞ ft.	2	A tubular glass rod.
J. Heddon's Sons	Mark IV	8455	8 ft.	2	An expensive rod with a fast tip.
True Temper Corp.	True Temper	1166	8½ ft.	2	When combined with No. 76 reel, it is a fine set.

REELS

Manufacturer	Model Name	Model No.	Length	No. of Pieces	Remarks
Enterprise Mfg. Co.	Pflueger Progress	N1774			An inexpensive single-action reel.
True Temper Corp.	Ocean City	76			A single-action fly reel.

WET FLY RODS

Manufacturer	Model Name	Model No.	Length	No. of Pieces	Remarks
Airex Corp.	Airex	193	8⅜ ft.	2	A medium-action rod.
J. Heddon's Sons	Mark I	8306	8¾ ft.	2	A fine rod for bass bugging.
True Temper Corp.	True Temper	1227	9 ft.	2	A long hollow-glass fly rod.

REELS

Manufacturer	Model Name	Model No.	Length	No. of Pieces	Remarks
Denison-Johnson Corp.	Johnson Magnetic	5			A fine, expensive reel. Guaranteed for life. Holds 100 yd. 12-lb. braided nylon line.
Enterprise Mfg. Co.	Pflueger Sal-Trout	1554			Inexpensive reel with large line capacity.
True Temper Corp.	Ocean City	90			Combination automatic and single-action reel. Line capacity 50 yds.

tip and line are released, and the snap of the rod springing back into position is enough to take the fly out. This method does not get great distance, but it comes in very handy in small, thickly covered brook-trout streams.

Fly fishing and fly casting takes practice. The motions should be effortless. When this is achieved and when a fish boils up at the fly, then the angler knows he is enjoying the finest of fishing.

Understanding Flies

There are thousands of fly patterns in existence, and it would take a highly specialized book just to list a small percentage of them. It is not my intent to do it here; instead I shall list the various types that are the basis of all flies. Variations are made by changing the color and materials used in constructing the fly.

The dry fly is the aristocrat of flies. It is made with the greatest skill because it is used by the fussiest of anglers—the purist— the dry-fly fisherman. These flies are tied on the smallest of hooks, and many designs are used exclusively for trout.

The smallest dry flies are spiders, which are tied on very small hooks and have large hackles that make them look like spiders riding on the water. A few spider patterns include the Black Spider, Brown Spider and a Blue Spider.

The variant fly is closely related to the spider, except that it usually has two small wings. The heart of this fly is the hackles that give it floating ability. The Light, Multi-color Variant and the Badger Variant are two variant patterns.

Bivisibles are tied with two-color hackles, and this contrast in colors makes them excellent attention-getters. Some designs include the Black Bivisible and the Brown Bivisible. These flies have black or brown hackles with white hackles.

The upright flies have the feathers placed in an upright position just as though the insect were about to fly away. Stiff hackles keep this fly above water. These patterns represent adult insects in the prime of life.

The spent-wing fly depends upon the spread of the wings of the fly to float it. Styles include the Spent-Yellow and Spent-Olive. This fly imitates a female fly after the mating season. It is productive on warm evenings.

The fan-wing flies have the feathers going outward from the body to aid in floating the fly. These feathers are usually large, indicating a large-winged insect. Some styles include the special Fan-Wing Royal Coachman or a Fan-Wing Green Coachman. I have found these good to use on breezy days when the water is rippled by the wind.

Dry flies are in their prime in late spring when insects are actively flying about. Then the trout are on the lookout for insects landing on the water, and the fish rise readily.

Another type of fly or bug that is basically a dry fly is the bass bug. It usually has hackles and a body constructed of balsa wood. The wood body is painted a variety of colors. This bug is used primarily in bass and sunfish fishing, although there is no rule that says other species of fish will not take them.

Wet flies will take fish earlier in the season than dry flies, and they will continue taking them later in the season. The basic difference between wet and dry flies is that wet flies are not treated to float and are not dressed with as many hackles.

The nymph is a fly designed to imitate immature insect life that starts in the water. The fly will have no wings and only a few hackles; the body of a nymph may be varnished, or it may be plastic or rubber. Some patterns include Stone-fly Nymph, Green Caddis and Hard-Body Nymphs. This fly is gaining in popularity every year because it has been found that trout will take some form of nymph almost any time. The problem is for the angler to match the fly to the young insects in the water.

The hackle fly closely resembles the nymph except that it has more hackle at its head. This is a classic fly, and it would be well if a beginner tried one of these before any other. Patterns include the Winters, Gray Marlow and the Bottle Imp. A variation is the Palmer Hackle Fly, which has a heavily hackled body.

The winged fly or standard wet fly has thousands of patterns, including such popular favorites as the Royal Coachman and

Cahill. The winged fly may closely resemble its dry-fly counterpart except that it is fished beneath the surface to imitate a drowned insect. Immediately after a spring or early summer rainfall is a wonderful time to try these flies.

The streamer fly is made of feathers which are generally tied

Various types of flies.

UPPER LEFT: *A streamer fly.* The Black Ghost.
UPPER RIGHT: *A nymph.* Hewitt.
MIDDLE LEFT: *A dry fly.* Winged Cahill.
MIDDLE RIGHT: *A Bucktail.* Edison Dark Tiger.
LOWER LEFT: *A Fan Wing.* Royal Coachman.
LOWER RIGHT: *A Bivisible.* Black Bivisible.

in such a manner as to imitate a small fish in the water. Some streamer patterns includes Wesley Special, Black Ghost, Nancy and the Maribou. The successful streamer-fly fisherman is the man who can closely imitate the action of a live fish with his fly.

The bucktail fly, like the streamer, imitates a small fish in the water. The only difference between the two is the material used in making them. The wing of a bucktail is made of hair, and it is a fine fly for taking really big fish. This fly can be trolled successfully, or it can be fished in wet-fly fashion. It is best when worked into the deep holes to tempt the big fish at the bottom. Designs include the Bucktail McGinty, the Edison Tiger and the Scott Special.

These are only the basic types of flies. For each type there are hundreds of thousands of patterns, and any one of them can be productive. When looking at some of the really well-constructed flies, one would almost expect them to crawl or fly away. No wonder the fish are fooled.

Fly Tying

Fly tying is an old art and craft. The first record of fly tying appears in the *Book of St. Albins,* which was published in the year 1496. It tells of fishermen going to the local trout streams of England and using feathers tied to hooks to catch fish. It was not until 350 years later, however, that fly fishing really began to grow as a popular sport. Today fly fishing is so popular that over 30,000 different kinds of flies have been tied, named and cataloged for the fisherman to use. Books such as Donald Du Bois' *The Fisherman's Handbook of Trout Flies* list and describe thousands of them.

Basically, fly tying consists in taking some feathers, or other material, and attaching them to a fishhook so that they resemble an insect or a small fish in the water. Most flies are small, for they must be made about the size of the insect they are to resemble. The more realistic the fly, the better the fishing —and consequently the better the fly.

Certain basic tools are needed for fly tying. A good fly-tying vise to hold the hook in place when the feathers and glue are being attached to it is essential. Fly-tying vises may be bought for $1.00 up to $25.00, and the most expensive is not necessarily the best. Remember that any vise is a good vise—no matter what its price—if it can hold the hook in place and allow you to work freely.

Fly tiers need hackle pliers to grasp the end of the hackle feather, which is then wound around the hook to form the hackles or fibers that project outward from the body of the hook. A stiletto, a fine needle-pointed instrument that picks out the hackle fibers that become tucked under the body of the hook, is also essential. Beeswax is needed to waterproof dry flies. Tying thread (sizes 2/0 to 4/0) attaches the feathers to the hook. After the thread has been thoroughly wound around the feathers, a little glue or varnish will keep the whole business together.

Complete fly-tying kits including all the above-mentioned materials plus an instruction book and a large selection of feathers may be bought for a few dollars.

The construction of a dry fly or a wet fly is a process of building feathers onto a hook. A very popular dry fly is the Royal Coachman. We will go through the construction of this fly step by step.

Insert a hook (size No. 6 to No. 8) into a vise and attach a piece of waxed thread to the shank. Then select a tail feather. The tail feather for the Royal Coachman is usually a golden pheasant-tipped feather, which is attached to the end of the hook and held fast by some thread twisted around it. Then twist some herl with red floss center around the body of the hook, and tie some brown hackle feathers around and into the body of the fly. These brown hackle feathers should be wound around the shank of the hook in front of the wings. Finally, dress your fly up nicely, glue down the ends, and you have a completed Royal Coachman dry fly.

Many variations of flies can be tied once the knack is acquired, and artificial lures can be made to resemble almost any

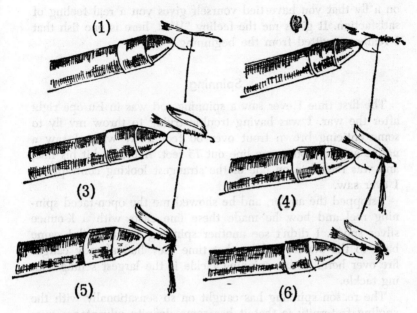

Constructing a Royal Coachman fly.

(1) Insert hook in vise and begin winding thread. Attach a golden pheasant tail feather, orange and black tipped. Tie on tail.

(2) Twist some herl around hook for body of fly.

(3) Tie on two white feathers (usually duck feathers) for wings.

(4) Tie scarlet floss on in center of body and tie brown hackle feathers around by making 2 or 3 turns with aid of hackle pliers.

(5) Cut end of hackle feathers and tie down with half hitches. Trim fly.

(6) Dress up fly and glue down the edges for the finished product.

bug in the area to be fished. Fly tying as a hobby becomes even more exciting when one starts to design his own flies and then goes out to see if they will work in the stream. Catching a fish on a fly that you have tied yourself gives you a real feeling of satisfaction. It gives me the feeling "Well, here is one fish that I really outwitted from the beginning."

Spinning

The first time I ever saw a spinning rod was in Europe right after the war. I was having trouble trying to throw my fly to some enticing brown trout over 50 feet away when I saw a native angler shoot some line out 75 feet. A brown hit his line, and was reeled in on one of the strangest looking contraptions I ever saw.

I stopped the angler, and he showed me the open-faced spinning reel and how he made these fine casts with a ¼-ounce silver spoon. I didn't see another spinning outfit until I came back to the States, and by that time they had already caught fire over here. Today spinning tackle is the largest selling fishing tackle.

The reason spinning has caught on so sensationally with the angling fraternity is that it has some definite advantages over standard equipment. First, the action on a light spinning rod of hollow-glass construction is as sporty as the action on any fly rod. Although a spinning rod is a foot shorter than the fly rod, it has lost none of the sportiness.

Another advantage of spinning tackle is that one can easily learn to use it. I have taught a 10-year-old boy to use a spinning rod in 10 minutes. I took the boy to a lake, gave him a demonstration, and let him try it. His first cast shot straight up in the air, and the next one dangled down at his feet, but on the third cast he was on his way. Within 10 minutes he was, by his own admission, an expert. I will vouch for him too, for he really did quite well that day; in fact, he picked up two nice bass and became a spinning addict.

Spinning rods are almost universally constructed of hollow glass. There are a few made of bamboo that are excellent, but they are for the specialist, and the average angler does well to use glass.

Some spinning rods weigh as little as one ounce, with the reels weighing only 2 ounces. This highly specialized equipment can make a bluegill or pumpkinseed feel like a 10-pound smallmouth.

The average angler will find that light rods weigh 2 to 4 ounces and come 6 to 7½ feet in length. These rods can flip a worm on a hook accurately and will handle lures from $\frac{1}{16}$ to ⅜ ounce in weight. The light rod is often used to work fly-spinner combinations for trout. This is fine equipment for trout and is a very big favorite with both metropolitan and mountain anglers. It is just as likely to be seen on a stream tucked away in the mountain that never knew a stocked fish as on a city stream with nothing but stocked fish. The rod is light, but in spite of its weight, it easily handles fish up to 5 pounds. Line for the rod is monofilament 2- to 4-pound test.

The medium rod by its very nature is the most versatile of spinning rods. It is the best size to buy for an angler having only one rod because it can handle almost any fish taken in fresh water, and can also do the more delicate work.

The medium rod is the same length as the light rod, 6 to 7½ feet, but it is more sturdily constructed and weighs 1 or 2 ounces more. This rod has a medium or medium-light action and uses 4- to 8-pound test monofilament. It will throw lures weighing ⅜ to 1¼ ounces. The rod is excellent for lake, stream or river fishing provided the fish only rarely exceed 15 pounds. There may be occasions when heavy-duty trolling requirements make it advisable to use a rod of solid-glass construction, which may be better suited to pull heavy lures at great depths.

A medium salt-water rod makes excellent heavy-duty fresh-water equipment. This rod is about 9 feet long and holds 200 yards of 10- to 20-pound test line which is capable of holding salmon, muskie, giant catfish and sturgeon. It will throw the bigger, heavier lures (½ ounce and up) and it is difficult for any fish to beat this.

The exact rod to buy of course, depends upon the angler's skill and where he lives, because a man living on the Snake River would want something completely different from someone living on Dale Hollow Lake.

Reels for spinning are all stationary-spool reels from which the line runs off without friction. Two very popular makes exist: the open-face, and the American type, or closed-face, reel.

The line on the open-face reel is visible to the eye, and as the line is rewound the wire hoop which winds up the reel can easily be viewed.

The closed-face reel has everything hidden from view with a housing to cover the line. In simplicity of use it ranks with the cane pole. The only thing that has to be learned is to press a button and cast and then to wind the reel. This is a fine reel for young boys because they will enjoy immensely the long, accurate casts that are possible; and it is so simple to use that they will attain a great sense of achievement.

Whether a person uses an open-face or a closed-face reel doesn't matter. Both are excellent, and the choice is strictly personal. I do suggest that only reels with star drags be purchased, for a star drag is important in handling big fish. The big fish wear themselves out fighting the drag, for one properly set will be just under the breaking point of the line; and even a fish twice the size of the tested strength of the line will soon be exhausted pulling against this brake.

An angler can set his drag with precision before going on a trip by rigging up and tying the line to a tree. Then the angler backs off 20 feet and starts to pull against the tree while he keeps strengthening the drag until he gets it to the desired strength. On a trip, hand-pull the line from the reel while adjusting the drag; this will give good results. On many occasions I have increased or decreased the drag while I played a fish. This, of course, can be dangerous until one knows his equipment well, for there is a tendency to overadjust, which means snapped lines and lost fish.

Line for spinning is almost exclusively monofilament. It is very thin, strong and almost invisible. It sinks (because it is heavier than the water it displaces) and is wonderful for casting and trolling. Only when the temperature is very low and the water extremely cold does monofilament act up; it then becomes stiff

SOME SPINNING TACKLE RECOMMENDATIONS

Manufacturer	Model Name	Model Number	Length	No. of Pieces	Remarks
		ULTRALIGHT RODS			
Garcia Corp.	Mitchell Gold Bond	475 lb.	5 ft.	2	Handles lures ¼ oz, to ⅜ oz, test line to 4 lbs.
J. Heddon's Sons	Heddon Mark III	7450	5 ft.	2	Handles fish up to 2 lbs.
Wright & McGill Co.	The Featherlight	LW 5	5 ft.	2	Handles lures to ¼ oz, fish up to 1 lb.
True Temper Corp.	True Temper	2000	5 ft.	2	2 ounce, hollow-glass rod.
		ULTRALIGHT REELS			
True Temper Corp.	Ocean City	310			Open-face. Capacity 100 yds. 6-lb. test Mono. line.
Zebco Co.	Zebco	101			Closed-face. Capacity 200 ft. 4-lb. test Mono. line.
		LIGHT RODS			
Garcia Corp.	Mitchell	475 NL	6¾ ft.	2	Can use very light lures $\frac{1}{16}$ to ½ oz.
True Temper Corp.	True Temper	2113	6¾ ft.	2	Rod has very light feel due to its fast tip action.
Wright & McGill Co.	The Ambassador	AML6¾	6¾ ft.	2	An expensive rod with fine workmanship.
Zebco Co.	Delux Spinning	6633	6 ft.	2	A balanced, hollow-glass rod.

LIGHT REELS

Manufacturer	Model Name	Model Number	Length	No. of Pieces	Remarks
Garcia Corp.	Mitchell	Cap			Open-face. Capacity 200 yds. 5-lb. test.
True Temper Corp.	Ocean City	300			Open-face. Capacity 225 yds. 6-lb. test.
Zebco Co.	Model	33			Closed-face spinning interchangeable spools. 150 yd. Capacity, 6-lb. test. Uses 4- to 10-lb. test line.

MEDIUM RODS

Manufacturer	Model Name	Model Number	Length	No. of Pieces	Remarks
Denison-Johnson Corp.	Johnson	11	6½ ft.	2	Designed for use with Johnson Citation Reel.
Garcia Corp.	Mitchell	475 LM	7 ft.	2	Handles lures ¼ to ⅝ oz., line to 10-lb. test.
J. Heddon's Sons	Mark I	6756	6½ ft.	2	Medium price. Fine quality rod.
True Temper Corp.	True Temper	2194	7 ft.	2	Rod has a fast tip for maximum sport.
Wright & McGill Co.	Delux	4A–7½	7½ ft.	2	This rod has a light tip and a heavy butt.
Zebco Co.	Spining	3300	6 ft.	2	An inexpensive solid-glass rod.

MEDIUM REELS

Manufacturer	Model Name	Model Number	Remarks
Airex Corp.	Apache	319	Open-face. Capacity 100 yds. 8-lb. test line.
Art Wire & Stamping Co.	RuMer	101	Open-face. Capacity 300 yds. 6-lb. test line.
Denison-Johnson Corp.	Johnson Citation		Closed-face spinning interchangeable spools. Can handle line from 8- to 15-lb. test. Capacity 125 yds. 10-lb. test Mono line.
Garcia Corp.	Mitchell	300	Open-face. Capacity 300 yds. 6-lb. test when using large capacity spool.
Garcia Corp.	ABU-Matic		Closed-face. Capacity 125 yds. mono with star drag.
Zebco Co.	Zebco	202	Closed-face. Capacity 100 yds. 10-lb. test line. Inexpensive.

Heavy Duty and Medium Salt-Water Tackle

Manufacturer	Model Name	Model Number	Length	No. of Pieces	Remarks
J. Heddon's Sons	Sturdy	7404	6¾ ft.	2	A sturdy rod. Fine for a slugging match.
Garcia Corp.	Mitchell	477 PM	6 ft.	2	Salt- and heavy-duty fresh-water rod. Casts lures 1 to 2½ ounces.
True Temper Corp.	Montague	2291	7 ft.	2	Hollow-glass rod. Weighs only 7½ ounces. Medium action.
Wright & McGill Co.	Granger	DF 8½	8½ ft.	2	For salmon-drifter fishing.
Zebco Co.	Heavy Duty Spinning	8955	8½ ft.	2	Tubular rod for muskie, etc.

Heavy-duty Reels

Manufacturer	Model Name	Model Number	Length	No. of Pieces	Remarks
Art Wire & Stamping Co.	RuMer Super				Open-face. Capacity 200 yds. 15-lb. test.
Garcia Corp.	Mitchell	306			Open-face. Capacity 200 yds. 15-lb. test. Good for salt or fresh water.
True Temper Corp.	Ocean City	320			Open-face. Capacity 200 yds. 15-lb. test.

and difficult to handle, and an angler running into such conditions might do well to take a spool of dacron line along.

Spinning in every phase is the most popular kind of fishing there is today. It is fine sport, and I suggest that the angler who is getting only one fishing rod get a medium spinning rod.

Disease in Fish

Many times an angler will take a sports fish and wonder if it's safe eating. The answer invariably is: if the fish is properly cooked and the meat is fresh, it is safe. Occasionally worms or other invertebrates will be found in or on a fish when it is caught; but these all die in cooking, and are not harmful.

One disease does come from fish, however—a tape-worm infection called Diphyllobothriasis. It comes from fish of the Great Lakes and nearby lakes, especially in the Minnesota-Michigan area. Some carriers of the disease are walleye pike, sand pike, northern pike and burbot. The disease can be transmitted only if an infected fish is eaten raw or inadequately cooked. The tapeworm is nonfatal, but it is long-lasting and difficult to eliminate. To insure prevention of the disease, fish from infected areas should be eaten only if it is thoroughly cooked at 122° Fahrenheit for 10 minutes or if it has been frozen for 24 hours at 14° Fahrenheit.

The tapeworm has an interesting life cycle; it begins with infected humans whose raw waste contains the eggs of the worm, which go into fresh water. These eggs then infect fish, who in turn infect any human who eats the fish raw. Tapeworms sometimes grow to the monstrous length of 30 feet in the human intestines.

This sickness is prevalent in Switzerland, Germany, France, Finland, Russia, Canada, and other countries. It is not nearly as prevalent in the United States, partly due to better sewage checks and partly to the American's reluctance to eat raw fish.

Gefüllte fish is often made from Great Lakes fresh-water fishes; and women making it must exercise extreme care not to sample the gefüllte fish until it is thoroughly cooked, or they risk the chance of getting a tapeworm.

An angler need never concern himself about the bad effects of eating fish, for it is a healthy, good-tasting food. Fish are carriers of far less disease than mammals, and fish is as healthy a food as anyone can ever hope to eat.

Caring for Fish

In primitive times fishing was a necessity to sustain life. Today, behind the façade of sport and pleasure, there still exists the desire for food, and the better the meal the angler brings home, the more he will remember his experience. Unfortunately, many fish are ruined before they ever arrive home and just do not taste as good as they should on the table.

The first rule is to clean and gut fish as soon as possible after they are caught. Then they must be washed and dried out. It is not a good idea to resubmerge a cleaned fish in water; it should be kept dry. Many trout anglers hang the fish up to dry thoroughly after cleaning. Anglers in primitive fishing camps who have to ship fish employ several methods to preserve fish. One way to ship fish while retaining their mountain-freshness for several days is to wrap each fish in oiled paper after it is cleaned. This paper is then wrapped in newspaper and further wrapped into a big bundle. A piece of wet newspaper can be wrapped around the outside of the bundle to keep the package cool and to help keep air away from the fish. The package is then put into a sack and transported.

Ice shipping is a more modern convenience, but it helps if the fish are individually wrapped in cool, soft grass or newspaper before they are shipped.

When fishing in warm areas, special care should be taken to get the fish on ice quickly. It is a good idea to keep the fish in the water on stringers until they are ready for cleaning, and then to ice them as soon as possible. Picnic ice boxes make fine containers for keeping fish on a relatively long drive.

All fish, no matter what species, will taste 100 per cent better if proper care has been given them, and nothing tastes as good as a fish that comes wriggling out of the water and is in the pan within five minutes.

Ice Fishing

When winter sets in and a deep freeze covers the land, fishermen know that this isn't the time to sit by the fireplace but the time to get out and catch fish. The league of sturdy ice fishermen is growing every year, and some are hardly able to contain themselves until the ice gets thick enough to get out there and get pickerel, perch, walleye, pike or lakers.

One reason for the rapid growth of ice fishing is that insulated, lightweight, warm garments make long stays on the ice comfortable. The most important point in successful ice fishing is the warmth and comfort of the fisherman. One absolute essential for comfortable ice fishing is warm feet; and the fisherman should wear arctic boots, ski boots or other insulated cold weather boots with warm socks. Warm outer garments and undergarments will make the ice fisherman more comfortable.

One point seldom made about ice fishing is that the coldest days are not necessarily the best fishing days. Water under the ice remains at a fairly constant temperature, a fraction over 32°, on cold as well as warm days; therefore, a fisherman can experience just as good fishing on a warm winter day as he will in a deep freeze. Diligent ice fishermen who build their own fish shanties will scoff at the suggestion of choosing warm days, because they are protected and will fish in any weather; but for many fishermen it's a point worth remembering.

Ice fishing has extended from its traditional center of New England and the Minnesota-Michigan area to other parts of the country. It is now common to see ice fishermen anywhere in the country where 4 inches of ice cover the water. In marginal areas anglers should keep away from ice under which there is likely to be moving water. A moving current or stream will melt ice away on the underside of the thickness, and these sections are the first to break. The danger of breakage lessens further north, but in early season and late season fishing it becomes a very real threat.

The basic materials for ice fishing begin with instruments with which to dig through the ice to reach the water. Choices vary according to the fisherman, with sundry forms of axes and ice chisels being the chief tools. Drills are used by other anglers. The hole dug is from 8 to 10 inches wide in ice up to 2 feet thick. Next on the list of essential tools is a plain ladle, which is necessary to keep ice from forming on the fishing hole. A few drops of kerosene dropped in the hole will stop the water from freezing over quickly.

There are a variety of fishing methods. The most popular is still by way of the tip-up. The simplest tip-ups are made at home from split shingles, and store-brought tip-ups will serve the angler well. He may buy the simplest or those with the reel built in and kept under water so the line will not freeze up. When a fisherman uses several tip-ups he usually sets them up in a circular pattern so that they may be serviced from a central point. Fishermen should check their state laws for the number of tip-ups and hooks permitted per line.

One of the fastest growing types of ice fishing is the quest for pan fish. Fishing for bluegill and crappie involves using a short rod in a method very similar to summer pan fishing. Sometimes a float is used on the line, but it has to be hauled in on the slightest wiggle on the float because the fish do not hit hard during the winter. A wire coat hanger that is straightened out and stuck in the ice will show the slightest nibble when it is used as a rod. Flies can be fished for bluegill. The usual flies are nymphs, which imitate the immature insects that are in the water during the winter. Other lures may be tiny spinners or spoons that are fished low and jigged from the bottom to a foot or two above the bottom. Best fishing for pan fish is in water less than 25 feet deep.

The yellow perch is the favorite of the Michigan ice-fishing fraternity. This fish stays active all year and gives anglers a fine time during winter months. The perch are school fish; therefore, action at a group of holes may suddenly get frantic.

Sometimes when a school is about it can be coaxed to stay longer by keeping a live fish on a hook in the water. It is best to set up shop along a sand bar for yellow perch. Perch are regular takers of minnows, which can be fished dead or alive. The small live ones are best. Perch also take spinners, jigged spoons, worms and a host of natural baits.

The walleye of the same area has to be taken right at the bottom. It is a minnow feeder, and the best waters are deep ones over sandy bottoms.

Throughout New England, the pickerel is the top ice fish. Good fishing is found in relatively shallow water over or near weed beds. Minnows or shiners are fine baits for pickerel just as they are for virtually any fish that remain on feed under the ice. Artificials and pork rinds take fish. Some of the best pickerel fishing takes place in winter when the fish are feeding in preparation for the early spring spawning.

An ice fisherman will take bass many times while he is fishing low and in the mud. These fish are usually protected by law and have to be thrown back, but the fact they are caught shows that some of the species will feed even under ice.

Lake trout can be taken in water as deep as 100 feet. Smelt and large minnows are the most popular baits for this species.

The American eel is a fish that can be captured in the dead of winter. These fish are usually taken in brackish water near the coast or in fresh water near the sea. Anglers cut holes through the ice and push long-handled rakes down into the water. They push the rake down into the mudholes where the eels congregate, and then pull up the eels that get stuck in the rake's teeth.

Northern pike are one of the big prizes of ice fishing. They are apt to be caught anytime at any depth. Many pike are speared as they curiously inspect a fishing hole in the ice. Sturgeon are a rare, worthwhile prize for ice fishermen, too.

Several surveys have shown that ice fishermen actually do better than their summer counterparts, both in total fish caught and in number of fish caught per hour of fishing. One reason for this is that there are few tourists among the winter fishermen, and the men who do go ice fishing know how to take fish. A survey like this shows that there are plenty of fish in the lakes that are hungry and waiting to attack a hook.

Now, whenever the temperature skids down to sub-freezing and all humanity hibernates, remember that there are fish stirring under the ice, with plenty of action to warm an angler's heart.

Index

Index—Latin Names of the Fish